AN ARIZONA CHRONOLOGY

STATEHOOD
1913-1936

Douglas D. Martin

Edited by
Patricia Paylore

THE UNIVERSITY OF ARIZONA PRESS
TUCSON

For Cecyl
as it surely would have been

The University of Arizona Press
www.uapress.arizona.edu

Printed in the United States of America
21   20   19   18   17   16   7   6   5   4   3   2

ISBN-13: 978-0-8165-0006-2 (paper)
ISBN-13: 978-0-8165-3534-7 (Century Collection paper)

L. C. No. 63-11975

♾ This paper meets the requirements of ANSI/NISO Z39.48-1992 (Permanence of Paper).

INTRODUCTION

This *Arizona Chronology*, 1913–1936, begins where the first Chronology ended, with statehood, and covers a span of nearly a quarter of a century. It was Mr. Martin's intention to carry it forward through another suitable period, perhaps through World War II, with later compilations to follow, but he died before he could complete more than is covered in the present work. It differs from the historical Chronology of Volume One chiefly in that its sources are almost exclusively from contemporary newspapers. This coincides with our coming of age, I am sure Mr. Martin decided, for he believed passionately in the ability of the public press to tell history's story.

I do not think that here Mr. Martin set out in any deliberate way to interpret this period of time. But although he took an across-the-board approach, something close to an interpretation emerges from the choice of the news he selected to delineate the events following statehood. Taking the thousands of cards which he left in rough unedited form, studying them, indexing them, as I did over a period of months, I realized that certain recurring themes began to stand out: the two depressions, the long dispute over the waters of the Colorado River, the prominence of Arizona's three C's — copper, cotton, cattle (no talk yet here about climate!) — the nagging growing pains as we tried to put our guns away and take up the pen and the book, and finally what became an abiding article of faith in Mr. Martin's own view of Arizona history, namely the persistence of the pioneer spirit of the nineteenth century as it was applied to the problems of the twentieth. He saw in the events here recorded not a quaint chronicle of a picturesque era but rather a testament to the strength and optimism of a young people determined to take its place in the Union.

Long ago, when Mr. Martin and I first began to talk about the idea of an Arizona Chronology, I asked him what use would ever be made of such a compilation. His patient explanation to one who had been nourished for half a century on Arizona history was quite simply that not everyone enjoyed such an advantage and that he thought it had a place in the education of newcomers, newcomers either to Arizona or to history. It was in such a spirit that I undertook after his death to finish what he had here begun. It must have been a difficult period to abstract, with none of the excitement attendant upon the previous period. Instead, it was characterized by politics, economics, a worldwide war, and the sobering business of unemployment, strikes, a troubled border, legislative conflicts. And yet, somehow, as a whole, the period is one of far more reality as a common experience than anything that went before. I believe Mr. Martin came to see it so, for he patently eschewed the sensational and the violent when it was news only in itself. The violence for the most part here recorded is inherent rather in the structure of our society as it attempted to grow up, become tamed, mature, responsible. The strains put upon it by the "Wobblies," the Communists, and yes, the Ku Klux Klan, often caused violence, but it was social violence, not personal, and because it was this way, Mr. Martin thought it was more important than Tombstone's feuds.

Fortunately for us, Mr. Martin came to history too late in his long and useful life to have been spoiled by the tendency of academic historians to footnote the life out of history. That had its place, he knew, but he knew too, perhaps better than many, that history was also life, was Sonnichsen's "poetry," was the commonplace monotony of Everyman's every day. And so here we have it all, a great slice of Arizona's adolescence, day by day, when its people could still get excited about simple things like the Graf Zeppelin, the speed record set in 1913 for the auto run from Tucson to Nogales, and the fact that ostrich feathers were going out of style.

There is a good deal of humor in this particular chronology: the University's anguish over the campus parking problem in Tucson in the '30s; Ed Echols' comments on the London rodeo; the thousands of gallons of illicit liquor poured on Arizona sands by prohibition agents.

And we had some unusual guests in the state during that quarter of a century: Jane Addams and Charles Lindbergh, Aimee Semple McPherson and John Dillinger, the two Roosevelts and John J. Pershing. At least one election was fought with the Townsend Old Age Pension Plan as the central issue. From 1915 to 1936, various attempts were made to establish an Arizona port on the Gulf of California, and as early as 1921, engineers were interested in a dam across Glen Canyon. In 1932 Phoenix took note of air pollution, and prospecting for oil went on stubbornly from 1913 forward.

One of the most astonishing series of events to manifest itself in this chronology was the early emphasis on aviation in Arizona. Beginning in 1919, though there are of course earlier records, Mr. Martin noted nearly half a hundred important references to flights, establishment of airports, use of air mail, mercy missions, and aerial surveys.

The one single figure who clearly dominates the period is undoubtedly George W. P. Hunt, seven-time governor of the state, and the architect of many of the issues which persisted throughout these years. Hunt was pro-labor, and his terms of office spanned some of the greatest labor disputes in our history, including the famous Bisbee Deportation and the prolonged strikes during the period of World War I. In retrospect his year-long struggle with Thomas E. Campbell over the outcome of the 1916 election is a yo-yo affair with overtones of humor, but at the time it had a deadly seriousness. Hunt's role in the continuing conflict over the Colorado River has yet to be assessed fully, but here is the raw data for him who cares to see.

For those who believe that the bracero problem is a new one, it may come as a surprise to learn that the importation of alien labor was an explosive issue in the early '20s. In its brutalizing aspects, with the citizens up in arms over the inhuman treatment of alien cotton pickers and their families, the grapes were being stored up against the days of wrath to come.

One day I stopped by the University Library's microfilm room to see how Mr. Martin was getting along. He pulled his head out of the microfilm reader and looked at me bleary-eyed. "It's amazing," he commented. "Change the dates and the names and we might be reading yesterday's *Star*." He said he couldn't understand why this kind of history was not being investigated, why the historian was in such a rut, why he was so afraid to come past the end of the nineteenth century, why he insisted on narrowing in on the same old business until the business just disappeared in a maze of repetitive documentation. He got up stiffly, and we went out in the hall and walked up and down awhile. "Take the Indians, for instance," he went on impatiently. "This Chronology has as many Indian stories as the first one, but it's practically untouched historically. These Indians are not scalping or going on the warpath. They've abdicated all that to television. These Indians are voting, they're dying as Arizonans in World War I, they're acting with more honor than the government in their efforts to see justice done and Washington's promises kept." He looked at me belligerently, and then we both began to laugh.

So here it is, Mr. Martin, as I've done my best to tell the world how you felt about some of these things. It was a labor of love, and my only regret is that I was the one who had to finish it.

PATRICIA PAYLORE

EARLY STATEHOOD

1913—1936

1913 JAN. 1. Sixty armed men guard oil claims in the Verde Valley on New Year's Eve, fearing claim jumpers. (8)

JAN. 2. City building inspector reports that Phoenix broke all records in 1912 by issuing building permits totalling $1,327,000. (2)

JAN. 3. People of San Simon excited over striking two artesian wells. (2)

JAN. 4. Flagstaff reports that northern Arizona sawmills are producing 68 million board feet of lumber a month. (2)

JAN. 7. Walter Douglas and other officers of El Paso and Southwestern railroad consult with Tucson officials over $60,000 gift for a Y.M.C.A. building. (2)

JAN. 7. Three hundred acres of land in the Salt River Valley reported as producing one bale of cotton per acre in 1912. (8)

JAN. 8. Arizona copper production in 1912 exceeds 350,000,000 pounds; largest production by any state in one year. (8)

FEB. 3. Second special session of the first state legislature convenes. Passes act appropriating $7,500 for sinking artesian wells in Sulphur Spring Valley; provides method of assessing property of railroad corporations; passes joint resolution asking federal government to participate in care of tuberculosis victims. (8)

FEB. 14. Phoenix celebrates first anniversary of statehood. Thomas R. Marshall, vice-president elect, is principal speaker. (8)

FEB. 27. Florence objects to appearance of convicts on its streets, and Governor Hunt orders state penitentiary to cease sending prisoners into town for business or pleasure. (8)

MAR. 6. Arizona Corporation Commission orders railroads to lower freight rates on cattle within state limits. (1)

MAR. 6. Governor Hunt orders quarantine on Cochise County cattle because of Texas fever tick. (1)

MAR. 14. Colonel Kosterlitzky, commanding the Federal garrison in Nogales, Sonora, surrenders to General Obregon's Sonora rebels after day-long fight in which flying bullets spray American side and one American soldier is shot and seriously wounded. (3)

MAR. 29. Legislature moves Industrial School from Benson to Fort Grant. (8)

APRIL 2. Prescott business houses and residences begin installing electric lights. (2)

APRIL 3. Act providing for police courts in incorporated cities and towns becomes a law. (14)

APRIL 7. Piqued at Governor Hunt, State Board of Control takes over his official car and says he can walk. (2)

APRIL 8. Tucson posts warnings that state speed laws limiting vehicles to 10 miles an hour in the business district must be observed. (2)

APRIL 11. New town of Chandler experiences a boom. Announces that it has 500 inhabitants and $40,000 in the two-months-old bank. (2)

APRIL 12. Governor Hunt vetoes penal code as adopted by the legislature because it limits pardoning powers. (2)

APRIL 14. General Pedro Ojeda and 100 survivors of his defeated troops flee from Naco to shelter on American side at Douglas and surrender to the U. S. Border Patrol. (1)

APRIL 24. Mexicans protest Arizona's anti-alien ownership law depriving them of prior rights to property. (2)

APRIL 25. Legislature passes three-cent-a-mile railroad fare law after hard battle. (8)

APRIL 29. Prospective women voters hold educational mock election in Phoenix and learn how to mark ballot. (2)

APRIL 29. Most of town of Maricopa is destroyed by early morning fire. (2)

MAY 2. Great Western Power Co's. government permit to water rights in Sabino Canyon expires. City of Tucson sends officials to file claim at midnight if the Power Company's claim is not extended. (2)

MAY 3. Two motorcycles set speed record for Tucson-Nogales run. Total time three hours and five minutes. (2)

MAY 17. Third special session of the first state legislature closes. After long wrangling it writes new legislation tripling the assessment of mines. Land commission is empowered to select one million acres of land granted by U. S. to pay off railroad bonds of Pima, Maricopa, Coconino and Yavapai counties. (8)

MAY 17. Legislature writes penal code providing for capital punishment. Hunt again vetoes measure but veto is overridden. (2)

MAY 22. State Board of Health rules that every case of tuberculosis must be registered with county or city health officer. (2)

MAY 30. Maricopa county votes dry but Phoenix remains wet. (2)

JUNE 2. Calumet and Arizona Co. starts the fires in the new $300,-000,000 smelter in Douglas. (1)

JUNE 2. Executive Order 1782 adds certain lands to the Gila River Reservation. (17)

JUNE 5. Secretary of State rules sufficient signatures are obtained to initiate anti-capital punishment law. (2)

JUNE 9. Douglas has a wild night; one dead and four wounded. It was payday. (2)

JUNE 17. Farmers of the upper Gila Valley carry fight to prevent copper mines polluting streams to the U. S. Supreme Court and win their case. (8)

JUNE 24. Striking streetcarmen plaster Phoenix police with eggs when company attempts to operate streetcars. (2)

JULY 4. Boys tear down Mexican flag flying above office of the consul in Tucson. International incident brews. (2)

JULY 17. Secretary of State Wm. J. Bryan orders investigation of Mexican flag incident in Tucson. Mayor of Tucson apologizes. (2)

JULY 18. Executive Order 1798 revokes Executive Order 1540 of May 29, 1912, reserving additional lands for the Hualapai Indians. (17)

JULY 21. Maricopa county estimates its expenditures for schools will reach a half-million dollars during the coming year. (3)

JULY 29. State Board of Equalization and representatives of county boards of supervisors open meetings in Phoenix in attempt to find system for equalizing property values throughout Arizona. (3)

AUG. 2. Seventeen Arizona investment companies are ordered by State Corporation Commission to stop doing business because of violations of the "blue sky" law. (2)

AUG. 9. Armed citizens are sworn in as special officers at Douglas and patrol the city at night to halt crime. (2)

AUG. 12. State Board of Equalization raises the estimates of county assessors by $10,000,000, making a grand total of $75,242,000 for the state. (3)

AUG. 14. Ten men are killed at Coronado mine near Clifton when two loaded ore cars break loose and dash down the steep grade. (2)

AUG. 15. Eight buildings are destroyed by fire at Ray, and citizens pull down several structures to prevent complete destruction of town. (2)

AUG. 19. Law establishing eight-hour work day for women goes into effect. (2)

AUG. 16. Mountain States Telephone and Telegraph company makes Phoenix principal toll station between El Paso and Los Angeles. (3)

AUG. 21. Chandler group begins plans for putting 12,000 acres under irrigation. (3)

SEPT. 2. Flood pours out of Paradise Valley into Arizona Canal, threatening homes and farms. (3)

SEPT. 4. Relatives of prisoner who froze to death in Douglas city jail sue the city for $10,000. (2)

SEPT. 6. Wholesale escape of boys from reform school at Benson causes sensation. (2)

SEPT. 8. Carl Hayden, Arizona congressman, gently rejects suggestion that he run for Governor and indicates he would prefer another term in Washington. (2)

SEPT. 17. Union and non-union men stage sporadic fights on Douglas business streets while citizens cheer. (2)

OCT. 1. Phoenix proves fertile recruiting ground for General Huerta of Mexico. Two groups leave city for Juarez. (3)

OCT. 3. Federal marshals are kept busy trailing gun-runners with headquarters in Tucson, Bisbee, and Douglas who ship material of war across the border to battling Mexican forces. (2)

OCT. 13. Governor Hunt of Arizona, Venustiano Carranza, provisional president of Mexican Constitutionalists, and other dignitaries meet on the American-Mexican border in Nogales and exchange felicitations. (2)

OCT. 13. Federal officials arrest justice of the peace at Washington Camp after finding 10,000 rounds of ammunition in his possession, and charge him with running arms over border. (2)

OCT. 22. Phoenix discovers its $250,000 bond election was illegal and must be held again. (3)

OCT. 23. Leading citizens of Douglas arrested and charged with gun running. (1)

OCT. 27. The biggest merchant in Tucson appears in district court to answer charge of smuggling arms into Mexico. (1)

NOV. 11. Board of governors of the Water Users Association turns down government's plan of a $60 per acre charge over 10 years. (3)

NOV. 13. Town of Mesa forms posses and turns out on a moonlit night to help officers hunt for killers of the town marshal. Manhunt ends successfully at Date Creek. (3)

NOV. 16. University of Arizona Experiment Station sends farm train through the state. Public is enthusiastic. (3)

NOV. 16. Phoenix sees and hears its first "talking movies." (3)

NOV. 22. San Carlos Hotel opens in Chandler. (3)

NOV. 26. Phoenix citizens vote $275,000 bond issue to fund floating indebtedness and enlarge city's services. (3)

DEC. 3. Mexican rebel forces seize Tucson man and demand $10,000 ransom from Washington. (2)

DEC. 3. Douglas, Bisbee and Tucson businessmen charged with selling war material in Mexico are discharged on technicalities. Court rules government did not prove actual destination of shipments. (2)

DEC. 6. U. S. District Court awards the 100,000 remaining acres of the Baca float in Southern Arizona to the heirs. (2)

DEC. 8. Governor Hunt files protest with General Venustiano Carranza of Mexico over wholesale executions of prisoners of war by Pancho Villa. Carranza replies it is necessary and humane. (2)

DEC. 11. Two Mexicans who pleaded guilty when indicted with Tucson-Bisbee-Douglas ring for shipping contraband war material into Mexico are fined $250 each in district court. Judge warns Arizona citizens that hereafter he will not be lenient. (2)

DEC. 11. Farmers of Bowie celebrate drilling of first deep well. (2)

DEC. 12. Eight men convicted of murder and reprieved by Governor Hunt await verdict of the public on capital punishment. (2)

DEC. 13. Yuma asks Governor Hunt for troops to protect border against Mexican marauders. (2)

DEC. 23. Phoenix is recommended as mobilization point for Arizona National Guard in case of war with Mexico. (3)

DEC. 23. Prescott Auto Club decides to fight new automobile tax as unconstitutional. (2)

DEC. 31. Total major metals production in Arizona for 1913 is $70,875,027. (16) Total number of cattle in Arizona, 1,145,000; value, $38,274,000. (24)

1914 JAN. 2. Globe miners support striking miners in Calumet, Mich.; accuse Department of Labor of being indifferent to bitter labor troubles in Michigan copper mines. (3)

JAN. 31. Papago Saguaro National Monument established. (26)

FEB. 9. Globe poised for boom as drillers prepare to explore for oil. (3)

FEB. 10. Mesa gets $27,000 advance on two weeks' shipment of cotton. (3)

FEB. 12. State Land Commissioner sells 14 million feet of standing timber from University lands for $41,355. (3)

FEB. 12. Cochise County Taxpayers Assn. reports floating debts paid and tax rate reduced. (3)

FEB. 13. Southern Pacific invites Governor Hunt aboard an engine and proves new state law establishing headlight candlepower creates serious hazard.(2)

FEB. 14. District Attorney of Yuma County uncovers deal to swindle Indians and government by sale of 200,000 acres of Colorado River Indian Reservation. (3)

FEB. 15. Tucson sinks a new well and gets a flow of one million gallons a day. (3)

FEB. 16. First Phoenix "Go-to-Church-Sunday" drive fills every church in city to its doors. (3)

FEB. 19. Arizona Supreme Court voids three-cent fare law passed by legislature. Says state has no right to make rates for public service corporations. (3)

FEB. 21. Verde River rises and pours flood down the Salt River, leaving farmers marooned. (3)

FEB. 26. Army engineers approve reservoir site on San Carlos Indian reservation for six million dollars. (3)

MAR. 2. Safford rejoices over its first electric lights. (3)

MAR. 4. Department of Agriculture announces that 2100 bales of the 1913 crop of Mesa cotton sold in London for 23⅓ cents a pound. (3)

MAR. 5. Phoenix city council establishes municipal free employment bureau to aid idle men. (3)

APRIL 5. Scandal breaks over treatment of boys and girls at Fort Grant. Discipline and morals are subject of lurid report. (1)

APRIL 8. Four troopers of U. S. Ninth Cavalry are wounded on American soil by wild bullets as Sonora state troops and Mexican federals fight for possession of Naco. (8)

APRIL 16. Military aides of Governor Hunt are stripped of their sidearms when they accompany him on a visit to Agua Prieta. (2)

APRIL 20. Guard placed over Tucson National Guard armory to protect rifles against possible seizure by Huertista refugees. (2)

APRIL 21. The U. S. takes Vera Cruz, and Governor Hunt asks permission to call out the Arizona National Guard. (2)

APRIL 22. The people of Bisbee and Governor Hunt ask War Department for 1400 rifles in storage at Fort Huachuca. General John J. Pershing moves his brigade across Arizona enroute from San Francisco to El Paso. (2)

APRIL 22. Quiet rules both sides of the border at Nogales despite landing of American troops at Vera Cruz. (1)

APRIL 23. One hundred and fifty homes are destroyed by fire in Bisbee. (1)

APRIL 23. As the U. S. and Mexico move toward war the Arizona National Guard at Yuma called out to patrol Colorado River border. (2)

APRIL 23. Three companies of U. S. regulars from Fort Huachuca are rushed to Yuma by special train to safeguard irrigation works. (2)

APRIL 24. Vigilance committee is organized in Tucson under leadership of the sheriff and the commandant of cadets at the University. (2)

APRIL 26. Special train arrives in Douglas from Nacozari bringing American citizens to safety. (2)

APRIL 27. Hundreds of Mormons, fleeing Mexico, unable to find accommodations in Douglas, camp in the fields near city water plant. (2)

APRIL 28. Governor Hunt withdraws state guard from Yuma when War Department fails to send regulars. Yuma citizens form a home guard. (2)

APRIL 28. Casa Grande suffers disastrous fire. (2)

MAY 6. Mormon refugees from south of the border get news that property they left behind has been seized by Mexicans. (2)

JUNE 8. Phoenix City Commission and school trustees sell land to Tucson, Phoenix and Tidewater Railway for depot. (2)

JUNE 18. Nogales, Arizona is alarmed by report that armed Yaquis are advancing for attack on Mexican garrison across the border. (2)

AUG. 1. Congressional Act appropriates $20,000 for the purchase of lands for Indians under jurisdiction of the Camp Verde Indian school, said lands to be held in trust and subject to the General Allotment Act. This is the Camp Verde Indian Reservation for Yavapai-Apache Indians. (17)

AUG. 8. Maricopa County Sheriff and Phoenix Chief of Police crack what they claim is a conspiracy planned by Mexicans and Indians to take Phoenix by force of arms, plundering banks and stores. (3)

AUG. 13. Federal Court in San Francisco rules that Arizona State Corporation Commission has authority to regulate rates of public utilities. (3)

AUG. 14. President Woodrow Wilson signs reclamation measure which gives farmers ten years of grace in repaying government loans used for construction of dams and canals. (3)

AUG. 19. Women are summoned for jury duty in Mesa. County attorney insists only males are qualified. (3)

AUG. 21. Law officers of Phoenix, Ray, Florence, and Superior fight four gun battles with Mexican woodcutters' gang. Five Americans and 12 Mexicans die. (3)

AUG. 22. Governor Hunt requests state highway engineer replace convict roadworkers in Cochise County with unemployed day laborers. (3)

AUG. 27. Executive Order reduces the size of the Gila River Indian Reservation. (17)

SEPT. 3. Farmers of Sulphur Springs Valley harvest huge crops of hay for first time in 10 years.

SEPT. 4. John O. Dunbar, Arizona editor, says Senator Eugene S. Ives claims to have proof that Mark Smith, Arizona senator, has been on the payroll of the Southern Pacific for 20 years. (2)

SEPT. 22. Two floods following a cloudburst sweep away homes in mining town of Ray which is still recovering from disastrous fire. (2)

SEPT. 29. Four troops of U. S. Cavalry are rushed to the border at Naco to help the Tenth Cavalry prevent violations of neutrality, as Mexican armies under Hill and Maytorena prepare for battle. (2)

OCT. 14. Governor Hunt announces he will send Arizona National Guard to Naco. Commander of U. S. regulars on the border asks that guard be kept at home. (2)

OCT. 17. Eight U. S. troopers are wounded by wild bullets from Maytorena forces across border at Naco. (2)

OCT. 30. Federal court jury in Phoenix convicts five Mexicans of having conspired to arouse Indians to revolt against whites. Maximum sentence is two years imprisonment. [see Aug. 8, 1914]. (3)

NOV. 4. George W. P. Hunt re-elected governor. Arizona votes for prohibition, three-cent fare law, old age and mothers' pension law, anti-blacklist law prohibiting interference with the rights of labor and 80 per cent law compelling employers to give preference to electors or native-born citizens. (3)

NOV. 6. *Nogales Daily Herald* established. (19)

NOV. 17. Arsonist runs amuck in Phoenix and city has seven fires in four days. (2)

NOV. 18. Feature story tells of ostrich farms at Yuma and Phoenix facing ruin as plumes on women's hats go out of fashion and birds and feathers become a drug on the market. (2)

DEC. 1. Teachers attempt to open public school in Naco but parents refuse to send children while Mexican bullets are flying. (2)

DEC. 8. Casualties at Douglas due to Mexican rifle fire cause Governor Hunt to make strong appeal for more U. S. military aid. (3)

DEC. 10. Three batteries of field artillery are ordered to Naco by War Department. (3)

DEC. 11. Mexican bullets sing about the head of General Tasker H. Bliss as he inspects American defenses at Naco. Washington warns Mexican chieftains that unless firing into American territory ceases, U. S. will reply with artillery. (3)

DEC. 13. Governor Hunt rescues six men sentenced to die on the gallows. It is his last act before losing power to commute or reprieve. (3)

DEC. 15. Governor Hunt issues proclamation announcing newly created Board of Pardons and Parole is in operation. (3)

DEC. 15. Deputy sheriff of Pima County seizes $50,000 shipment of gold and silver bullion brought into the state illegally. (3)

DEC. 20. Rain falls in Phoenix for 72 consecutive hours, and reservoir behind Roosevelt Dam gains 40,000 acre feet flow in one day. (3)

DEC. 23. Swollen by week of rain the Santa Cruz River floods valley and runs one and one-half miles wide at Amado where destruction is heavy. (3)

DEC. 24. Arizona liquor dealers attack constitutionality of state prohibition in federal court. (3)

DEC. 26. Maricopa is flooded and miles of railway track are under water as floods continue. Eight hundred passengers are marooned on Southern Pacific trains. (3)

DEC. 31. Three hundred Arizona saloons do a rush business as they prepare to obey prohibition amendment and close at midnight. (2)

DEC. 31. Phoenix reports by wire: "The reservoir is filling rapidly; the Valley Bank is ready for business; the holding company has declared a 20 per cent dividend; the cattle and sheep ranges are in the best condition within the memory of man; the country is at peace; business is good, prosperity is at hand." (2)

DEC. 31. Reorganized Valley Bank opens on last day of the year. (3)

DEC. 31. Deposits in Arizona banks total $31,213,642. (27)
Total major metals production in Arizona, $59,956,029. (16)
Total number of cattle in Arizona, 1,300,000; value, $46,232,000. (24)
Town of Winkelman, Gila County, incorporated. (18)
City of Yuma, Yuma County, incorporated. (18)

1915 JAN. 2. Phoenix welcomes New Year with huge parade, celebration, and dollar dinner. (8)

JAN. 7. Federal court declares unconstitutional the new Arizona law making it illegal for employers to use more than 20 per cent alien labor on their payrolls. (8)

JAN. 11. Second regular session of state legislature convenes; establishes a state library, makes Sunday barbering illegal, and appropriates $17,000 for drilling artesian wells in Greenlee and Mohave Counties. (14)

JAN. 30. Prolonged rains bring floods which break holes in Arizona Canal. Cave Creek cuts hole in the Eastern and Consolidated canals. Gila rises seven feet at Florence. (3)

FEB. 1. Roosevelt Dam reports month-end storms add 180,000 acre feet of water to reservoir. (3)

FEB. 3. City of Casa Grande is incorporated.

FEB. 14. Supreme Court of Arizona upholds the new dry law. (3)

FEB. 15. Ground is broken in Nogales for a modern electric light and ice plant. (9)

FEB. 20. L. W. Mix. mayor of Nogales, takes lead in proposing that Governor Hunt appoint a committee to raise funds for a sterling silver service which will be a gift from the people of Arizona to the battleship named for the state. (9)

FEB. 25. Legislature completes joint resolution to Congress asking that all mines and mineral lands on Indian reservations be reopened to entry by the white man. (14)

MAR. 4. Bureau of Mines is established and placed under direction of Board of Regents by act of legislature. Senate joins House in asking Congress to build a barbed wire fence along the U.S.-Mexican border. (4)

MAR. 6. Legislature empowers superintendents of Indian agencies to issue marriage licenses and perform the marriage ceremony. (14)

MAR. 12. Constitutionality of new state Board of Pardons is upheld by Supreme Court. Deluge of applications for pardon follow. (3)

APRIL 2. Franklin K. Lane, Secretary of the Interior, makes survey of Roosevelt Dam and Salt River Valley and applauds spirit of the people. (3)

APRIL 6. Tucson City Council adopts ordinance which denies streets to jitneys. (3)

APRIL 15. First spillage over Roosevelt Dam draws thousands of Arizonans "as to Mecca the holy" for epochal celebration. Exodus from entire Salt River Valley. State offices closed. (3)

APRIL 16. Melting snows of White Mountains take out two dams on Little Colorado near St. Johns. Eight people are drowned. Damage over half a million dollars. (3)

APRIL 23. Two deputy sheriffs hang three Mexican prisoners near Greaterville in effort to force confessions in killing case. One dead, one dying, one missing. Deputies confined in Pima County jail without bail. (3)

APRIL 28. State Land Commission receives permission to sell 42,000 acres of land and use receipts to pay off railroad bonds issued by Maricopa, Pima, Yavapai, and Coconino Counties. (3)

MAY 1. Tucson lists municipal construction and private buildings to be completed in coming summer at total cost of $75,000. (3)

MAY 18. Casa Grande lets contracts for water and electric lights. (1)

MAY 24. Arizona and California celebrate opening of the new "Ocean to Ocean" Highway Bridge at Yuma. (1)

MAY 28. Board of Pardons reprieves sentences of five prisoners condemned to hang. (1)

JUNE 19. "With water and wine" Battleship *Arizona* is launched in N. Y. Navy Yard, christened with bottle of first water to flow over Roosevelt Dam, and champagne. Seventy thousand see ceremonies. Cost of ship: $13,000,000. (3)

JUNE 20. Nogales city council decrees that all business houses must close at 6 p.m. (9)

JULY 2. Aroused by efforts of Maricopa County to move University's agricultural college from Tucson to Tempe, Pima County citizens threaten a referendum seeking removal of the state capital from Phoenix to Bisbee, Douglas, or Globe. (2)

JULY 19. Executive Order 2222 modifies the boundaries of the Gila River Reservation. This final executive order laid the groundwork for modern tribal management of the 55,527-acre reservation. (17)

JULY 21. Tempe school trustees decide to segregate Mexican children in first three grades. (8)

JULY 25. U. S. Secretary of State asks Arizona to delay execution of five Mexicans at state penitentiary because of political situation in Mexico. Arizona agrees. (8)

JULY 29. Attempt is made to dynamite Miami reservoir. (8)

AUG. 11. State Land Commission files on lands of Fort Grant military preserve donated by U. S. government for a boys' school. (8)

AUG. 13. Stock company organizes at Los Angeles to hunt for the fabled buried treasure of Tumacacori. (8)

AUG. 27. Four passengers are killed and sixteen injured when Santa Fe, Prescott, and Phoenix train crashes through Date Creek Bridge. (8)

SEPT. 15. Town of Florence and state penitentiary are placed under heavy guard as rumor spreads that 300 Mexican troops are invading Arizona to rescue friends of the revolution from their cells. (3)

SEPT. 19. Sheriff takes over Clifton mines to protect them during strike. (3)

SEPT. 20. Supreme court upholds new eight-hour work-law for women, thus reversing verdict of lower court. (3)

OCT. 1. Governor Hunt threatens to call out troops if labor troubles at Clifton are not settled. (3)

OCT. 4. Mine managers at Clifton leave the camp and Governor Hunt orders in small detachment of state guard to aid sheriff in maintaining order among striking miners. (3)

OCT. 17. Food is distributed to 2300 miners' families in the Clifton-Metcalf-Morenci district as strike drags on. (3)

OCT. 21. University of Arizona students serving as members of the National Guard at Clifton are sent back to their studies. (3)

OCT. 28. U. S. Department of Labor orders probe into strike in the Clifton-Morenci mining district. (3)

NOV. 2. U. S. Supreme Court knocks out Arizona's alien labor law. Cook in a Bisbee restaurant is the complainant. (3)

NOV. 5. Aviatrix Katherine Stinson drops Arizona's first official air-mail letters near Tucson postoffice. (1)

NOV. 6. Million-dollar fire of unknown origin destroys Arizona Copper Company's new concentrator system at Clifton. (3)

NOV. 10. Arizona Supreme Court knocks out the sale of two per cent near beer. (2)

NOV. 18. Sheriff of Cochise county says that for every bottle of liquor seized by his force, a dozen bottles escape. (2)

NOV. 20. State Board of Trade is organized at Phoenix. Slogan is "I am for Arizona." (2)

NOV. 22. Executive order redefines the boundaries of the Colorado River Indian Reservation to correct an error in the original survey, resulting in a loss to the reservation of 13,440 acres. (17)

NOV. 26. Twelfth U. S. Infantry at Nogales, Arizona, under Colonel W. H. Sage, and Obregón forces seeking to drive Villa out of Nogales Sonora, engage in 30-minute small-arms battle across International line. Both commanders meet at line and apologize. (10)

NOV. 30. Political enemies of Governor Hunt launch organization to conduct statewide recall petitions. (3)

NOV. 30. Walnut Canyon National Monument established. (26)

DEC. 9. Preliminary survey for a Mt. Lemmon road begins in Pima County. (2)

DEC. 10. First execution since Hunt became governor takes place in Florence. Executed man had been reprieved three times. (2)

DEC. 10. One hundred and fifty striking miners hold up a freight and a passenger train three miles from Clifton in search of strike-breakers. (2)

DEC. 11. University of Arizona students build a gigantic letter "A" on Sentinel peak. (2)

DEC. 24. Federal court issues injunction restraining striking Clifton miners from interfering with Detroit Copper Co., which seeks to continue assessment work on its unpatented claims. (2)

DEC. 24. Phoenix Business Association opens campaign to sell Congress on the idea of buying land from Mexico on the Gulf of California so that Arizona may build a seaport. (2)

DEC. 28. Governor Hunt breaks silence on recall charges and says movement was started because he refused to order militia to shoot hungry men at Clifton. (2)

DEC. 31. Deposits in Arizona banks total $37,832,305. (27)
Total major metals production in Arizona, $90,806,349. (16)
Total number of cattle in Arizona, 1,450,000; value $51,167,000. (24)
City of Casa Grande, Pinal County, incorporated. (18)
City of Willcox, Cochise County, incorporated. (18)

1916 JAN. 3. Five feet of snow falls in Flagstaff, foils claim jumpers who ordinarily seize unimproved claims on New Year's Eve. (4)

JAN. 5. Sheriff Harry Wheeler of Cochise County admits that he cannot control bootlegging but is successful with robbery, arson, murder, and other felonies because the people now believe such offenses to be crimes. (4)

JAN. 6. Clifton strikers vote to sever affiliation with Western Federation. (4)

JAN. 19. Last rail of track is laid connecting New Cornelia mine at Ajo with the world markets. (4)

JAN 23. Four feet of water covers Yuma when levee breaks, and Colorado runs wild destroying 100 homes and business places. Residents forced to flee to high ground. (2)

JAN. 25. Long and costly strike of miners in the Globe-Morenci district is ended. New wage scale gives laborers $2.50 a day while miners get $3.41. (4)

FEB. 13. Arizona Supreme Court rules that liquor may be brought into the state for personal use. Court says the law does not make drinking illegal. (4)

MAR. 10. Following Villa's raid on Columbus, N.M., Douglas citizens form volunteer motor corps to hurry U. S. troops to any threatened spot. (4)

MAR. 21. Governor Hunt is ordered to bring the Arizona National Guard up to war strength. (4)

MAR. 26. Farmers of the Sulphur Springs Valley rejoice over the promise that the Douglas smelter will soon be rebuilt and no longer will kill crops and drench the land with poisonous fumes. (4)

MAR. 31. Despite recall movement, Governor Hunt announces he will be a candidate for renomination. (4)

APRIL 6. Phoenix Union High School and Globe High are first in the state to be accepted by the North Central Association of Accredited Schools and Colleges. (3)

APRIL 16. Federal Grand Jury indicts newspapers on charge that they carry paid advertising from mining interests as news matter. (3)

MAY 7. Yuma game warden reports that civil war in Mexico is scaring big game across the line into Yuma and Mohave mountains. (3)

MAY 9. Tucson motorists set a new record to Phoenix; make the trip in three hours and 35 minutes. (3)

MAY 10. Government orders out Arizona National Guard for service on the Mexican border. (3)

MAY 12. Salt River Valley cantaloupe growers plan a record-breaking crop of 900 carloads. (3)

MAY 16. Town of Pima is incorporated.

MAY 19. Arizona private citizens let contract for solid silver service to be presented to the battleship *Arizona*. Price approximately $8,000. (3)

JUNE 1. Mexico files suit in Tombstone for duties which it alleges were lost when Americans smuggled 3,500 head of cattle across the border. Amount involved is $35,000. (3)

JUNE 8. Pima County supervisors provide financial assistance for needy families of Tucson Guardsmen. (3)

JUNE 17. Hard-fought arguments over whether liquor may be imported for personal use of Arizonans end when railroads announce they will handle such shipments. (3)

JUNE 18. Elroy Irvine of Phoenix is first Arizona boy to graduate from West Point. (3)

JUNE 19. Sonora authorities seize Southern Pacific of Mexico and cut telegraph lines at Nogales. (3)

JUNE 20. Arizona National Guard regiment is mustered into federal service at Douglas. (3)

JUNE 22. U. S. Army troops on border are deployed in Santa Cruz valley between Nogales and Tucson to halt rumored Mexican cavalry thrust. Nothing happens. (3)

JUNE 23. Mayor of Nogales, Ariz., wires President Wilson asking that town be placed under martial law. No action follows. (3)

JUNE 24. Dixie National Forest in Mohave County is practically eliminated by executive order opening 22 townships of reserved land to entry and settlement. (3)

JUNE 27. Devasting forest fire rages in the National Forest Reserve, southwest of the San Francisco Peaks. Hundreds of acres of choice timber destroyed. (3)

JUNE 28. Organization of home guards holds its first drill in Phoenix. Will operate as police reserves. (3)

JUNE 29. First Arizona Chapter of American Red Cross is organized in Phoenix. (3)

JULY 1. Phoenix Red Cross harvests carload of fruit and melons to feed national guard units passing through city enroute to Mexican front. (3)

JULY 2. State Supreme Court holds old age and mothers' pension acts are invalid. (3)

JULY 3. Twelve hundred members of California militia reach Tucson, and city has difficulty setting up a commissary to feed them. (3)

JULY 5. U. S. Geological Survey reports that Arizona is producing copper at practically twice the rate of any other state. (3)

JULY 5. Eight thousand U. S. troops take up active duty on the Arizona border. (3)

JULY 11. Mexican military commander of Sonora holds conference with American mine owners and operators and assures protection if they will return to Mexico and resume operations. (3)

SEPT. 7. Robbers hold up Golden State Limited at Apache. (1)

SEPT. 10. Glendale and Phoenix flooded when Arizona, Grand, and Maricopa canals are breached by flood waters. (3)

SEPT. 22. Eugene Caruthers, 18, son of President of Yuma bank, shot and killed in pistol duel by Russell Johnson, prominent young Gila Bend cattleman. Bad blood over fences said to be cause. (3)

SEPT. 22. National Bureau of Education begins survey of Arizona schools. (3)

OCT. 3. Tucson women report to supervisors that Pima county jail, food, and accommodations are not fit for human beings. (2)

OCT. 17. Tucson Chamber of Commerce effort to abolish Papago Reservation fails. (2)

OCT. 19. University of Arizona receives gift of $60,000 for purchase of 36-inch reflecting telescope. (1)

OCT. 21. Theodore Roosevelt campaigns for Charles E. Hughes in Phoenix before a cheering audience of 8,000. (3)

OCT. 31. Federal officials uncover conspiracy in Nogales to sell arms to warring Mexicans. (1)

NOV. 5. Arizona Corporation Commission reports heavy buying of stocks as scores of new mining companies are incorporated. (1)

NOV. 5. Sixteen-year-old Zeckendorf-Steinfeld lawsuit originating in Tucson is finally settled by stipulation. (1)

NOV. 7. Thomas E. Campbell, Republican, is declared to have defeated G. W. P. Hunt, Democrat, for governor by 30 votes. (2)

NOV. 7. Electors adopt constitutional amendments providing for prohibition and eliminating death penalty from the penal code. (2)

NOV. 7. Santa Cruz deputies choose election day to raid "blind pigs" in Nogales area; fifteen resorts closed. (1)

DEC. 16. Governor Hunt's effort to contest the election of Thomas E. Campbell as governor is denied by Superior Court in Phoenix. (2)

DEC. 20. Two companies of infantry are sent to Ajo on representation that Villa bandits are menace. This relieves sheriff who has been busy arresting striking miners for disturbing the peace. (2)

DEC. 25. Tucson has a blizzard on Christmas Day. (2)

DEC. 27. Phoenix, Tucson, Douglas, and Bisbee plagued by intense cold weather and coal shortage. Demand for mesquite is heavy. (2)

DEC. 30. Thomas E. Campbell, Republican and G. W. P. Hunt, Democrat, take oaths of office as governor of Arizona. (2)

DEC. 31. Deposits in Arizona banks total $53,902,559. (27)

Total major metals production in Arizona, $190,806,170. (16)

Total number of cattle in Arizona, 1,650,000; value $63,310,000. (24)

1917 JAN. 3. Hunt refuses to vacate governor's office and Campbell opens temporary office at his home. State treasurer and state auditor say they will not honor checks signed by Campbell. (1, 3)

JAN. 3. New city council of Tucson holds first session and discovers it lacks funds to meet current bills. Decides to raise water rates 30 per cent. (1)

JAN. 3. City council of Bisbee makes it unlawful to have liquor on the person or in the home. (4)

JAN. 4. Arizona Press Club completes formal organization in Phoenix. (3)

JAN. 5. City of Douglas, suffering coal shortage, asks Arizona Corporation Commission to compel Santa Fe to stop confiscating its shipments at Gallup, N. M. (3)

JAN. 6. Tucson city council decides to sell municipally owned real estate to meet its overdrafts. (1)

JAN. 6. Riot staged by I.W.W. Mexicans carrying red flags in Ajo is subdued by sheriff and deputies. (1)

JAN. 9. State legislature approves present design of state flag, establishes minimum wage of $10 a week for women, and bans the public drinking cup and common towel. (1)

JAN. 13. State Legislature petitions Congress to abandon newly created Papago Indian Reservation of 3,100,000 acres in Pima, Pinal, and Maricopa Counties. (3)

JAN 23. Phoenix hotels and lodging houses agree to give credit to members of legislature until a governor is authorized to pay them their fees. (4)

JAN. 24. Revolt breaks out in the Arizona National Guard at Naco. Company M charged with parading up and down company street shouting that it wants to go home. (3)

JAN. 25. G. W. P. Hunt carries his fight to retain governorship into the Superior Court in Phoenix. (3)

JAN. 25. Attorney General rules that Arizona's dry law is valid. (4)

JAN 26. Postal authorities decide official mail for governor will be delivered to Sidney P. Osborn, secretary of state, until Superior Court decides issue. (3)

JAN. 27. American and Mexican troopers clash on border south of Arivaca. (1)

JAN. 27. Legislature's House Committee on Education disapproves of proposed Arizona flag on ground it resembles Japan's banner. House does not sustain objection. (1)

JAN. 27. Supreme Court declares Thomas E. Campbell to be Governor, de facto, of Arizona. (1)

JAN. 29. Hunt agrees to turn his office over to Campbell. (4)

JAN. 30. Superior Court sitting in the Hunt-Campbell trial rules that ballots marked as straight party vote and marked again opposite the name of opposition party candidate for governor are illegal. (3)

FEB. 3. State Senate (House not in session) sends official expression of confidence to President Wilson following severance of diplomatic relations with Germany (3)

FEB. 5. Arizona Red Cross Chapters are told to prepare for war efforts. (2)

FEB. 7. Publication of Superior Court rulings on disputed Hunt-Campbell ballots raises so much acrimonious discussion that Judge Stanford declares future rulings will be reserved until end of the contest. (3)

FEB. 13. Executive order reduces Papago reservation in Pima County by 475,000 acres. (2)

FEB. 28. Governor Campbell offers to raise troops of rough riders if U. S. enters World War. (1)

MAR. 2. Federal court sentences two robbers who held up Golden State Limited to 25 years. (1)

MAR. 9. Third Legislature passes anti-gambling redlight abatement bills at last minutes of session. (4)

MAR: 15. Overruling the national reclamation commission, Franklin K. Lane, Secretary of the Interior, rules that the Salt River Valley reclamation project is completed, that the Roosevelt Dam is part of the project and that the federal government should turn the completed job over to the Water Users Association. (3)

MAR. 15. State Attorney General rules that Arizona "blue sky" law, framed to prevent sale of questionable securities — especially mining stocks — is legal. (3)

MAR. 21. Copper Queen Consolidated Mining Co. changes its name to Phelps Dodge Corporation. (4)

MAR. 24. Recount of ballots in Hunt-Campbell election results in Douglas precinct number one being thrown out. Hunt loses 153 votes. (2)

MAR. 27. First Arizona Infantry ordered to continue in active service as border guard. (2)

MAR. 29. University of Arizona is advised that it will train reserve officers. (2)

MAR. 29. Phoenix reports last horse drawn cab in the city has been replaced by an automobile. (3)

MAR. 30. All officers of the Arizona guard regiment stationed on border sign pledge to drink no alcoholic liquors during their active service. (3)

APRIL 1. Seven thousand Tucson citizens march in loyalty parade and pledge allegiance to the flag. (2)

APRIL 4. Fire destroys all but two buildings in the mining town of Ajo. Citizens save phonograph from one store. It plays, "There'll Be a Hot Time in the Old Town Tonight," as buildings burn. (3)

APRIL 6. Board of Regents offers University buildings, grounds and plant to the Federal government and grants degrees to seniors who enlist before end of the academic year. (2)

APRIL 7. Fort Huachuca is made mobilization point for armed forces in Arizona. (2)

APRIL 13. Town of Florence turns on its first electric street lights. (3)

APRIL 19. Governor's State Council of Defense meets in Phoenix and appoints prominent citizens to 14 committees ranging from public defense and security to federal and interstate relations. (3)

APRIL 19. Phoenix stages Loyalty Rally on 142nd anniversary of the Battle of Lexington. Gov. Campbell rebukes young men of the state for their failure to enlist in the First Arizona Infantry and bring it up to war strength. (3)

APRIL 19. The term "Boches" appears in Tucson newspaper headlines. Heretofore the common term has been "Teutons." (2)

APRIL 21. Agricultural conference at U of A is startled when Dr. A. E. Vinson recommends slaughtering 25,000 burros and grinding meat up for bologna. (2)

MAY 22. Superior Court Judge R. C. Stanford rules that examination of the ballots shows Thomas E. Campbell defeated George W. P. Hunt for governor. Five month legal battle ends when court declares Campbell's majority is between 30 and 50 votes. (3)

MAY 3. First prisoner of war captured in Arizona is a Phoenix baker who is arrested on a Presidential Warrant. (3)

MAY 6. Mob of 50 citizens takes prisoner accused of murder and assault from deputy sheriffs in Maricopa County and lynch him in Pinal. Coroner's jury finds killer was "the victim of justifiable homicide committed by persons unknown to the jury." (2)

MAY 18. The Tucson *Citizen* reports that a group of 100 prominent men are informed that the city is under consideration as a site for an army cantonment of 30,000 men and says, "A greater, bigger, richer Tucson, grown overnight with a host of armed men tramping her streets and a golden stream of commerce filling her life rose as a picture." Descriptions of what the coming of such a body of men would make to the growth and prosperity of the city were reiterated on every side until a sobering speech from Federal Judge W. H. Sawtelle pointed out that the spirit of commercialism should be stilled in these days of war and that patriotism should be the paramount consideration. [Deming, N.M., got the cantonment.] (2)

MAY 24. International Union of Miners calls strike in the Jerome district. United Verde asks government to take over mine. (2)

MAY 25. Twenty-five picked non-coms from Arizona National Guard reach Presidio for officer training. (2)

MAY 29. Two United Verde mine employees are killed, a third man fatally wounded, as shots are fired in labor struggle at Jerome. (3)

MAY 30. Schoolhouse meetings of farmers are held throughout state to preach necessity for harvesting bumper crops of foodstuffs. (3)

JUNE 2. Food survey shows both seed and labor are short in the Salt River Valley. (3)

JUNE 5. Registration boards in Arizona are swamped as 34,814 young men register for military service. (3)

JUNE 5. Governor Campbell reports that strike troubles at the Jerome mines are over. (2)

JUNE 14. Flag Day is observed in Arizona communities; features drive for the Liberty Loan. (3)

JUNE 26. Metal Mine Workers Union calls strike in Bisbee an idles 1,000 workers in the great copper mines. (2)

JULY 2. Arizona supreme court upholds constitutionality of the employers' liability law. (3)

JULY 2. Miners go on strike, completing the tieup of the Clifton-Morenci-Metcalf district which normally produces eight million pounds of copper a month. (2)

JULY 5. Four troops of U. S. cavalry and one machine gun troop are withdrawn from the Mexican border and rushed to Globe. Governor Campbell report state authorities cannot control rising disorder among miners. (2)

JULY 6. International Workers of the World move into Arizona strike zones and seize leadership of striking miners. (2)

JULY 8. Egyptian Cotton Growers' Assn. in the Salt River Valley agrees to pay pickers 2½ cents a pound. (3)

JULY 11. Jerome drives out 63 mob leaders and sends them to Needles where armed citizens send them back to Arizona. (2)

JULY 12. Armed citizens of Bisbee, acting as deputy sheriffs, round up 1,100 local strikers, load them in freight cars and ship them into the New Mexico desert. (2)

JULY 13. Governor Campbell receives the following telegram from President Woodrow Wilson:

"Secretary of War has instructed General Parker to send officers to Arizona at once to report to him on conditions there with a view to cooperating in the maintenance of order.

"Meanwhile, may I not respectfully urge the great danger of citizens taking the law into their own hands as your report indicates their having done. I look upon such actions with grave apprehension. A very serious responsibility is assumed with which precedents are set." (3)

JULY 13. Washington notifies Arizona that its first quota for the national army will be 3,427 men. (2)

JULY 13. Tucson Citizen publishes list of producing mines of Arizona and gives detailed figures of their worth. Total value, according to Citizen, is one-third of a billion dollars. (2)

JULY 13. Adjutant General's department announces that 99 members of the Arizona National Guard regiment have deserted at Naco. (2)

JULY 14. U. S. Cavalry from Douglas escorts deported I.W.W. men to Columbus, N.M., where they are placed in detention camp under army orders. (2)

JULY 14. Live Stock Sanitary Board reports that it has 18,500 cattle brands on file at the State Capitol. (3)

JULY 17. With armed civilians guarding the roads to prevent return of deported I.W.W., Bisbee mines resume production. (2)

JULY 17. Executive order sets apart 125,000 acres in Arizona for Kaibab and other Indians now residing thereon and revokes departmental order of October 16, 1907. (17)

JULY 20. National lottery, with numbers drawn from a fishbowl in Washington selecting draftees to be called for army service, begins at 9:45 a.m. (2, 3)

JULY 22. Governor Campbell warns citizens of Globe that U. S. troops will resist efforts to deport I.W.W. strikers from that city. (4)

AUG. 1. Governor Campbell protests that Arizona's draft quota is unfair, being based on greatly overestimated population of state. (2)

AUG. 5. First Arizona Regiment is drafted into the United States Army. By the close of World War I, 8,113 men in Arizona had entered the National Guard, 1,854 were in the regular Army, 1,269 in the Navy and 147 in the Marine Corps. Three hundred and twenty-one died in service. (23)

AUG. 7. Globe's giant smelter, closed for five weeks by labor troubles, resumes production. (3)

AUG. 9. Pima County sheriff pours $20,000 worth of contraband liquor on the courthouse lawn. (2)

AUG. 12. Heavy rainstorm strikes Bisbee, flooding the gulches, smashing automobiles and homes and washing tons of rock and debris into business section. (3)

AUG. 15. Washington rules that men holding mining claims need do no assessment work while in military service. (3)

AUG. 28. Pima County draft board posts its first list of "slackers." It contains 194 names. (2)

SEPT. 6. Federal Marshall and deputies raid I.W.W. headquarters in Phoenix. (3)

SEPT. 9. First Arizona contingent of selective service men leave for Fort Riley. (2)

SEPT. 16. Bisbee cleans up remnants of I.W.W. troubles by arresting returning deportees for vagrancy and offering them choice between moving on or standing trial. (3)

SEPT. 21. Government pegs price of copper at 23½ cents and mines agree not to reduce wages or slow production. (3)

SEPT. 22. Nogales jail overflows with prisoners as draft dodgers from many states are trapped in this border city. (2)

SEPT. 29. Many Arizona merchants limit credit to 30 days. (2)

OCT. 1. Sheriff and four deputies face 250 striking Mexicans enroute from Morenci to Clifton and break up their invasion. (3)

OCT. 5. Presidential commission arrives in Arizona to spend two weeks studying labor situation. Wm. B. Wilson, secretary of labor, heads the inquiry. (3)

OCT. 5. Main building of Sisters' Hospital burns in Phoenix. All patients are saved. (3)

OCT. 10. Globe-Miami miners place labor dispute in hands of the President's Labor Commission. (3)

OCT. 19. Pima County is first in the nation to oversubscribe Liberty Bond allotment. (2)

OCT. 20. Attorneys for G.W.P. Hunt, former governor, attempt to establish rules for a rehearing of the Hunt-Campbell election contest before the Supreme Court. (3)

OCT. 22. Secretary Wilson announces that the Globe-Miami strike is over. Further strikes barred for period of the war. (3)

OCT. 25. Arizona cities hold Liberty Day parades in great drive to put over the second Liberty Loan — "The loan which will end the Kaiser." Arizona exceeds its quota. (3)

OCT. 29. Arizona joins national food pledge drive. Forty thousand state families asked to sign promises to save food. (3)

NOV. 1. First four days of pledge card drive show 8,500 Arizona housewives signed promise to conserve food. Tucson leads with 2,300. (3)

NOV. 7. U. S. Council of defense report shows 491,867 acres of land under cultivation in Arizona. Maricopa County has more than half of this with 266,362 acres. Yuma is second with 35,234 and Cochise third with 30,931. (3)

NOV. 8. Federal administrator is appointed for the duration of the war in the Warren district over the protest of the mine owners who object to regulation of its relations with workers. (3)

NOV. 9. Tucson and Pima County lawmen sweep up 15 bootleggers and huge caches of forbidden liquor in swift operation. (2)

NOV. 10. Arizona Council of Defense completes crop survey and plans for expansion of production through distribution of state crops on a percentage basis. (3)

NOV. 12. Stage line operating between Phoenix and Mesa gets permission to advance round trip fare from one dollar to $1.25. (3)

NOV. 17. Dr. R. B. von KleinSmid, president of the University of Arizona, is elected first president of the League of the Southwest. (3)

NOV. 20. First appearance of the term "Hun" noted in the Arizona press. (2)

NOV. 22. Advisory boards being named in every Arizona community to aid drafted men who need legal help. (3)

NOV. 24. President Wilson's Special Labor Commission, appointed to investigate Bisbee deportations, denounces heads of mines and Bisbee citizens, and says act "was wholly illegal and without authority in law, either state or federal." (3)

NOV. 25. Arizona Cattle Growers Assn. asks State Food Administration to take over handling of all cattle feed stuffs to insure fair prices and equitable distribution. (3)

NOV. 26. Washington informs Arizona that hereafter Tuesday will be "meatless day" and Wednesday will be "wheatless." (3)

NOV. 29. Arizona Council of Defense and U. S. Food Administration tell growers that Arizona wheat crop is not large enough to feed the people of the state and that there should be a fifty percent increase in acreage. (3)

NOV. 30. Phoenix citizens "go over the top" in providing Christmas gifts for men in service. (3)

DEC. 1. U. S. Food Administration charges that Arizona is a "sugar slacker" and must trim consumption at once. (3)

DEC. 4. Department of the Interior returns 27,700 acres of grazing lands in the Monzano National Forest in Arizona to the public domain. (3)

DEC. 7. Fifty-six of Arizona's 300 doctors and surgeons reported as serving as officers in the National Army. (3)

DEC. 7. Federal Food Administrator for Arizona rules that hotels and restaurants using 10 barrels of flour a month must have a federal license. (3)

DEC. 11. Arizona Red Cross sends 100 warm woolen outfits to Arizona soldiers training without proper clothing in below zero temperatures at Camp Funston. (3)

DEC. 14. Arizona's three superior court judges decide that confiscated liquor must be turned over to Red Cross for redistillation, thus saving alcohol for hospital purposes. (3)

DEC. 18. Governor Campbell urges Cato Sells, commissioner of Indian Affairs, to grant plea of Arizona cattlemen and open the ranges of Indian reservations. Claims drought has swept other ranges clean. (3)

DEC. 19. Stirred by incendiary fires which destroy hay fields of Salt River Valley and by two attempts to burn new Phoenix Y.M.C.A. building, Governor Campbell offers $250 reward for perpetrators of such acts. (3)

DEC. 22. Supreme court reverses the verdict of the trial court and declares G. W. P. Hunt was legally elected governor. Campbell served 11 months and three weeks. (3)

DEC. 25. Governor Campbell turns back his office to Governor Hunt on Christmas morning. (2)

DEC. 31. Deposits in Arizona banks total $60,832,283. (27)
Total major metals production in Arizona, $209,393,802. (16)
Total number of cattle in Arizona, 1,750,000; value $72,521,000. (24)
Town of Holbrook, Navajo County, incorporated. (18)

1918 JAN. 8. Former Governor Campbell appeals to the supreme court for a rehearing of the gubernatorial contest. (2)

JAN. 19. Governor Hunt appoints H. A. McCloskey, organizer for the Western Federation of Miners, to fill vacancy on the University of Arizona Board of Regents. (2)

FEB. 3. Warned by Washington that the U. S. must save food if it is to win the war. Arizona flour mills begin making barley and corn flour to conserve wheat. (3)

FEB. 13. Fifty-five percent of Arizona schools show 100 percent enrollment of school children in the Junior Red Cross. (1)

FEB. 14. Board of army officers surveys Tucson and suggests that prostitution be wiped out. (1)

FEB. 16. Health officers close all public places in Globe when smallpox develops. (1)

MAR. 5. Town of Miami is incorporated.

APRIL 1. Arizona goes on new national wheat saving diet; one and one-half pounds a week to each person. (3)

APRIL 2. Maricopa County supervisors decide convicted bootleggers must work out their sentences on county roads. (3)

APRIL 11. Arizona farmers release 800,000 pounds of wheat at the request of Herbert Hoover. (3)

APRIL 13. Federal Food Administrator closes store of Willcox merchant who sells wheat flour disguised in barley sacks. (3)

APRIL 19. William G. M'Adoo visits Arizona and appeals to the people to support Third Liberty Bond drive. (3)

APRIL 21. Mesa is the first city in Arizona to sell its quota of Third Liberty Bonds. (3)

MAY 6. Government announces that it will cancel summer tourist rates to the coast and to northern resort spots. Arizona Corporation Commission files immediate objection. Says state's summers are so hot people must find relief. (3)

MAY 10. Radical "blacklist law" passed by First State Legislature is declared unconstitutional by Superior Court of Gila County. (3)

MAY 21. Third State Legislature meets in special session; defines sabotage and sets up penalties for same; makes it illegal to "aid, comfort or employ" slackers or deserters from military service. (3)

MAY 24. State Legislature completes resolution ratifying proposed prohibition amendment to the Constitution of the U. S. (14)

MAY 28. Matthew Rivers, a Pima Indian, is killed at Catigny, France. He is the first Arizonan to die in World War I. (23)

JUNE 1. Statewide classes in canning and drying vegetables scheduled. (3)

JUNE 9. Cattlemen are still settling arguments with guns. Three Maricopa pioneers fight over a calf. Two die. (3)

JUNE 19. Arizona families face sugar rationing and one delivery a day from food stores. (3)

JUNE 20. Office of Dairy Commissioner created with powers over dairy and creamery industries. (14)

JUNE 21. Harry Wheeler, former sheriff of Cochise County, and John C. Greenway of Phelps-Dodge Co., are indicted in connection with deportation of Bisbee miners. Both are overseas. (3)

JUNE 23. State Tax Commission reports that decrease in production of copper, due to strikes, cuts Arizona tax revenues $1,000,000. (1)

JUNE 29. German-born foreman of a Tucson dairy is indicted on charges of disloyalty and espionage. Federal court convicts him and judge sentences him to two years for saying U. S. will lose the war and Liberty bonds will be worthless. (1)

JULY 7. Suits for damages totaling $3,000,000 are filed against Arizona copper companies by 160 Bisbee deportees. (1)

JULY 11. Arizona copper mines raise all mining, milling and smelting wages 50 cents a day. (1)

AUG. 2. Prescott lawyers offer to defend, free of charge, all mining operators in their district being sued by I.W.W. deportees. (1)

AUG. 10. American Mining Congress reports that Arizona copper mines set new record by producing nearly 77,000,000 pounds during month of July. (1)

AUG. 17. U. of A. campus is declared to be military establishment and prostitution and gambling are outlawed within a ten mile zone. (1)

AUG. 20. U. S. Employment Service in Arizona receives urgent request to furnish unskilled labor for war work. (1)

AUG. 25. Tucson has no difficulty in raising fund to buy wrist watches for men leaving for service. (1)

AUG. 28. Comparatively quiet conditions at the Nogales border explode into a battle in which two Americans are killed and 20 wounded. Mexican government expresses regret. (1)

SEPT. 12. Tucson's mayor declares a holiday and business houses close as 5,000 Pima County men register for national army. (1)

SEPT. 13. One cent a pound profit is allowed on sugar sold in Arizona. (1)

SEPT. 14. Thirty-three of the principal cities and towns of Arizona organize fair price boards. (1)

OCT. 3. Deadly "Spanish influenza" epidemic which swept the East reaches Arizona. Many cities report deaths. Theaters and schools are closed. University is quarantined for two weeks. (1)

OCT. 4. Ranges of Southern Arizona are dry and stockmen report cattle are starving. (1)

OCT. 18. Phoenix opens an emergency hospital to care for growing number of influenza sufferers. Appeal is made for Spanish speaking volunteers. Nurses, bedding and clothing needed. (3)

OCT. 20. Arizona meets its quota of Fourth Liberty Bonds. (3)

OCT. 31. Acting on advice of State Health Department the State Fair Commission cancels plans for annual fair. Entire state in grip of influenza epidemic. (3)

NOV. 5. Thomas E. Campbell is first Republican elected governor of Arizona. Carl Hayden is returned to Congress. (1)

NOV. 8. Phoenix Chapter of the Red Cross issues desperate appeal for nurses and workers as number of influenza cases soar and deaths mount. (3)

NOV. 11. All Arizona goes made with joy as the word comes that Germany has capitulated to demands of the Allies and World War I is over. (3)

NOV. 11. Their classes suspended because of influenza, Phoenix high school scholars study by mail. (3)

NOV. 13. State councils of defense are notified by Washington that ban against non-war types of construction is lifted. (3)

NOV. 21. Relief is in sight for sorely pressed cattlemen of the Southwest when government cuts freight rate on feed. (1)

NOV. 22. Tucson authorities order face masks worn in public by all citizens. (1)

NOV. 22. After concealing statistics on the influenza epidemic from its beginning, committee of Phoenix citizens and doctors decide to make full reports daily. (3)

NOV. 26. Phoenix citizens are warned not to appear on the streets or in public places unless wearing a face mask. City has more than 600 cases of influenza. (3)

NOV. 30. Phoenix police arrest citizens who fail to wear masks on the street. (3)

DEC. 9. Citizens of Mesa agitate for separation from Maricopa County. Would take in Chandler, Gilbert, Egypt and Tempe. (1)

DEC. 14. Nogales reports 500 cases of influenza. (3)

DEC. 15. The 158th (Arizona) Infantry is chosen as the guard of honor for President Wilson while he attends peace conference in Paris. (1)

DEC. 17. Tucson police arrest scores of citizens who fail to wear flu masks as prescribed by city ordinance. High school is ordered closed. (1)

DEC. 24. Superior court rules that Tucson's flu mask ordinance is illegal. (1)

DEC. 31. Tucson and Phoenix reopen public schools. (1,3)

DEC. 31. Deposits in Arizona banks total $64,643,964. (27)
Total major metals production in Arizona, $202,134,880. (16)
Total number of cattle in Arizona, 1,645,000; value, $73,071,000. (24)
Town of Somerton, Yuma County, incorporated. (18)

1919 JAN 1. Phoenix opens the year with a drive to collect clothing for suffering Belgians. (3)

JAN. 6. Thomas E. Campbell is sworn in as Governor Hunt does the unexpected and introduces his rival. (1)

JAN. 7. Governor Campbell closes state offices and orders all flags at half mast to mark death of Theodore Roosevelt. (3)

JAN. 7. Senator Henry F. Ashurst of Arizona carries fight to the floor of the senate in support of his resolution recommending that U. S. purchase Baja California. Mexico is silent. (3)

JAN. 8. Phoenix newspaper exposes spread of influenza; 200 cases in 2 days. (3)

JAN. 8. Sabotage closes mill of Old Dominion and Arizona Commercial mine at Globe and throws 1,500 men out of work. (3)

JAN. 9. Tucson reports no new cases of influenza for a week but Phoenix admits epidemic is growing and closes schools again. (1)

JAN. 10. Phoenix reports 700 cases of influenza; Tucson continues to minimize situation. (3)

JAN. 13. Fourth State Legislature meets. Sets up a State Water Commission, makes fraudulent advertising illegal, and passes joint resolution expressing confidence in President Wilson. (4)

JAN. 21. By joint resolution State Legislature requests Congress to pass National Woman Suffrage amendment. (14)

JAN. 28. Five hundred advocates of good roads from all sections of the state meet in Phoenix and demand action. (3)

JAN. 29. Lower house of legislature defeats measure providing minimum pay of $20 a week for women. (1)

FEB. 1. By joint memorial, Legislature urges Congress to buy State of Lower California, Coronado Islands and 10,000 square miles in the State of Sonora from Mexico. (14)

FEB. 4. Protests flood Governor's office when public learns Utah wants to buy Arizona territory north of the Grand Canyon. (1)

FEB. 6. State legislature goes on record as supporting self-determination for Ireland. (1)

FEB. 6. General Enoch H. Crowder, provo marshal general and head of the selective service system in World War I, reports that Arizona and Rhode Island men led the nation in physical fitness. (3)

FEB. 6. Governor Campbell reports to the legislature that an audit shows every state fund is bankrupt except that of the University. (1)

FEB. 7. Copper, pegged at 26 cents during the war, drops to 18⅜ cents a pound. Jerome mines announce 75 cent wage cut but rescind order before it takes effect. (1)

FEB. 10. Phoenix holds memorial services in three churches to honor memory of Theodore Roosevelt. (3)

FEB. 13. Jerome mines close when continued I.W.W. agitation results in walkouts. Federal agents arrest seven men. (1)

FEB. 15. Union of Mine, Mill and Smelter workers is told in Phoenix meeting that market is glutted with a billion pounds of copper, produced for war use, and the industry faces grave crisis. (1)

FEB. 16. Legislature passes measure which wipes out 10,000 obsolete cattle brands. (1)

FEB. 17. State Senate votes to appropriate $5,000 for Arizona troops as they land in New York. House concurs.

FEB. 19. With the state deep in the post war depression, legislature slashes the budget. University barely stays alive. (1)

MAR. 5. Publishers of Arizona daily papers meet in Tucson and form State organization. (3)

MAR. 11. Governor Campbell vetoes legislative act providing bonus of $10,000 for first owners to bring in an Arizona oil well. Legislature overrides the veto. (1)

MAR. 12. Federal Reserve reveals that women sold 45 percent of the Liberty Bonds purchased in Arizona. (1)

MAR. 16. Five Douglas business men and one woman are sentenced to two years imprisonment and fines of $10,000 each for smuggling $100,000 worth of Mexican whiskey into Arizona. (3)

MAR. 17. Arizona Resources Board created by the Legislature is approved by the Governor. (14)

MAR. 20. State Legislature provides for establishment and maintenance of kindergartens in connection with elementary schools. (14)

MAR. 23. Last piece of furniture in the last draft board office is sold and Arizona wires Washington that the job is finished. (3)

MAR. 25. Legislature passes joint resolution approving of League of Nations. (14)

MAR. 25. Governor Campbell vetoes bill providing for the reading of the Bible in public schools. (3)

MAR. 26. Legislature appropriates $100,000 to co-operate with U. S. Dept. of Interior on surveys and preliminary studies for construction of storage or diversion dams, etc., to increase productivity of the land. (14)

APRIL 11. State Corporation Commission cancels permits of Arizona companies which unload oil stocks without submitting financial reports of their condition. (2)

APRIL 19. Plant of Union Oil Co. in Phoenix is destroyed by $100,000 fire. (3)

APRIL 21. State Prison, Pioneers' Home and State Hospital for the Insane are without funds. Governor orders emergency drafts. (2)

MAY 4. Eight high school teachers in Tucson, including the principal, resign in a body as a protest against attempt by Superintendent F. A. Nims to embroil them in school bond election. (2)

MAY 4. Tucson boys from "Arizona's Own," the 158th Infantry, reach home from France. (1)

MAY 9. Phoenix, Yuma and Tucson officially designated as government landing fields on transcontinental air route. (2)

MAY 14. Arizona keeps her Liberty Loan record bright and oversubscribes the Fifth Loan. (3)

MAY 16. Four Arizona copper companies fail to pay regular dividends. (2)

MAY 17. Gambling in oil stocks booms. Newspapers carry glowing promises of rich wells being sunk in Arizona, and full page advertisements excite the gullible from Benson to Holbrook and from Yuma to Tucson. (2)

MAY 17. Maricopa County votes $4,000,000 bond issue for good roads and a week later defeats $700,000 bond issue for new high school buildings. (3)

MAY 23. Secretary of the Arizona Livestock Sanitary Board reports that Cochise County swarms with cattle rustlers. (2)

MAY 24. Advertising and promotion of doubtful oil stock in Arizona and Texas reaches such a point that Governor demands State Corporation Commission do its duty. Commission refers him to the attorney general and district attorneys. (2)

MAY 25. Twelve hundred Arizona men from the 89th Division land in New York and are royally entertained. (3)

JUNE 16. G. W. P. Hunt, long time governor of Arizona, starts for Bangkok where he will serve as U. S. minister to Siam. (2)

JULY 1. State Tax Commission places valuation of railroads for assessment purposes at $100,000,000. (1)

JULY 3. Race riot erupts in Bisbee's Brewery Gulch between Negroes of 10th U. S. Cavalry and Bisbee police. Three are shot. (1)

JULY 11. Returned veterans organize state unit of the American Legion in Tucson. (1)

JULY 11. Five million dollars in damage suits are filed by 272 men deported from Bisbee. (3)

JULY 12. Abnormally rapid ripening conditions ruin 700 carloads of cantaloupes in the Salt River Valley. (3)

JULY 14. City of Globe is swept by flood which puts main street two feet under water. Property damage estimated at $100,000. (1)

JULY 22. Two hundred and fifty Bisbee and Douglas citizens are arrested on charges of "kidnapping" in connection with the Bisbee deportation. All are released on bond. (1)

JULY 26. Tucson is first western city to donate land for aviation field to war department. Gift covers 82 acres on South Sixth Ave. (1)

AUG. 10. First government action to check high cost of living in state comes to Arizona when U. S. Attorney General sends agents to check prices asked by Tucson wholesalers. (1)

AUG. 12. Two thousand citizens of the Casa Grande Valley attend mass meeting in Florence and pledge $50,000 to finance campaign for San Carlos Dam. (1)

AUG. 14. Arizona Attorney General orders county attorneys to gather evidence and prosecute merchants and wholesalers who set high prices on food in defiance of anti-trust laws. (1)

AUG. 15. National and state attack on high food prices begins in earnest in Arizona. U. S. Agents and district attorneys meet in Phoenix and formulate plans. (1)

AUG. 16. Governor Campbell urges conference of western governors to adopt a plan for jailing profiteers, seizing their foodstuffs, and then worrying about convictions. (1)

AUG. 18. Tucson city council offers to take orders from citizens for government surplus foodstuffs. Carload of food is sold in three days. (1)

AUG. 25. Preliminary hearings of 200 Bisbee citizens on charge of kidnapping are moved to Douglas theater and Bisbeeites board special train at noon each day to attend afternoon court. Train is called "Deportation Special No. 2."

AUG. 25. Government surplus army foods go on sale at the Chamber of Commerce in Tucson. (1)

AUG. 26. Commanding officer of the 25th Infantry charges Nogales merchants with "outrageous profiteering"; says the Town Council "passes the buck" and the Chamber of Commerce ignores his letters of protest. Result is that he buys outside the city and puts Nogales off limits for two days. (1)

AUG. 30. Tucson opens public market for farm products in San Augustine Plaza and buyers clean it out in three hours. (1)

SEPT. 9. Two hundred Bisbee citizens charged with kidnapping, waive further examination at Douglas and ask to be bound over for trial in Superior Court. (1)

SEPT. 16. Harry C. Wheeler, former sheriff of Cochise county, insists on being bound over for trial on kidnapping charge and claims he alone was responsible for deportation of I.W.W. at Bisbee. (1)

SEPT. 20. Charging Swift & Co. with hoarding canned food stuffs, United States Marshals seize company storehouses at Bowie and Douglas. (1)

SEPT. 21. U. S. postoffice in Phoenix discontinues selling government surplus food when sales drop as low as $10 a day. (3)

OCT. 4. Representatives of all industries meet in Phoenix to consider means of halting decline of the dairy industry due to increasing cotton acreage. State Dairy Commissioner reports production of milk and butter in Salt River Valley does not meet local demands. (3)

OCT. 14. Bisbee reports selling eight carloads of surplus army food in successful attack on the high cost of living. American Legion sparks move. (3)

OCT. 14. U. S. Department of Justice Agents make six arrests in Globe in campaign to wipe out dope ring operating from Nogales. (1)

OCT. 23. University of Arizona professors warn farmers to rotate their crops and not to abandon dairying. (1)

OCT. 23. Tucson places cigar boxes at street corners as depositories for contributions to Theodore Roosevelt Memorial Fund and Colonel James H. McClintock, noted historian, blasts city for "undignified methods." (1)

OCT. 30. Arizona State Federation of Labor endorses nation-wide coal strike and wires President Wilson not to use troops. (1)

NOV. 2. Thirty-seven autos start road race from El Paso to Phoenix and 16 reach Bisbee. Six cars finish in Phoenix. (3)

NOV. 6. R. B. Von KleinSmid, president of the University of Arizona, tells Phoenix Teachers' Institute there would be more teachers if they were paid on a 12-month schedule. (1)

NOV. 11. Department of Justice special agents open drive on Globe's moonshining industry; issue 115 warrants and seize 10,000 gallons of moonshine. (1)

NOV. 12. Federal Judge W. H. Sawtelle tells Arizona, "I'm going to stop private distilling if I have to fill the penitentiary." (1)

NOV. 18. U. S. Department of Agriculture foresees Arizona cotton production for the year at 46,000 bales of Egyptian and 24,000 bales of short staple. (2)

NOV. 22. Phoenix citizens meet and form organization to "combat radicalism in Arizona." Tucson follows action the next day. (1)

NOV. 26. Calumet & Arizona Mining Co. at Douglas follows general movement among copper companies of U. S. and cuts production 50 per cent. (1)

NOV. 29. Heavy floods sweep down the Hassayampa and Verde Rivers. Fourteen foot head of water passes Jerome. (1)

DEC. 6. Federal Fair Price Commissioner wants to know just what profits Tucson merchants consider fair. (1)

DEC. 15. U. S. Marshal captures 8,000 gallons of wine in Globe district and pours the supply into Pinal Creek. (1)

DEC. 20. State Tax commission reports Arizona mines produced $174,529,388 in 1919. (1)

DEC. 27. Phoenix experiments with a municipally operated store selling government blankets, underwear, beans and corned beef, in attempt to combat high cost of living. (3)

DEC. 27. Historian James H. McClintock reveals that the East-West Arizona border is one mile out of true North and South order. (1)

DEC. 28. City Building Inspector of Phoenix shows building permits for 1919 totalled $3,000,000; Tucson City Engineering Department puts its figure at $1,040,000. (1, 3)

DEC. 29. Fire breaks out in 96th Aero Squadron camp at Douglas and 250 aerial bombs explode causing $100,00 damage. (1)

DEC. 31. Deposits in Arizona banks total $84,379,087. (27)
Total major metals production in Arizona, $111,157,872. (16)
Total number of cattle in Arizona, 1,620,000; value $68,040,000. (24)

1920 JAN 1. Government report on Arizona crops of 1919 places total for everything except livestock — which is at low ebb — at $61,758,000. This is a gain of $20,000,000 over 1918. (1)

JAN. 2. 1919 saw the peak of the cotton boom that started in 1917. Prices went as high as $625 a bale for Pima long staple resulting in a tripling of cotton acreage. At year's end three fourths of the irrigated land in the Salt River Valley was in cotton. (21)

JAN. 10. Superior Court in Maricopa County upholds the law which makes it illegal for cattlemen to obtain more than one section of land by renting additional sections from relatives and employees. (1)

JAN. 16. Arrival of vagrants for the winter season drives Phoenix City Council to organize a chain gang. (3)

JAN. 20. Phoenix welcomes General John J. Pershing. He visits the Salt River Valley, proceeds to Tucson where he dedicates a memorial fountain for university students who died in World War I, then proceeds to Douglas where he lauds Bisbee deportation as a necessary act of war. (1, 3)

JAN. 20. Four hundred Arizonans from all parts of State attend "Farmers' Week" at University of Arizona. (1)

JAN. 21. Two hundred and ten defendants, including millionaire mine owners, shift bosses, deputy sheriffs and plain citizens plead "not guilty" to Bisbee kidnapping when case opens in Superior Court at Tombstone. (1)

JAN. 22. Phoenix *Republican* tries, with news stories, to stop the menace of what it calls "one crop economy" in the Salt River Valley. (3)

JAN. 23. Tucson Luncheon Club is told that many citizens who failed to co-operate with government census takers would be jailed as slackers except for the fact the city does not have enough cells. Phoenix has similar trouble. (1, 3)

JAN. 29. State Board of Health reports that careless physicians and parents fail to register births of babies. (3)

FEB. 3. University of Arizona enrollment passes the thousand mark for the first time when 1,046 students enter second semester. (1)

FEB. 7. "Kidnapping" trials in Tombstone recessed. County attorney announces he will try only ringleaders of Bisbee deportations. (1)

FEB. 8. Health department announces that influenza has hit Tucson again and says an epidemic cannot be avoided if public refuses to report cases in their families. (1)

FEB. 11. Last of the military guards on the international line at Nogales are withdrawn. Army reports cordial relations between the two cities. (1)

FEB. 12. Fourth State Legislature holds one-day special session and votes to ratify 19th amendment to U. S. Constitution establishing women's suffrage. (3)

FEB. 13. Women's Board of Home Missions of Presbyterian Church gives $125,000 for additional school buildings at Ganado. (3)

FEB. 17. With Roosevelt Lake filled to the brim, first drops trickle over the spillway at 2 a.m. Engineers report 1,370,000 acre feet of water behind the Dam. (3)

FEB. 17. City of Chandler is incorporated.

FEB. 18. Phoenix casts an overwhelming vote in favor of a $50,000 bond issue for new high schools. (3)

FEB. 19. Heavily armed robbers enter Camp Verde bank and leave with $1,000 and the cashier. Posses take to the trails. (1)

FEB. 20. Dr. A. J. Chandler is elected the first mayor of the city he founded. (3)

FEB. 21. Despite appalling shortage of good roads, Arizona stands ninth in per capita ownership of automobiles of the nation. (1)

FEB. 26. After spending four weeks drawing a jury, the state and defense announce they are satisfied and Bisbee deportation trial opens at Tombstone. (1)

MAR. 2. Bisbee deportation trial is again delayed at Tombstone when a juryman discovers he has formed a strong opinion and is dismissed. A new panel is drawn, bringing the number summoned to 2,500. (1)

MAR. 3. Tempe bridge is declared dangerous and closed to the public, after a 6¼ inch sag develops. (3)

MAR. 4. Juror asks to be excused from sitting in deportation case, returns to ranch, writes note asking that his family be left in peace, and shoots himself. (1)

MAR. 5. Jury box at the Bisbee deportation case is again filled. (1)

MAR. 6. U. S. Senate sub-committee begins inquiry into border troubles between U. S. and Mexico but bars the press. Harry C. Wheeler, former Cochise sheriff, on the stand. (1)

MAR. 6. Senator Albert B. Fall charges publicly that businessmen of Nogales, Ariz., are afraid to testify against Mexicans. Chairman of Nogales Chamber of Commerce and Young Men's Business Club resent the charge and are promptly subpoenaed. (1)

MAR. 9. The Bisbee deportation case — actually the trial of H. E. Wooten, one of the defendants — finally opens in Tombstone. Future legal action depends on outcome of this trial. (1)

MAR. 9. Phoenix joins Tucson in drive for the open shop and holds mass meeting. One thousand citizens attend, 200 of whom try to break up the gathering by creating disturbance. (3)

MAR. 12. Defense in the Wooten case develops the argument that deportation was a necessary act of patriotism and that the community had a right to protect itself. (1)

MAR. 19. Phoenix spends $844,000 on redwood pipe to bring water from the Verde River. (3)

MAR. 20. Urging home vegetable gardens, Phoenix Chamber of Commerce says yield in vegetables and small fruits in Salt River Valley 40 percent below 1919. (3)

MAR. 24. Phoenix cavalry unit is mustered in and made Troop A of the National Guard. (3)

MAR. 24. Judge Samuel L. Pattee, sitting in the Wooten case, makes important ruling; says in effect that when a people have called on state and federal authorities for protection in vain, they have a right to protect themselves. This becomes known as "The law of necessity." (1)

MAR. 29. Capt. Harry C. Wheeler, sheriff of Cochise County at time of Bisbee deportations, testifies that patriotism and necessity of forestalling bloodshed on Bisbee streets justified kidnapping of I.W.W. Takes full responsibility. (1)

MAR. 31. Salaries in Phoenix schools are raised. Instructors in five first grades are paid $1,125 in first year. Teachers in upper grades are paid $1,250. Salaries are paid in nine installments and in state warrants. (3)

APRIL 6. Mexican strikers abandon freight train loaded with tomatoes 25 miles south of Nogales and every truck in the twin towns is requisitioned to salvage the freight and unload it in Nogales, USA. (1)

APRIL 8. Arizona Livestock Commission warns that stockmen face loss of a million dollars unless malady known as "blackleg" can be wiped out promptly. (3)

APRIL 10. Arizona views with mixed emotions the revolution of the State of Sonora against the corrupt Republic of Mexico. (1)

APRIL 11. Governor Campbell announces that he has appealed to seven western state legislatures to contribute funds for an educational campaign on Colorado River basin project. (1)

APRIL 11. Confident of a big year, Salt River Valley growers refuse $1.20 a pound for 101 bales of long staple cotton. (3)

APRIL 13. Hundreds of head of cattle are rushed out of Sonora to Douglas because of growing fear of battles between forces of Republic of Sonora and Mexican Federal Government. (1)

APRIL 14. Delegates attending district meeting of State Women's Clubs in Phoenix have hot words over medical inspection of students in public schools. Opponents say it is "Unamerican." (1)

APRIL 19. City of Douglas relieved when U. S. refuses Mexico's request for Federal troops to cross American border in campaign against Sonora forces. (1)

APRIL 20. Gasoline famine grows so acute in Arizona that many stations close. (3)

APRIL 30. Grand Canyon National Park dedicated. (3)

APRIL 30. Superior Court jury in Tombstone acquits H. E. Wooten, key defendant in Bisbee deportation case, on the first ballot. (1)

MAY 1. President von KleinSmid of the University is fined $10 in Tucson for speeding. (2)

MAY 5. Pima and Pinal Counties accept bids for new highway from Tucson to Casa Grande. (2)

MAY 8. Huge supply of machine gun ammunition, destined for Mexican revolutionists, is shipped from Tucson to Nogales in coffins but is tracked to undertaking parlor and seized by U. S. Marshal. (2)

MAY 10. Cochise County officials estimate that county paid $90,000 in legal fees in Bisbee deportation trials and hearings. (1)

MAY 10. Political enemies reveal that Mulford Winsor, former secretary to Governor Hunt, is conducting mail campaign for Democratic nomination for governor on official letterhead of the State. (2)

MAY 12. Maricopa signs record-breaking $4,500,000 contract for good roads. (3)

MAY 13. Tucson hurls charge that Phoenix is holding up its census figures — with assistance of Senator Ashurst — until it can discover how many "additional uncounted residents" must be reported to put city ahead of Tucson. (2)

MAY 18. Farmers ask city council of Tucson to establish hitching posts on South Sixth Ave. (2)

MAY 20. Phoenix Chamber of Commerce decides to accept reports of the census takers. Its population is 29,052. (2)

MAY 23. Tucson joins Sisters of St. Joseph in celebrating 50th anniversary of their arrival in the Old Pueblo. (2)

MAY 27. Pumping plant for the Yuma citrus experiment station is installed by the University. (2)

MAY 28. Federal government notifies Arizona that it has no rights or interests in the Parker Indian Reservation. (2)

MAY 30. State Tax Commission urges that ten acres of public lands be given to every white child born in the State. (2)

JUNE 4. University of Arizona opens first summer school. (1)

JUNE 11. Disaster strikes Phoenix bootleggers when Mohave County officers capture 180 cases of high grade whiskey enroute to the capital city. (3)

JUNE 23. Board of Health urges all citizens of Tucson to boil drinking water 10 minutes. Contaminated well has filled the mains. (2)

JUNE 24. Salt River Valley Water Users Assn. announces it will irrigate an additional 200,000 acres of land on the Agua Fria. (2)

JUNE 26. Electrical Workers Union attempts to close Tucson Power Co., but fails. Business men form what is called "Open Shop Association." (2)

JUNE 27. Labor unions threaten to boycott every Tucson bank and pull men off work of employers who join Open Shop Association. (2)

JUNE 30. Tucson Chamber of Commerce wants strikes among public utility employes made illegal. (2)

JULY 1. Federal government makes $430,000 in aid available to Arizona for completion of Superior-Miami highway. (2)

JULY 6. Nogales Catholics file a strong written protest claiming they were deliberately ignored during Fourth of July ceremonies. (2)

JULY 6. Town of Gilbert is incorporated. (Personal letters)

JULY 7. Arizona Cattle Growers and Arizona Wool Growers Associations petition President Wilson to shut off imports of beef, mutton and wool or wages of cowboys and herders must drop. (1)

JULY 8. Arizona cattlemen, meeting in Flagstaff, condemn England for cancelling its orders for western beef. Charge this is costing growers from $30 to $60 a head on fat steers. (2)

JULY 9. To the dismay of many Southern Arizonans the Governor of Sonora closes gambling houses and outlaws hard liquor. (2)

JULY 9. Prescott's hospital is crowded when collision on the Santa Fe, Prescott and Phoenix Railway kills two and injures 16 persons. (1)

JULY 10. Because copper mines are hard hit by depression the State Tax Commission drops valuation $25,000,000 below figures of 1919 and fixes total at $389,029,918. (2)

JULY 10. Fire sweeps Grover Canyon in Globe, destroying 100 homes. (1)

JULY 11. Tucson suffers from a water famine. Irrigation of lawns barred in daytime. (1)

JULY 12. Governor Campbell of Arizona and President Obregon of Mexico meet under a "Welcome" arch at the international line in Nogales. Event marks first fraternizing since revolution placed Obregón in office. (2)

JULY 12. Fighting the efforts of cattlemen and sheepmen to acquire huge grants of Arizona lands, Gov. Campbell tells them, "You are riding for a fall if you insist on tying up the heritage of the people for your own purposes. State lands belong to the people and not to any one group." (2)

JULY 13. Special committee reports to the city council that all Tucson wells are either contaminated or subject to contamination. (2)

JULY 20. Phoenix warns tourists gasoline supply in the state is so short that it is unsafe to leave for the next stop west without 20 gallons in tank or cans. (3)

JULY 20. Rabbits damage Safford cotton fields and county organizes a hunt which wipes out 2,000 bunnies. (2)

JULY 24. New Cornelia mine at Ajo is added to list of mines which reopen as business improves. (2)

JULY 28. Two hundred Mexican laborers employed in Arizona cotton fields are turned adrift without pay and gather at Nogales. Governor Campbell begins investigation of charges that workers have been abused. (2)

AUG. 5. Depression drives price of wool so low that Navajos stop selling it and go back to making blankets. (3)

AUG. 7. State Board of Health completes survey of Arizona. Reports housing conditions among poorer families in Phoenix and Tucson as bad as anything in New York slums. (3)

AUG. 17. Maricopa County Board of Supervisors calls for an election on question of issuing a second $4,500,000 bond issue for good roads. (3)

AUG. 22. Governor Campbell and representatives of other western states visit Warren G. Harding, Republican candidate for President, and try to sell him on a policy of increased funds for reclamation of barren lands. (2)

AUG. 28. Cotton growers meet in Mesa and agree to set the wage scale for cotton pickers at four cents a pound. (3)

AUG. 30. Border breathes easier as Mexican government claims end to a 40-year guerilla war with Yaquis. (2)

SEPT. 4. John Dunbar, stormy petrel of Arizona journalism, is arrested for the seventh time in two years on charges of criminal libel. As usual, he is released on his own recognizance and goes back to publishing *Dunbar's Weekly*. (2)

SEPT. 13. Shortage of dormitory space compels students at University to canvass Tucson, house by house, for board and room. (2)

SEPT. 21. Tucsonans find they are stuck with thousands of dollars worth of worthless stock in an airless tire company. (2)

SEPT. 21. Opening his campaign for re-election, Governor Thomas E. Campbell denounces State Land Commission which, he charges, has leased 1,000,000 acres of public domain to 25 cattlemen. (3)

SEPT. 26. To aid stockmen who cannot afford to sell cattle at going prices, U. S. Forest Service plans to provide pasturage over the winter. (2)

SEPT. 27. Customs inspectors at Nogales crack Mexican smuggling ring and capture large supply of opium. (2)

SEPT. 28. State Board of Education finds it cannot get qualified school teachers at the going wages and issues temporary certificates in order to staff public schools. (3)

SEPT. 30. Dean G. M. Butler, head of the University School of Mines, says mining men will back bill to compel government to open coal fields on Indian reservations. (2)

OCT. 9. Delegation of Yaquis calls on the governor. Declare they are neither Indians nor Mexicans but American citizens. They ask for schools and clothing for their children. (2)

OCT. 10. Tucson Gas, Electric Light and Power Co. gas plant destroyed by fire and city is without gas for three weeks. (2)

OCT. 11. Fire destroys more than half the town of Lowell, a suburb of Bisbee. Damage set at $750,000. (3)

OCT. 14. Because of collapse of the cotton market Arizona growers find themselves faced with ruin. Maricopa County bankers persuade California institutions to raise reserve fund of $2,500,000 and extend credit to growers. (3)

OCT. 20. Phoenix celebrates its 50th anniversary mildly. (3)

OCT. 23. Ralph Cameron, Republican candidate for Congress, has a new idea about Colorado River Indian reservation. He would give it to ex-service men. (2)

NOV. 2. Republicans win bitter political campaign in Arizona. Campbell is re-elected governor and Ralph H. Cameron defeats Mark Smith for Congress. (2)

NOV. 19. Because the mayor of Nogales surrendered a Mexican accused of murder in Tucson, 3,000 of his countrymen hold mass protest. (2)

NOV. 24. Arizona banks give hard-pressed cattlemen extensions on their loans. (2)

NOV. 25. Declaring acts of God have created emergency conditions, Governor Campbell orders the state auditor to honor warrants to the amount of $100,000, thus providing for the repair of Tempe and Agua Fria bridges. (3)

NOV. 27. Bisbee reports closing of Cananea Consolidated Copper Co., largest American owned copper company in Sonora. (3)

NOV. 28. Pima County farmers harvest their cotton but keep it off the market because of low prices. (2)

NOV. 30. Arizona's highway expenditures for the year will total $3,285,000. (2)

DEC. 1. Nogales, Ariz., Chamber of Commerce presents Alvaro Obregón, newly inaugurated President of Mexico, with a solid gold paperweight which is a replica of the Sonora border between the U. S. and Mexico. (2)

DEC. 2. Arizona raises the salaries of teachers in one room schools from $80 to $100 a month — and pays them in state warrants. (2)

DEC. 3. State adjutant general's department reports that the Tucson High School cadet corps is the poorest in the state. (2)

DEC. 7. Arizona Gas and Electric Co. at Nogales refuses gas to citizen who does not use its electricity and State Corporation Commission orders it to serve the petitioner. (2)

DEC. 11. Business and Professional Women's Club make survey and find that over 200 skilled office women are out of employment in Phoenix. (3)

DEC. 15. All Tucson turns out for a day of volunteer labor on the Pastime Park site where federal government is erecting tent city sanatorium for tubercular soldiers. (2)

DEC. 16. State Game Wardens report senseless killing of game in the Fort Huachuca area by soldiers. (2)

DEC. 17. Fifty planes and 400 mounted troopers search deserts and mountains for two lost army fliers for 10 days without result. (2)

DEC. 17. State leaders hold banquet in Phoenix and form Arizona unit of Boy Scouts. (3)

DEC. 21. Educational circles of the state are scandalized when only five applicants pass the teachers' examination in Maricopa County and none pass in Pima. (2)

DEC. 23. Governor Campbell urges Congress to place high tariff on Egyptian cotton. Suggests 20 to 30 cents a pound. (2)

DEC. 24. Federal Power Commission outlines suggestion for 3,000,000 horsepower hydro-electric project on the Colorado in Utah and Arizona. (3)

DEC. 29. First shipment of army surplus goods arrives in Phoenix and is sold at "community store." Eight hundred and fifty customers spend $5,571. (3)

DEC. 31. Last act of Wiley Jones, State Attorney General, is to bar extract of sweet oranges from Arizona. Charges extract contains alcohol. (2)

DEC. 31. Total assessed valuation of all property in Arizona is placed at $886,000,000 for year 1920 by State Tax Commission. (3)

DEC. 31. Deposits in Arizona banks total $75,225,813. (27)

Total major metals production in Arizona, $114,628,584. (16)

Total number of cattle in Arizona, 1,575,000; value, $58,275,000. (24)

U. S. Census reports population of Arizona as 334,162; gain of 63.5 percent since 1910. Phoenix passes Tucson. (25)

Average daily attendance in elementary schools 41,983; in high schools 4,438. (15)

1921 JAN. 1. Maricopa County votes $4,500,000 bonds to complete road building program. (3)

JAN. 6. U. S. Department of Agriculture reports that Arizona farmers sales in 1920 fell $20,000,000 below 1919. (3)

JAN. 12. Governor Campbell's message to the legislature calls for laws making cotton gins public utilities; recommends survey of Arizona's educational needs and strengthening of compulsory school laws. (3)

JAN. 12. Tucson brick masons voluntarily lower their wage rate from $11 to $10 a day. (2)

JAN. 13. Southern Pacific reduces passenger fares 25 percent between Chicago and points west. (2)

JAN. 13. James S. Douglas, identified by press as "millionaire mine owner," engages in controversy with Tom Maddock, state engineer, over highway program. Douglas says Arizona highways cost too much. (2)

JAN. 13. Two Mexican bandits accused of killing three men in robbery of Tempe store shoot it out with U. S. Immigration Inspectors near the Nogales border and are fatally wounded. (2)

JAN. 18. James S. (Rawhide Jimmy) Douglas, owner of the United Verde Extension Mine, warns that unless state cuts its operating costs in two this year it will have serious trouble. (3)

JAN. 21. Salt River Valley Cotton Growers meet and go on record against State control of cotton gins. (3)

JAN. 22. Mexican consul protests that from 15,000 to 20,000 Mexican laborers are stranded in Arizona because cotton growers have not paid them their wages. (2)

JAN. 23. Superintendent of Tucson High objects to girls wearing levis in school. (2)

JAN. 24. California asks Arizona to stand with her in opposing citizenship for Orientals. (2)

JAN. 24. Southern Pacific agrees to transport 10,000 hungry and unpaid Mexican cotton pickers in the Salt River Valley back to Mexico. (2)

FEB. 3. Tucson carpenters cut their daily scale from $9 to $8 a day. (2)

FEB. 3. State Highway Department exhausts funds and closes work camps throwing 1,500 men out of jobs. (3)

FEB. 6. Governor Campbell in conference with Mexican consuls and Arizona cotton growers learns that 8,000 Mexican cotton pickers are destitute and 2,000 in dire need. Agreement reached to deport between 2 and 3 thousand indigent. (2)

FEB. 8. Frank O. Lowden, former Governor of Illinois, addresses the Fifth Arizona Legislature and urges adoption of Governor Campbell's plans for reorganization of state government. (3)

FEB. 10. Tucson opens campaign to get one of proposed U. S. hospitals for ex-service men. (2)

FEB. 13. Phoenix merchants report they are taking a $1,000,000 loss to meet drop in prices. (3)

FEB. 16. Merchants and Manufacturers' Association in Phoenix absorbs the Open Shop Association. (3)

FEB. 23. Declaring that the State of Arizona has no money, Pima County goes on record against $1,025,000 omnibus highway bill. (2)

FEB. 24. Organized labor establishes soup and bread line in Phoenix and feeds 1,000 Mexican men, women and children a day. Fifth State Legislature considers problem of hungry and unemployed cotton pickers and suggests the U. S. should take over since Immigration Bureau admitted the workers to the Salt River Valley. (3)

FEB. 25. U. S. Immigration Bureau says it permitted Mexican laborers to enter U. S. and work in Salt River Valley because the cotton men demanded them. Suggests cotton growers do their duty. (2)

FEB. 26. Governor Campbell signs anti-alien land bill, effect of which is to prevent Japanese from owning farms in Arizona. (2)

MAR. 5. Legislature gives governor authority to appoint an Arizona Commissioner who will meet with appointees from California, Colorado, Nevada, New Mexico, Utah and Wyoming and join in forming a Colorado River Commission. Purpose of commission will be to frame a compact for apportionment of Colorado River waters. (14)

MAR. 5. Phoenix newspaper says "depression is only skin deep in Salt River Valley and there is no cause for alarm." (3)

MAR. 11. Despite depression and condition of State Treasury, good roads advocates push $1,100,000 omnibus road bill through Legislature. (2)

MAR. 13. Emergency legislation enabling state to issue bonds based on anticipation of payment of taxes, enables Arizona to meet its running expenses. (2)

MAR. 17. State employees complain that they have great difficulty in cashing state warrants at face value. (2)

MAR. 19. Governor Campbell delivers scathing attack on divorce when he vetoes senate bill which would permit easy divorce where either party is found incurably insane. (3)

MAR. 20. Campaign develops in Phoenix to bring back the dairy herds and plant alfalfa again. Think it will be the "salvation of the valley." (3)

MAR. 24. Worried by failure of small banks in the valley, depositors start runs on Phoenix banks. Shipments of cash are hurried from the coast and run is broken on second day. Central Bank of Phoenix, however, does not re-open. (3)

MAR. 30. Engineers report that Lyman Dam is sinking into the mud of the Little Colorado even while work of building goes on. (2)

MAR. 31. Cotton acreage in the Salt River Valley drops from 185,000 to 75,000 acres as result of losses taken by cotton growers. (3)

APRIL 3. The cotton market is in a state of collapse and hundreds of growers are ruined. The copper mines have been forced to close. The state is paying its employees, including school and university teachers, with warrants of doubtful value. But on this date Tucson *Citizen* assures readers all is well. (2)

APRIL 3. One hundred and five cotton growers, including many with heavy acreage, sign up with newly organized firm-contract marketing association on first day. They are to be followed by many others. (3)

APRIL 5. Bisbee post office is robbed of $50,000 by two Mexican renegades. (3)

APRIL 10. U. S. Reclamation Service announces that it will erect the highest dam in the world — 500 to 600 feet — in Boulder Canyon, joining Nevada and Arizona. (3)

APRIL 11. State agrees that it will redeem $1,150,000 in outstanding warrants. (3)

APRIL 19. After a long battle Tucson votes favorably on $750,000 bonds for new high school. (2)

APRIL 20. Phoenix man has plan to make Arizona a seaport state. Claims he has concession from Mexican government for strip of land 3 miles wide and 90 miles long along the lower Colorado River and the eastern coast of the Gulf of California. Would establish a harbor 60 miles below the international line. (3)

APRIL 20. State Supreme Court tells cities to let waterways which pass through them alone or be prepared to pay damages from floods. (2)

APRIL 26. Mexican nationals at Tempe are given a choice of working for $1.25 a day or getting a free ride to the border. Two hundred go home in trucks furnished by the county. (2)

APRIL 28. Federal Grand Jury looks into the campaign expenses of newly-elected Senator Ralph H. Cameron. No action follows. (2)

MAY 1. Eighty Mexicans, impoverished when thrown out of work by closing of mines at Ray, camp in the open while waiting passports and transport from their government. Tucson feeds them. (2)

MAY 4. State Supreme Court rules that Arizona law taxing sheep, cattle and horses owned by non-residents of state is invalid. (2)

MAY 11. Governor Campbell heads committee of seven western governors which draws up compact on use of Colorado River water and visits President Harding to ask co-operation of federal government. (2)

MAY 18. Arizona cotton growers who have carried on a long fight to get lower freight rates to the cotton mills of the East are angry when Interstate Commerce Commission establishes higher rates. (2)

MAY 19. Glendale State Bank, one of many to meet financial troubles during depression, is forced to close. Receiver says failure due to a generous loan policy. (2)

MAY 19. Governors of seven Colorado River states meet in Denver and request the national government to appoint a representative of the United States to sit on the new Colorado River Commission. (22)

MAY 21. State Immigration Inspector announces that before Mexican laborers are again imported to pick cotton, American citizens will be given preference. (2)

MAY 28. Phoenix voters ratify six bond issues by heavy vote. Bonds, totalling $450,000, will provide water from the Verde, contribute to control of Cave Creek floods, build an armory, pave streets, and create a city park. (3)

JUNE 1. State law requiring both parties to a marriage contract to appear before county clerk becomes effective. (2)

JUNE 1. Indication that the dairy business is recovering is seen in reopening of creamery plant which has stood idle at Tempe for two years. (3)

JUNE 3. Southern California Edison Co. files application asking right to build dam at Glen Canyon and Diamond Creek which would operate huge power plant. (3)

JUNE 5. Ku Klux Klan burns fiery cross at Telegraph Pass near Yuma. (3)

JUNE 8. Posses with bloodhounds set out to trail 13 prisoners who escape from Nogales, Ariz. jail. (2)

JUNE 9. As of this date every Arizona real estate salesman is required to have a license. (3)

JUNE 11. Judge of the Imperial County Superior Court in California rules that Yuma is located in the State of California. Yuma Water Users had threatened to tear out Imperial Valley diversion works on the Colorado. (3)

JUNE 17. Arizona cattlemen appear before Commissioner of Indian Affairs in Washington. They ask that grazing fees on San Carlos and Apache Reservations be cut from $2.20 to $1.20 a head a year. They also want government to discontinue leasing land to the highest bidders. (2)

JUNE 22. Phoenix Republic finds 2,100 people in the city are suffering from hunger. Most of them are Mexican workers. Associated Charities pass out free food daily but supply is inadequate. (3)

JUNE 23. Phoenix Ministerial Assn. meets; churches will combine in effort to feed starving Mexicans. (3)

JUNE 24. Every woman in Phoenix is asked to contribute a pound of food to the needy Mexicans. Associated Charities distribute supplies. Two babies die of malnutrition in the organization's office. (3)

JUNE 27. Fire destroys the busy mining town of Oatman. Estimates of losses run as high as $500,000. (3)

JUNE 29. Citizen with experimental turn of mind flips a cigarette into pool of tequila which Maricopa sheriff is pouring into drain. Fire department is summoned. (2)

JUNE 30. Mad dogs become a problem in Tucson. Police kill five. (2)

JULY 1. Central Bank of Phoenix is reorganized and reopens. (3)

JULY 1. Governor Campbell holds meeting with representatives of long staple cotton organizations and promises he will try to convince Congress that only a 20 cent tariff can save the industry in the West. (2)

JULY 1. Heavy rains in the Catalina Mountains swell Rillito River, wash out two piers of Oracle bridge, and hold up heavy holiday traffic. (2)

JULY 2. Maricopa County employees chant "When do we eat?" as they discover county won't cash their salary warrants. (2)

JULY 3. Seven hundred men work day and night to finish main slab of the new Florence Diversion Dam before summer rains and floods come. (2)

JULY 4. Independence Day merrymaking and celebration of progress on Florence Dam is interrupted by three foot wall of water. Picnickers scramble for high ground. (2)

JULY 6. Arizona wool growers protest that high freight rates to eastern mills will more than wipe out any benefits from increased tariffs. (2)

JULY 8. Phoenix is informed by bond experts that $70,000 issue voted for a Phoenix armory cannot be approved. (3)

JULY 14. Arizona Pima Cotton Growers' Association is incorporated under the law passed by Fifth Legislature. Seven hundred farmers join this marketing organization. (3)

JULY 19. State Supreme Court declares Arizona's Workmen's Compensation Act is invalid and directs State Treasurer and State Auditor not to permit commission to spend state money. (2)

JULY 25. First edition of *Arizona Highways* comes off the press and begins astounding career. (2)

JULY 26. A. O. Neal, registrar of the University of Arizona, explains to Tucson Rotary Club that business depression will do the institution more good than harm. He says that young men out of work will now go to school. (2)

JULY 30. Governor Campbell cancels state fair to save taxpayers $90,000. (2)

AUG. 1. Department of Agriculture estimates Arizona cotton crop for the year is 89 percent of normal. (2)

AUG. 2. Pima County and State Highway Department argue over which owns the Rillito bridge and which should repair flood damages to structure. (2)

AUG. 2. Mt. Lemmon in the Catalinas gets 15.79 in. of rain in July. Six hundred feet of Tanque Verde road are washed out. (2)

AUG. 3. Reporting on the conditions of roads after heavy rains, all that Arizona can say is "They're passable." (2)

AUG. 4. Snowflake reports that heaviest rains in many years are making it impossible for dairy farmers to get their milk to Tucson. They are considering selling their herds. (2)

AUG. 4. Southern Pacific announces that it will reduce freight on copper bullion and cottonseed oil from Arizona east. (2)

AUG. 5. Tucson Chamber of Commerce demands that Pima County supervisors cut their budget $50,000. Supervisors eliminate $32,000. (2)

AUG. 6. State Highway Department offers to split cost of repairs of Rillito bridge with Pima County. (2)

AUG. 6. Congress passes bill which gives seven western states right to negotiate for use of Colorado River water. (3)

AUG. 8. Governor Campbell refuses appeal from tax conference committee to call a special session of Legislature and cut $1,500,000 from institutional budgets. (2)

AUG. 11. Increase in drunk driving impels Tucson judge to establish penalties of $200 and 20 days in jail. (2)

AUG. 18. Mad dog plague reaches such proportions in Tucson that police officers cruise city and kill every dog running loose on streets. Ten killed in Yaqui settlement and more in Tucson. (2)

AUG. 22. Cave Creek floods entire west end of Phoenix. Capitol stands in two feet of water. (3)

AUG. 25. Half a million dollars in cattle loans approved for Arizona cattlemen by advisory committee of the National Livestock Finance Corp. (3)

AUG. 26. Postmaster and wife are murdered at Ruby, apparently by Mexican bandits. (3)

SEPT. 2. University of Arizona cuts board and room fee to $25 a month. (3)

SEPT. 4. Arizona newspapers filled with big advertisements announcing cut prices on leading passenger cars. Ford Roadster sells for $550.78. (1)

SEPT. 14. Glendale district reports having shipped 55,000 cases of melons in 1921 season. (3)

SEPT. 16. It is finally decided by Arizona State Tax Commission that Pima County supervisors may incur liabilities of $8,000 and proceed with repairs of Rillito Bridge. (1)

SEPT. 22. Dallas Reserve Bank Agent informs Arizona bankers that War Finance Corporation will aid hard-pressed cattlemen. (1)

SEPT. 23. Early morning fire destroys huge storehouse of the Arizona Egyptian Cotton Co. at Phoenix. Loss is $50,000. (3)

SEPT. 27. Orville S. McPherson, secretary of the Tucson Chamber of Commerce, tells U. A. Alumni that certain large business interests and James Douglas in particular, are spreading propaganda against the University which may result in loss of President R. B. von Klein-Smid. (1)

SEPT. 28. Cotton picking is about to begin and again Mexican and Yaqui families are rushed to the Salt River Valley. Farmers want 5,000 pickers. (1)

OCT. 1. Federal officers say that campaign against drug peddlers in Southern Arizona has driven them to Globe and Prescott. (1)

OCT. 4. Despite recent difficulties over non-payment of Mexican cotton pickers, 270 Mexicans are shipped to Tucson in trucks of Arizona Cotton Growers' Assn. (2)

OCT. 8. R. B. von KleinSmid resigns as President of the University. *The Citizen* speaks of "marplots who have made a waspish and unjustifiable attack on the University." Charges also that "certain men have set out to destroy the University." Faculty calls it all a "calamity." (1)

OCT. 9. Railroad police of the Tucson division pluck 3,373 hoboes off Southern Pacific trains in one month. (1)

OCT. 11. Pima and Maricopa County continue angry feud over location of paved highway from El Paso to Yuma. Phoenix wants traffic west to come there and be routed to California by the Ehrenberg cutoff. Tucson wants Ajo-Tucson route. (1)

OCT. 16. Cattle which were starving on dry Pima County ranges in July are now knee deep in grass and well watered as result of heavy rains. (2)

OCT. 22. Anticipating nationwide rail strike, Washington asks Arizona cities to survey food stocks available. (2)

OCT. 23. Cattle rustling becomes so common in Salt River Valley that cattlemen decide to lay in wait for raiders, "shoot them where they stand and leave them when they fall." (3)

OCT. 24. Ralph H. Cameron, senator from Arizona, is indicted by a grand jury on a charge of perjury. (3)

NOV. 3. Tombstone bank reopens. State press never announced it had been closed. (1)

NOV. 8. War Finance Corporation announces opening of $200,000 finance board in Tucson which will lend money to agriculture and livestock interests. (1)

NOV. 9. Nogales business district suffers a $150,000 fire. (1)

NOV. 11. Arizona celebrates Armistice Day with elaborate parades and pageants as America pays honor before the Tomb of the Unknown Soldier in Washington. (3)

NOV. 12. Ku Klux Klan said to be organizing in Tucson. (2)

NOV. 16. Highway holdup costs woman rider her life. Wounded husband drives on from Stoval to Yuma, remains in critical condition. Assassin is captured. (2)

NOV. 20. Arizona gets $154,000 from U. S. Dept. of Agriculture for construction of forest roads and trails. (1)

NOV. 26. Forty carloads of Pima cotton start east. Largest single shipment to leave valley. (3)

DEC. 6. Yuma business section is gutted by $250,000 fire. (2)

DEC. 8. Five states attending League of the Southwest Conference on Colorado River problems announce they will withdraw unless all members have equal votes: they are Arizona, Colorado, New Mexico, Utah and Wyoming. (3)

DEC. 9. U. S. Department of Labor reveals that lumber operation in Arizona is 25 percent of normal. (3)

DEC. 14. Governor Campbell and Dwight B. Heard appear before Senate Finance Committee and plead for 20 cent tariff on Egyptian cotton. (3)

DEC. 15. Pima County man who purchases 6,000 head of steers and then discovers they are diseased sues for half a million in Superior Court. (2)

DEC. 16. One hundred and seventy-five representative men from all sections of Arizona gather for two day industrial conference which is pledged to statewide co-operation. (3)

DEC. 17. U. S. Supreme Court rules that Arizona courts have the right to prohibit picketing. (1)

DEC. 17. Organization of the Colorado River Commission is completed when President Harding grants request of six of the seven states and names Herbert Hoover to act as the representative of the United States. Only California dissents. (22)

DEC. 18. Arizona protests what it calls unfair railroad rates in the West at Interstate Commerce Commission hearing in Phoenix. (3)

DEC. 29. Pima County sheriff denounces Tucson police who confiscate 175 gallons of white mule and a still outside the city limits. (1)

DEC. 31. Tucson reports total building costs for the year are $2,500,000. (1)

DEC. 31. Deposits in Arizona banks total $64,051,324. (27)

Total major metals production in Arizona, $29,563,472. (16)

Total number of cattle in Arizona, 1,492,000; value, $41,179,000. (24)

1922 JAN. 1. Official line in Tucson as expressed by the press is that while 1921 was a depression year conditions here were better than in remainder of the state. (2)

JAN. 3. Residents of northwestern sections of Phoenix ordered to abandon their homes when Cave Creek flood waters rise for second time in six months. (2)

JAN. 4. Sixty educators apply for post of president of the University of Arizona. (1)

JAN. 10. Arizona Cattlegrowers' Association considers making demand for revisions in the State Constitution. Favors economies in administration of Arizona's affairs. (3)

JAN 13. First double hanging takes place in the penitentiary at Florence. Two Maricopa murderers die. (3)

JAN. 15. Tucson argues for months over site of $750,000 high school. Voters finally settle it. (1)

JAN. 17. Federal judge tells citizens of Arizona that hereafter those who violate the dry laws can expect to go to jail. (2)

JAN. 18. President Obregón of Mexico cancels rule demanding Americans carry passports when entering country. President Harding returns the courtesy, does same for Mexican visitors. (2)

JAN. 20. Jerome is heartened by the news that its mines will reopen in 40 days. (3)

JAN. 22. Tucson police begin new year drive on gambling with raid which nets 35 men. (1)

FEB. 5. Corporation formed in Phoenix to raise table grapes in the Salt River Valley. (3)

FEB. 6. Hog cholera decimates herds in southern Arizona. (2)

FEB. 6. Construction of Cave Creek Dam begins. (3)

FEB. 7. Arizona receives $878,911 from National Forestry Highway Fund, $598,000 of which is for roads of primary importance to the state. (2)

FEB. 10. U. S. Bureau of Public Roads favors building Tucson-Phoenix highway via Casa Grande. (2)

FEB. 11. Maricopa County Chamber of Commerce holds first meeting at Phoenix. (3)

FEB. 14. Pima cotton is shipped to Czechoslovakia at premium rates. (3)

FEB. 16. First act of the legislature is to pass appropriation bill of $51,880 to pay salaries and other expenses of session. (3)

FEB. 17. State learns it has been loaning money illegally. State Loan Board failed to get signatures of Governor, State Treasurer and Secretary of State. (2)

FEB. 22. State Superintendent of Public Instruction recommends that a campaign against illiteracy be opened in Arizona. Statistics show that illiteracy count in 1920 was above 31,000 which was 7,000 greater than in 1910. (3)

FEB. 25. Governor Campbell and entire legislature take the oath and are made Boy Scouts. (2)

FEB. 25. Department of Agriculture eases distress of cattlemen by permitting them to graze stock in forest reserves without paying fees in advance. (3)

FEB. 26. Farmers see hope as 2,500,000 pounds of wheat from Salt River Valley are sold for $60,000. (3)

FEB. 27. Legislature discovers counties have borrowed $250,000 from state to build bridges but have repaid nothing. Repeal of the law is suggested. (2)

MAR. 4. University professors happy when legislature passes concurrent resolution authorizing state to redeem the warrants with which they have been paid. Week later Governor Campbell vetoes act as unconstitutional. (2)

MAR. 7. Proposals to amend Arizona State Constitution are denounced in the legislature as a Wall Street "assault upon the hopes of the oppressed." (2)

MAR. 12. Governor forbids importation of cattle from New Mexico. Epidemic of scabies alarms Arizona stockmen. (3)

MAR. 13. Storm buries campus of the University at Tucson under seven inches of snow. (2)

MAR. 14. Legislature votes 15 to 4 not to hold a joint session in the Shrine Club to hear Herbert Hoover. (2)

MAR. 15. Seven Colorado River states represented in Phoenix when Herbert Hoover opens hearings on water problems. (3)

MAR. 15. Interstate Commerce Commission cuts the freight rates between Arizona and the long grass country in the Northwest by $151 a carload. Cattlemen are jubilant at success of long fight. (3)

MAR. 16. Herbert Hoover addresses joint session of Arizona Legislature and says he endorses the Boulder Canyon project. (3)

MAR. 18. G. W. P. Hunt returns from Siam and announces he will campaign against proposed amendments to state constitution. (2)

MAR. 22. Arizona finds it necessary to pay 8 percent interest on its registered warrants to protect its credit at home and abroad. (3)

MAR. 23. Ku Klux Klan admits it whipped principal of Lehi school for crime of which a jury had found him innocent. Governor Campbell offers $250 reward for capture of the guilty ones. (3)

MAR. 23. Governor Campbell approves legislative memorial urging Congress to act favorably on soldiers' bonus. (2)

APRIL 1. Legislature rejects measure to kill the mill tax which supports University. (2)

APRIL 2. Twelve new buildings and five additions go up at Fort Whipple which will become government hospital. (2)

APRIL 7. Tucson Chamber of Commerce lets it be known that it will oppose any through highway which by-passes Phoenix. (2)

APRIL 8. Phoenix press uses blackface type and long news story to hail spirit of Tucson which "binds the two cities more firmly in the bonds of fellowship and co-operation." (3)

APRIL 9. Record lettuce yield in the Salt River Valley brings from $400 to $1,000 an acre. (3)

APRIL 12. Governor Campbell signs war finance bill making $1,500,000 available for loans to Arizona stockmen. (3)

APRIL 13. State treasurer discovers that Arizona lost $20,000 on deposit in the closed Bank of Willcox. (2)

APRIL 14. Arizona Industrial Congress reveals that it has 10,000 members. (3)

APRIL 15. Special session of the Legislature adjourns, claiming to have shaved state expenditures by $1,000,000. Session also created County Highway Commissioners, amended marriage and divorce acts, provided for regulation of migratory livestock and authorized State Loan Commissioners to anticipate collection of taxes. (14)

APRIL 24. United States Good Roads Assn., Bankhead National Highway Assn., and the U. S. Good Roads show open five day session in Phoenix. Speakers of national and state importance address 500 delegates. (3)

APRIL 25. Bishop of the Episcopal Diocese of Arizona tells annual church convention in Nogales, "Lack of reverence for law lies at the root of most of our evils of today." (3)

APRIL 27. Governor Campbell vigorously rebukes those who call Arizona "The land that God forgot." (2)

APRIL 28. Governor Campbell signs general appropriations bill but not before he chops out another $72,600. (2)

APRIL 30. Phoenix, Miami, Globe railroad connecting Salt River Valley with Gila Valley and mining camps, comes alive at celebration attended by thousands in Miami. (3)

MAY 1. Senator Ralph H. Cameron of Arizona appears in office of U. S. Marshal in Phoenix and demands information on his indictment for perjury, voted by grand jury a year ago. Marshal has no warrant. (3)

MAY 1. Tucson sets up vaccination centers in efforts to check growth of smallpox cases. (2)

MAY 5. Phoenix, Globe and Douglas have best milk in the state. Tucson scores next to lowest, which is Clifton. (2)

MAY 9. Last Federal troops leave Fort Apache just as first mission church (Lutheran) is dedicated there and baptizes 100 Indians. (2)

MAY 10. Long awaited Florence diversion dam which harnesses the rolling Gila River is dedicated before Arizonans from all sections of the state. (3)

MAY 13. Masked train robbers continue to operate in state. Arizona-New Mexico Railroad train held up near Clifton and mail car robbed. (3)

MAY 14. Undelivered letters of 60 years ago are found with skeleton of pony express carrier in cabin cellar near Oatman. Mail sack discovered after recent dynamiting to rout nest of rattlesnakes. (3)

MAY 15. Outlaws attempt hold up of Southern Pacific's Golden State at Jaynes Station near Tucson. One dies and others flee fusillade from express messenger's shotgun. (2.

MAY 17. Indictment against Senator Ralph H. Cameron on charge of perjury is dismissed. (2)

MAY 20. Former Governor George W. P. Hunt denounces platform adopted by the state Democratic party. Becomes candidate for Governor again. (2)

MAY 27. Governor Campbell gains list of state membership of the Ku Klux Klan and publication reveals names of many prominent citizens. (3)

JUNE 1. Five thousand farmers gather at State Fairgrounds to celebrate organization of agricultural, industrial, commercial and business interests into co-operative marketing group. (3)

JUNE 3. Grand Jury is called in Phoenix to investigate actions of the Ku Klux Klan. (3)

JUNE 9. U. S. Department of Agriculture predicts Arizona will have 103,000 head of cattle ready for June market. (2)

JUNE 21. KFAD, Arizona's first licensed broadcasting station, goes on the air in Phoenix. (3)

JUNE 21. Herbert Hoover, Secretary of the Interior, pleads in Congress for construction of a dam and reservoir on the Colorado River at Boulder Canyon. (2)

JUNE 23. The states of Arizona and California agree to change course of the Colorado River and thus relieve flood conditions in Palo Verde Valley. (2)

JUNE 24. Grand Jury in Mesa calls residents in probe of Ku Klux Klan activities. (2)

JUNE 25. For the second time in two days Yuma is shaken by earth tremors. (2)

JULY 1. Phoenix gets its heart's desire as contract is signed for a new armory. (3)

JULY 2. Grand Jury at Phoenix is busy issuing indictments against officials of closed banks. (2)

JULY 6. Department of the Interior gives Salt River Valley Water Users Assn. exclusive and prior rights to all power sites, rights of way and dam sites on Salt River between Phoenix and Roosevelt Dam. (3)

JULY 7. Tax Commission cuts 1921 valuation of railroads by $776,000. (3)

JULY 8. Thirty business places are flooded, power plant fails, three bridges are washed out and many Mexican adobe dwellings dissolve into mud when twin cities of Nogales are swept by worst flood in 12 years. (3)

JULY 10. Federal and state agencies agree to join in campaign to eradicate bovine tuberculosis in Arizona. (3)

JULY 14. Two felons, convicted of the 1921 murder of Ruby postmaster and his wife, escape while enroute to state prison after killing Cochise sheriff and seriously wounding his deputy. (2)

JULY 17. Huge 36-inch lens for the University's Steward Observatory is finished. (2)

JULY 17. Carload of 75 Negro strike breakers being hurried to Needles, Cal., is halted at Seligman on receipt of warning that Needles citizens will not let workers leave the train. Train returns to Winslow where it is warned to keep going and backtracks to Gallup, N. M. There National Guard hurries it back east. (3)

JULY 18. A dozen posses hunt Ruby murderers for five days and corner them at last near Amado. (3)

JULY 21. State Tax Commission lowers the assessed valuation of Arizona $81,650,000. (3)

JULY 29. State Board of Regents and State Treasurer quarrel over $50,000 from the Morrill Fund. Treasurer wants to handle the money. (3)

JULY 30. Eastern banks finance 1922 cotton crops with $1,500,000 to be loaned at 5½ percent. (3)

JULY 31. Pima County finally gets $150,000 proceeds from land grant given it by Congress to pay off worthless bonds sold to build narrow gauge railroad. (2)

AUG. 5. Idea of building great dam at Glen Canyon on the Colorado River continues to attract attention. Governor Campbell and party make three day visit to possible site. (3)

AUG. 10. Bank records show Arizona is emerging from depths of depression. (2)

AUG. 13. Nationwide railway strike halts Santa Fe service. Passengers are marooned at junction points. President Harding offers Governor Campbell federal aid. (3)

AUG. 15. Santa Fe resumes overland passenger service. Mohave County suffers from food shortage as freight trains fail to move. (3)

AUG. 17. Railroad Brotherhoods at Prescott vote to return to work, reopening service to all Arizona points. (3)

AUG. 18. Mexican cowboys raid ranches near Ruby and Nogales rushes armed force of deputy sheriffs and city police to the scene. (2)

AUG. 22. Cloudburst sweeps Bisbee. Every street in the business district turns into mountain torrent. Property damage is high. (3)

AUG. 30. Rancher destroys joys of motoring by fencing off three miles of new road between Globe and Payson. (2)

SEPT. 13. Former Governor Hunt is renominated by Democratic party. (3)

SEPT. 15. Tucson Sunshine Climate Club is formed. Campaign for $50,000 started. (2)

SEPT. 17. Silver Bell copper mines are reopened. (2)

SEPT. 23. Governor Campbell protests to President Harding against order replacing U. S. cavalry at the border with infantry. Harding revokes the order. (3)

SEPT 27. Fresh battle between old opponents open as Governor Campbell throws his hat in the ring and begins to campaign against Hunt. (3)

OCT. 3. Four Tucsonans are indicted for complicity in land frauds by U. S. grand jury. (2)

OCT. 4. Criminal indictments charge former tax commissioner and Tucson citizen with plot to carry on land steal of 100,000 acres in northern Yuma and Southern Mohave counties. (2)

OCT. 4. Arizona finally lifts its quarantine against New Mexico cattle. (3)

OCT. 5. Former Secretary of State indicted on charge of conspiracy to defraud Arizona on land deals. (2)

OCT. 5. Governor Campbell says it is "utterly futile" to attempt to develop Arizona's full potential without bringing in more outside capital. (3)

OCT. 6. Grand juries continue to indict officials of defunct banks. (3)

OCT. 9. Report of 57 Arizona financial institutions show bank deposits have increased by $4,217,000 in the last year. (3)

OCT. 11. Inheritance tax collection in Arizona during 1921 totalled only $65,000. (3)

OCT. 17. Engineering survey of practicality of Boulder Dam begins. (3)

OCT. 19. Delegations from Southern Arizona counties unite to kill bond issue for Ehrenburg-Hassayampa highway. Call it "week-end trail." (2)

OCT. 30. Federal officers arrest western leader of I. W. W. at Phoenix on charge of promoting sabotage in Santa Fe walkout. (2)

NOV. 3. Federal government and state combine in four month drive against pests and predatory animals. Eight thousand coyotes, 247 mountain lions, 205 lobo wolves and 18,000 gophers are destroyed. Maricopa County school boys handled the gophers. (3)

NOV. 4. Reductions in federal taxes save Arizona over $1,000,000 in current year. (3)

NOV. 5. One hundred and nineteen thousand acres of Arizona land ordered opened to settlement by veterans. (2)

NOV. 7. Democratic party sweeps Arizona in state election. Hunt defeats Campbell for governorship. (2)

NOV. 8. Governor Campbell signs proclamation declaring Rucker Range country in Apache County quarantined because of prevalance of dread cattle plague. (2)

NOV. 16. [After procedural meetings, Colorado River Commission, meeting with Herbert Hoover, discussed suggested compacts, voted on each section and accepted those receiving majority vote.] Reports it has now agreed on major points of what becomes known as the Colorado River Compact. (2, 22)

DEC. 1. Arizona and New Mexico halt autos at state borders in search for contraband cotton, boll weevil, pink boll worms, and poor seed. Action necessary to protect pure strains of long staple. (3)

DEC. 6. U. S. Geological Survey reports that Colorado River flow during the fiscal year of 1921-22 was 17,600,000 acre feet at Yuma. This is below 20 year average. (2)

DEC. 9. Herbert Hoover visits Phoenix and makes appeal as Secretary of the Interior for the ratification of the Colorado River project. Says Arizona is well protected. (3)

DEC. 13. Phoenix Chamber of Commerce sounds out possibility of changing the name of the Salt River Valley to something like, "Sunny Green Spot of the West," or even "Happy Valley." (3)

DEC. 23. State's delinquent taxes reach $3,471,000. Maricopa alone shows $1,632,000. (3)

DEC. 31. Deposits in Arizona banks total $67,051,324. (27)
Total major minerals production in Arizona, $62,902,725. (16)
Total number of cattle in Arizona, 1,454,000; value, $45,946,000. (24)

1923 JAN. 1. Stockman's State Bank of St. Johns closes doors. (3)

JAN. 5. Shareholders of the Salt River Valley Water Users Assn. vote 14 to one for $1,800,000 bond issue to finance Mormon Flat project. (3)

JAN. 18. Wyoming Colorado River Commissioner reports to his legislature that plan to divide use of the river among the states as originally planned is abandoned in favor of a division into two groups: the upper basin states of Colorado, Utah, New Mexico, and Wyoming, and the lower basin states of Arizona, California, and Nevada. Arizona's opposition to the compact begins here as she casts only dissenting vote. (22)

JAN. 19. Phoenix postmaster announces that first class mail now reaches him from New York in three days. (3)

JAN. 23. Governor Hunt demands legislature go slow about ratifying Colorado River Compact. (2)

FEB. 2. American Hereford Assn. reports that Greene Cattle Co. of Patagonia, with 825 head of purebred Herefords, has the largest herd of registered cattle in the Association. (3)

FEB. 3. Tucson business and professional women bombard legislature with objections to proposed minimum wage law for women. Want equal wage with men. (2)

FEB. 9. Fight opens in Arizona Legislature on proposal to adopt Santa Fe Compact. House loads bill with reservations. (2)

FEB. 13. Governor Hunt signs act raising minimum wage for women from $10 to $16 a week.

FEB. 13. Joint legislative investigation committee reports that Arizona Highway Department is "hopelessly bankrupt." (4)

FEB. 14. State employees are notified by elected state officials that they must contribute two percent of their salary until Democratic party deficit is paid up. Governor Hunt signs the letter. (2)

FEB. 16. *Holbrook News Tribune* established. (19)

FEB. 25. Army announces it will open summer military training school for citizens at Fort Huachuca. (4)

MAR. 5. Arizona accountants denounce State Legislature for importing Chicago accountants to search for waste in state funds. (2)

MAR. 6. University of Arizona uses radio for first time in Extension courses. (2)

MAR. 6. New Cave Creek dam saves Phoenix from flood. (3)

MAR. 7. Legislature defeats bill calling for unreserved ratification of the Santa Fe Compact, passes act forbidding corporations to prevent employees from joining in political activities, makes drunk driving a jail offense, petitions Congress to permit cattlemen to graze herds in National Forests and on Indian Reservations. (14)

MAR. 14. Arizona copper mines announce a ten percent increase in wages. (2)

MAR. 20. Governor Hunt vetoes three cent tax on gasoline. (2)

APRIL 7. U. S. Department of Agriculture finds that Pima County is one of 13 counties in the United States where dairy herds are completely free of tuberculosis. (1)

APRIL 12. New financial code is established by special session of the Legislature.

APRIL 20. Nogales, Arizona, fire department crosses international line to fight $50,000 fire in Nogales, Sonora. (1)

MAY 2. Tucson National Bank fails. Bankers say it will not affect Tucson's business stability. (2)

MAY 4. First State Bank of Patagonia fails. (2)

MAY 22. Four die in explosion at Apache Powder Plant near Benson. (2)

MAY 31. University of Arizona proudly graduates largest class in its history — 139 students. (3)

MAY 31. Pipe Spring is made a National Monument. (26)

JUNE 2. Bisbee's unwritten law, "No Chinaman ever stays here overnight," is broken when Chinese student enrolls in UA branch summer school. (3)

JUNE 3. Automobile sets new record for San Diego-Phoenix run; 14 hours and 10 minutes. (3)

JUNE 21. Rt. Rev. Monsignor Daniel J. Gercke is named Bishop of the Diocese of Tucson. (2)

JUNE 22. Sparks from a moonshiner's still cause a fire which sweeps 400 acres of land in the Huachuca forest district. (2)

JUNE 24. Federal agents seize four wagon loads of I.W.W. propaganda in Globe-Miami zone where strikes are brewing. (2)

JULY 1. Governor Hunt's Arizona committee of nine, appointed to establish a policy for the use of Colorado River water, meets in Tucson and keeps discussions secret. (2)

JULY 11. Arizona Cattle Growers Assn. meets at Flagstaff and votes to incorporate. (3)

JULY 13. Mad dogs frighten Tucson. Authorities kill 13 and pound-master is ordered to carry a shotgun. (2)

JULY 15. Visiting government nurse complains that many infants die in Tucson during summer because price of ice is so high families cannot afford to keep milk fresh. (2)

JULY 25. Tucson cracks down on speeding autos. Picks up 21 cars and drivers first day. (2)

JULY 28. Cashier of Tempe Farmers' and Merchants' Bank burns many of bank's records. State examiner closes the institution. (3)

JULY 29. Board of Health closes 10 Tucson restaurants as unsanitary. (2)

AUG. 2. President Warren G. Harding dies suddenly on return trip from Alaska and Arizona cancels plans for huge cavalcade to the Mexican border. (2)

AUG. 2. After five day delay marked by growing crowds of citizens around closed doors of Tempe Farmers' and Merchants' Bank, county attorney issues warrants for arrest of bank's officials. (3)

AUG. 10. Thousands gather at University of Arizona to pay final tribute to President Harding. (2)

Aug. 21. Southern Arizona sportsmen learn that first trout fry of 18,000 Colorado mountain fingerlings will be planted in the Catalina Mountains. (2)

AUG. 29. State Supreme Court rules that Governor Hunt had no legal authority to veto three-cent gasoline tax and that it must be collected. (3)

AUG. 31. Obregón government of Mexico is recognized by U. S. and Tucson sees marked business advancement. (2)

SEPT. 1. Forest rangers near Prescott sell wood at 50 cents a cord. (5)

SEPT. 4. Governor Hunt informs Federal Power Commission that Arizona will not subscribe to Santa Fe Compact and that state intends to own, operate and control all Colorado water projects within its borders. (2)

SEPT. 11. Governor Hunt gains control of the Board of Regents and announces that man and wife may no longer serve on faculty at same time. (2)

SEPT. 12. Town of Hayden suffers heavy damage from hail and wind storm. Ten houses washed away. (3)

SEPT. 19. U. S. Biological survey reports 100 mountain lions killed in one year in drive to wipe out predatory animals. (2)

SEPT. 19. Entire northeastern section of Arizona, east of Flagstaff, is isolated and all Atchison, Topeka and Santa Fe traffic is tied up by heavy two-day rain. (3)

SEPT. 21. Crack California Limited train leaves Santa Fe tracks north of Phoenix. Four dead, scores injured. (3)

OCT. 1. Phoenix holds high carnival as its new railroad station is opened by Southern Pacific and the Atchinson, Topeka and Santa Fe. (3)

OCT. 10. State Engineer makes a survey of auto traffic on all Arizona roads for one day. Finds total number of cars on the highways to be 18,954. (3)

OCT. 13. Federal Prohibition Director makes two raids on alleged sellers of liquor and arrests 88 for "witness sales" in Yavapai County. (3)

OCT. 13. Fire destroys a square block of residences and business places in Nogales, Arizona. (3)

OCT. 18. *Tucson Citizen* gives 8 column head to arrival of 17 winter visitors in one day. (2)

OCT. 25. Inspired by one of Harold Bell Wright's novels, New Yorkers organize $100,000 corporation to back hunt for lost "Mine with the Iron Door" in Catalina Mountains. (2)

OCT. 27. Arizona copper mines and smelters announce they will discontinue recent raise in wages. (3)

OCT. 30. Arizona produced $58,772,906 in gold, silver and lead in 1922, by according to Arizona Tax Commission. (3)

NOV. 3. Maricopa and Yavapai Counties agree to stop feuding over boundaries and Supreme Court orders that old lines be resurveyed by U. S. Geodetic Survey and county engineers. At stake are taxes from the Santa Fe. (3)

NOV. 10. One hundred samples of bootleg liquor are seized by federal men in Arizona. Government laboratory tests show all are poisonous. (3)

NOV. 12. Mormon notables lay cornerstone of $500,000 temple at Mesa. (3)

NOV. 16. Teaching of evolution at UA creates controversy in Tucson. (2)

NOV. 23. Prohibition agents pour 1,000 gallons of captured liquor into the Salt River. (3)

NOV. 27. U. S. Army Remount Service says most Arizona horses are worthless "nags" and recommends that half of them be killed off. (2)

DEC. 1. Abandonment of that portion of Salt River canal which flows through Phoenix — known as the "town ditch" — is approved by Water Users Assn. (3)

DEC. 3. Arizonans pass million mark in income taxes in 1923. Total is $1,164,000. (3)

DEC. 5. First 200 cases of the new crop of grapefruit from Salt River Valley are sold in England. (3)

DEC. 12. Snowstorm holds Tucson in its grip for two days. (2)

DEC. 14. U. S. Department of Labor finds all cotton gins in Arizona are working at full capacity. (3)

DEC. 17. Figures for the year ending June 30 show Arizona leads nation in effectiveness of prohibition enforcement. Convictions estimated at 97 percent. (3)

DEC. 20. Assessment of 100 percent is levied on stockholders of Tucson National Bank. (2)

DEC. 22. In face of refusal of Federal Power Commission to authorize work, construction under state license is begun on $36,000,000 Diamond Creek Dam. Promoters expect it to develop 200,000 horsepower of electrical energy. (3)

DEC. 27. Globe mob threatens prisoner accused of killing UA student and assaulting Globe girl. Officers rush suspect to state prison in Florence. (2)

DEC. 28. Arizona's persistent fight for 3.6 cent-a-mile passenger fare pays off at last when Interstate Commerce Commission rules favorably. Will mean an annual $2,000,000 saving to train-traveling public in Arizona. (3)

DEC. 31. Deposits in Arizona banks total $71,328,053. (27)
Total major minerals production in Arizona, $104,301,200. (16)
Total number of cattle in Arizona, 1,411,000; value, $40,637,000. (24)
City of Mesa, Maricopa County, incorporated. (18)

1924 JAN. 1. Valley National Bank announces deposits in Phoenix banks increase $5,000,000 in last three months of 1923. (3)

JAN. 3. One hundred and seventeen touring cars with passengers are mired in a muddy highway near Casa Grande. Hauled to Southern Pacific tracks they bump over ties for more than a mile before passable road is reached. (2)

JAN. 6. U. S. Dept. of Agriculture places value of Arizona's 1923 cotton crop at $14,000,000, double the figure for 1922. (3)

JAN. 8. One hundred and eighty-four defendants charged with violations of the prohibition laws appear before Federal Court in Prescott. Cases are transferred to Phoenix by the judge who says he was cursed and abused by drunken citizens. (3)

JAN. 11. Three year restriction against raising cotton in Tucson and Flowing Wells district because of boll weevil blight is vigorously attacked by farmers. Claim pest has been eradicated. (2)

JAN. 12. Arizona refuses to join California in making a survey for a bridge across Colorado at Ehrenberg. (3)

JAN. 16. Congress gives UA title to 160 acres of land near Yuma where Experiment Station is located. Value $50,000. (2)

JAN. 19. United Verde Extension Mining Co. decides to withdraw its suit protesting tax valuation and agrees to pay Yavapai County $243,000. (3)

JAN. 21. U. S. Dept. of Agriculture opens drive to wipe out cotton rats which do great damage to orchards in Salt River Valley and Flowing Wells district. (2)

JAN. 23. Secretary of State announces that new gasoline tax laws enriched Arizona by $422,692 in 1923. (3)

FEB. 2. Prof. J. J. Thornber, Dean of the UA's College of Agriculture, says value of Arizona crops reached a total of $36,000,000 in 1923. (3)

FEB. 6. Arizona cities mark death of Woodrow Wilson, war-time President, with memorial services. (2)

FEB. 17. President Coolidge asks Congress to approve $300,000 appropriation to complete Sacaton Dam on the Gila. (3)

FEB. 19. Federal prohibition agents find 100-gallon-still hidden in White Tank Mountains. Still is reached by burro trail. (3)

FEB. 20. Southern Pacific announces cut of approximately 25 percent in passenger fares through Arizona. (2)

FEB. 28. Tucson Chamber of Commerce boasts city has annual payroll of $10,000,000. (2)

MAR. 1. State Veterinarian rules that prevalance of hoof and mouth disease in California justifies Arizona in taking steps to disinfect all cattle, freight cars and automobiles crossing the border to points within this state. (3)

MAR. 8. U. S. Dept. of Commerce finds total amount of Arizona's principal forms of wealth reached $1,300,000,000 in 1922. This is a gain of 190.8 percent in ten years. (3)

MAR. 12. Arizona Supreme Court approves sale of bonds financing power line from Roosevelt Dam to Casa Grande. (2)

MAR. 26. Agitation for dividing Pima County and creating a new county containing Ajo is opposed by New Cornelia Copper Co. Proposal dies. (2)

MAR. 30. Drillers start sinking well in search for oil near Benson. (2)

APRIL 5. Congressional committee makes two requests for Governor Hunt to appear and justify his charges that Colorado is being favored by the government in efforts to utilize Colorado River water. Hunt backs away. (2)

APRIL 6. State Veterinarian closes all but two entry points from California and halts auto passengers. (3)

APRIL 7. Arizona livestock men and veterinarians consider asking that National Guard be called out to prevent entry of cattle from California and New Mexico. (2)

APRIL 13. Seventy east-bound California motorists try to rush river bridge at Yuma and are pushed back by Arizona armed guards. (2)

APRIL 9. Governor Hunt issues a formal proclamation halting all auto traffic from California at the border. (3)

APRIL 18. California reports that 1600 motorists are stranded at points of entrance into Arizona because of embargo on vehicular traffic due to hoof and mouth quarantine. Occupants of 115 cars at Needles threaten to overpower Arizona guards. Governor Hunt orders National Guard readied for duty. (2)

APRIL 18. Chiricahua National Monument established. (26)

APRIL 19. Seven hundred destitute, hungry and desperate California motorists attempt to break the quarantine line at Yuma. Guards drive leaders back with streams from fire hose. (2)

APRIL 21. Federal government refuses Arizona's request for regular army troops to enforce quarantine along the California-Arizona border. (2)

APRIL 22. Governor Hunt tightens embargo. Rules that California passengers on railway trains cannot alight in Arizona without a certificate from the Arizona Board of Health. (3)

APRIL 24. State Commission of Agriculture and Horticulture establishes safety zone in Pima County on which planting of cotton is forbidden because of boll weevil plague. Farmers estimate their loss will be $1,500,000. (2)

APRIL 25. New edict limits Californians entering Arizona to hand luggage. (3)

APRIL 29. After holding east-bound Californians and their cars as long as a week, Arizona establishes stations and begins disinfecting the travelers at Yuma, Wickenburg, and Kingman. (2)

MAY 1. Indians on the Yuma Reservation take a hand in enforcement of quarantine regulations and drive 75 stranded tourists off their lands. (3)

MAY 7. J. W. (Uncle Billy) Spear, managing editor of the *Arizona Republican,* criticizes a decision by Pinal County Superior Court judge and is fined $300 for contempt of court. Spear refuses to pay, goes to jail and is finally released on bail. (2)

MAY 10. Pima Indians appeal to Congress to restore their rights to water from the Gila which the white man has stolen. (3)

MAY 11. One company of U. S. Infantry is sent to the Chiricahuas to help forest rangers fight serious forest fire. (3)

MAY 15. Representatives of industry, finance and agriculture confer with Governor Hunt over possible modification of California quarantine and demand rigid controls be continued. (3)

MAY 17. Declaring that no contempt of court has been committed, superior court frees editor J. W. (Uncle Billy) Spear of the *Arizona Republican.* (7)

MAY 18. Charges that farmers and dealers in the Salt River Valley are taking advantage of embargo to raise price of fruits and vegetables is denied by Phoenix Chamber of Commerce. (3)

MAY 19. Judge of Pinal County Superior Court is arrested on charge of carrying a concealed gun. (2)

MAY 21. Superior Court at Phoenix holds that judges are peace officers and therefore can carry concealed weapons. (3)

MAY 22. Arizona Federal Courts acquit only three defendants in 124 prohibition cases during April. (3)

MAY 27. Nine hundred Pinal County citizens sign petition seeking recall of Superior Court judge who presides with "a pistol in his hip pocket, has a bad temper and suffers from hallucinations." (3)

JUNE 5. Congressional approval of San Carlos dam on the Gila at cost of $5,500,000 ushers in big celebration at Casa Grande. Project expected to irrigate 80,000 acres. (2)

JUNE 17. Pima County cotton growers go to Federal Court to try to free their cotton crop, now restricted by Arizona Commission of Agriculture. (2)

JUNE 30. Arizona Industrial Congress announces survey which shows one-quarter of Arizona's people live in communities that depend on mining industry for existence. (1)

JULY 1. First parcel post package is sent airmail from Tucson to New York. (1)

JULY 2. Washington closes the border at Douglas, Naco and Nogales from 9 p.m. to 7 a.m. daily, and gambling ceases in Sonora towns. (1)

JULY 11. Fiscal year 1923-24 shows 100 percent increase in recorded Arizona crime over previous year due to vigorous prosecution of bootlegging. (2)

JULY 20. Pima Cotton farmers win a delay in proposed destruction of their crops, giving them time to pick a million dollar yield. (2)

JULY 22. Murder suspect being returned by officers from Calexico to Yuma escapes from car by leaping into Colorado, but is imprisoned by quicksand and disappears. (1)

JULY 22. Order closing the U.S.-Mexico border is revoked, mainly through the efforts of Congressman Carl Hayden. (1)

JULY 26. Arizona lifts restrictions against California's eastbound rail passengers. Disinfection ceases. (3)

JULY 27. "It's no place for a cowboy — it's too far east. There's not much coffee and too much tea," declares Ed Echols, back from the rodeo in London, in describing his experiences in England. (1)

JULY 29. Shareholders of the Salt River Valley Water Users Assn. vote twenty to one in favor of $2,000,000 bond issue for Horse Mesa Dam on the Salt River. (3)

JULY 31. Effects of depression are shown in assessed valuation of the state which drops $51,500,000. Low price of copper brings down assessed valuation of productive mines $41,600,000. Sheepmen are angry because valuation of their flocks is increased $1 a head. (1)

AUG. 17. Salt River Valley has its greatest cantaloupe crop and sends approximately 2,200 carloads to market. (3)

AUG. 31. U. S. Senator Ralph Cameron is cited for contempt in Federal Court. He refuses to recognize Supreme Court ruling that his claims to strategic sites on Bright Angel Trail in Grand Canyon are spurious. (1)

SEPT. 4. First Arizona Indian casts his ballot under provision of act of Congress granting citizenship to the red man. (3)

SEPT. 9. G. W. P. Hunt is again candidate for the Democratic nomination for Governor. (2)

SEPT. 17. Federal court gives Senator Cameron two weeks in which to vacate the sites he continues to hold on Bright Angel Trail. (1)

SEPT. 28. Arizona bars cattle from four Texas counties due to outbreak of hoof and mouth disease. (1)

SEPT. 30. Interstate Commerce Commission approves Southern Pacific's plan to acquire control of El Paso and Southwestern Railway and build main line through Phoenix. (3)

OCT. 1. Senator Cameron surrenders his Bright Angel Trail claims and federal judge dismisses contempt action. (1)

OCT. 2. Thousands of Phoenix citizens gather at Union station to celebrate coming of the Southern Pacific main line. (3)

OCT. 7. State Supreme Court rules that National Guard has the power to court martial and punish soldiers for disobedience of orders. (3)

OCT. 22. Attempt to strike oil at Benson is abandoned. Fresh capital views prospect of further drilling. (1)

OCT. 24. Arizona has what it calls "A week of wonders." Navy dirigible "Shenandoah" crosses the state and people hear first nationwide radio broadcast of a presidential speech, as Coolidge talks to National Chamber of Commerce. (2)

OCT. 29. Federal prohibition agents stage battle in the Huachuca Mountains with guards of pack train loaded with liquor. (1)

NOV. 5. Catholic Church of Santa Cruz in Tucson seriously damaged by explosion of bomb. (1)

NOV. 6. G. W. P. Hunt declared winner in close gubernatorial contest with Dwight B. Heard. Will be his fifth term as Governor. (3)

NOV. 15. Order for destruction of Pima cotton crop is declared illegal by special master in chancery. Decided victory for the cotton growers. (1)

NOV. 19. Forestry Service throws open Kaibab Game Preserve to hunters with permits good for three deer. Governor Hunt tells county prosecutors to arrest all hunters found with dead game. (3)

NOV. 20. Electric power flows through new lines in the Casa Grande-Florence Valley district and irrigation of 100,000 acres begins. (3)

NOV. 29. Verbal war over hunting deer in Kaibab forest fizzles out when state gives its approval to reduction of the vast herd. (3)

DEC. 1. Town of Benson is incorporated.

DEC. 6. Congressman Carl Hayden persuades appropriations committee of the House of Representatives to name the San Carlos project, "Coolidge Dam." (7)

DEC. 9. Wupatki prehistoric ruins made a National Monument. (26)

DEC. 10. One hundred indictments are found against officers of defunct Tucson National Bank; charges are conspiracy to misappropriate funds. (3)

DEC. 11. American Association of University Professors probes dismissal of teachers at the University of Arizona. (3)

DEC. 12. Labor commissioner brings charges against Yuma cotton planters alleging they paid off workers with bad checks. (3)

DEC. 17. Hundreds of Phoenix residents view the latest example of luxurious transportation — the new Golden State Limited of the Southern Pacific. (3)

DEC. 18. Elaborate plans for spectacular drive of 5,000 Kaibab deer across the Colorado to new grazing lands are frustrated when the wild animals stampede in a blinding snowstorm and disappear. (3)

DEC. 22. Florence suffers a disastrous pre-Christmas fire which destroys half a block of business buildings. (3)

DEC. 23. Auto and gasoline taxes for 1924 yield Arizona $1,000,000 in taxes for the first time. (3)

DEC. 26. Governor Hunt and state's business men draft a message to Congress announcing that the sovereign State of Arizona will uphold her rights in any legislation bearing on use of Colorado River water. (1)

DEC. 29. Strict quarantine is put on importation of poultry into Arizona from other states. Epidemics have practically destroyed industry in middle west. (3)

DEC. 31. Deposits in Arizona banks total $71,231,463. (27)
Total major minerals production in Arizona, $99,610,379. (16)
Total number of cattle in Arizona, 1,300,000; value, $31,590,000. (24)

1925 JAN. 2. Phoenix records largest real estate transaction to date as Phoenix National Bank pays $200,000 for half-block in center of business district. (3)

JAN. 5. Actual construction of the new main line of the Southern Pacific begins at Picacho before group of municipal and railroad officials. (1)

JAN. 6. U. S. agrees to permit Sonora cotton to pass from Nogales to El Paso under bond for fumigation. (2)

JAN. 8. Federal court jury hears pleas of Papago Indians that "Tiswin" is not whiskey but a ceremonial drink made sacred by time and custom and therefore legal. The jury finds defendants guilty of manufacturing intoxicating liquor. (1)

JAN. 12. Seventh State Legislature opens. Changes names of normal schools to State Teachers Colleges; establishes code of vital statistics; makes study of U. S. and Arizona constitutions compulsory in all public schools; passes workmen's compensation law; ratifies child labor amendment to Federal Constitution. (14)

JAN. 16. Salt River Valley cotton harvest for 1924 is estimated at 65,000 bales. (3)

JAN. 25. Fire in Yuma wipes out headquarters of U. S. Reclamation Service and County Water Users Association; damage $150,000. (3)

JAN. 27. Deputy sheriff of Gila County is fined $250 by Federal court for taking U. S. prisoners to the polls on election day. (2)

FEB. 19. U. S. Senate debates possibility of denying Mexico the right to any Colorado River water, stored or impounded, in Arizona. (3)

FEB. 20. Main structure of Mormon Flat Dam is completed and reservoir with capacity for 90,000 acre feet of water begins to fill behind it. (3)

FEB. 20. Federal prohibition agents and Tucson police dry up the city temporarily when they seize 15 stills, 200 gallons of whiskey, and make 40 arrests. (2)

FEB. 21. Arizona House of Representatives votes to keep lobbyists off the floor. Step is aimed at advocates of Colorado Compact. (3)

FEB. 27. U. S. House of Representatives finally votes to ratify the Colorado Compact. (3)

FEB. 28. California and Arizona stage celebration at Yuma over opening of the Phoenix-Yuma-Imperial Valley highway. (3)

MAR. 1. Phoenix booms; building records show total of $750,000 in first two months of year. (3)

MAR. 5. Arizona cattlemen told that federal government will cut grazing fees during 1925 on U. S. lands in districts where drouth conditions have worked hardships. (2)

MAR. 9. Tucson city council revives old curfew law and orders all children off the streets by nine o'clock. (2)

MAR. 11. U. S. Senate approves the Colorado River Compact. (3)

MAR. 20. Governor Hunt establishes quarantine on Arizona cattle and requires state permit for all movements; scabies have broken out again. (3)

MAR. 23. Penniless tourists returning to homes in East from California present so great a demand for aid that Tucson's organized charities declare they can care only for children. (2)

MAR. 25. Governor Hunt scornfully rejects a legislative resolution ratifying Colorado River Compact. (3)

MAR. 30. State asks federal government to help fight epidemic of scabies among Arizona cattle herds. (2)

MAR. 31. Cattlemen in vicinity of Prescott use gasoline blow torches to burn spines off cactus and provide fodder for starving herds. (2)

APRIL 18. Right of the voters to recall Superior Court judges for misconduct in office is upheld by State Supreme Court. (3)

APRIL 18. Governor Hunt imposes quarantine on large herds of cattle in Pima and Santa Cruz counties to prevent spread of scabies. (2)

APRIL 20. Two die and between $50,000 and $100,000 worth of property is lost in fire originating in a restaurant at Cottonwood. (2)

APRIL 22. Year long drouth in Southern Arizona is broken by heavy rains. Northern counties are covered with snow. (2)

APRIL 24. Phoenix Chamber of Commerce circulates straw ballot on proposition that name of Salt River Valley be changed to Roosevelt Valley; meets strong opposition. (3)

APRIL 25. George Lynn, editor and publisher of *Yuma Evening Herald,* is charged with criminal libel and goes to jail rather than make bond. (2)

APRIL 26. Monument honoring Charles D. Poston, "Father of Arizona," is dedicated on Poston Butte near Florence. (3)

MAY 17. Six-months campaign to raise $340,000 for a tourist hotel in Tucson ends with a victory dinner. (2)

MAY 23. Bisbee citizens form volunteer fire fighting force to battle blazes in forest reserves near the city. (3)

MAY 24. Globe reports 500 acres of timber afire in Crook National Forest. (3)

MAY 31. Fire which has destroyed 2,500 acres of forest lands in the Huachuca Mountains is brought under control. (2)

JUNE 4. Arizona cattlemen ask for extension of waiver fees in national forest reserves until end of 1926. Want per acre instead of per head principle to govern future charges. (3)

JUNE 10. U. S. Senate sub-committee investigates administration of National Parks and Public Domain in Arizona. (3)

JUNE 15. Phoenix tries to buy street railway system. Corporation Commission refuses permission. (3)

JUNE 16. U. S. Government and State of Arizona enter into agreement to begin engineering study of irrigational and power possibilities of the Colorado River in Arizona. (2)

JUNE 18. Jury fails to agree in libel suit brought against George W. Lynn, editor of *Yuma Herald,* who charged prominent dairymen with doping tubercular milk with formaldehyde. (3)

JUNE 19. Land owners on the Gila river are given right to take six acre feet from river yearly for irrigation purposes. (3)

JUNE 20. Arizona Supreme Court reverses ruling of Superior Court that judges are peace officers and therefore are free to carry concealed weapons. (3)

JUNE 21. Chief Forester of the U. S. announces in Flagstaff hearing that he favors extension of free grazing rights in nationally owned forests. (2)

JUNE 24. Landholders of the Roosevelt Water Conservation District vote $1,000,000 bond issue for further development of their project. (3)

JUNE 30. Arizona cities wire offers of aid to city of Santa Barbara which is hard hit by earthquakes. (3)

JULY 1. Cantaloupe growers in Salt River Valley break all records with $2,800,000 crop and lettuce growers follow with yield estimated at $1,968,000. (3)

JULY 3. Arizona State Tax Commission sets value of state's producing mines at more than quarter-billion dollars. (1)

JULY 4. Two days of rainstorms flood Tucson, wash out Nogales road and bring down telephone and telegraph lines. Santa Cruz River goes on rampage. (1)

JULY 8. Maricopa County sheriff's men seize 52 stills with a capacity of 5,000 gallons a week in sustained three months' drive on violators of prohibition laws. (3)

JULY 21. President Mulford Winsor of the State Senate and Speaker MacMillin of the House name a board to participate in the deliberations of representatives of Lower Basin States at Phoenix. Governor Hunt declares he will refuse to approve members' expense warrants. (3)

JULY 23. Tucson citizens raise a purse of $62 for policeman who killed a burglar. (1)

JULY 31. Board of directors of new hotel financed in Tucson selects the name "Conquistador" from 6,000 suggestions. (1)

AUG. 3. Disregarding Winsor's committee, Governor Hunt names his own delegates to the Tri-State River Conference. (3)

AUG. 9. U. S. border patrol, organized July 1, 1924, reports capture of 1310 illegal entrants into Arizona in one year. Forty men cover 320 mile beat from New Mexico line to point 35 miles east of Yuma. (1)

AUG. 12. State Tax Commission slashes assessments of New Cornelia Mine and Tucson Gas, Electric Light & Power Co. by $4,000,000. (1)

AUG. 16. State Highway Department announces that tourists spend $10,000,000 a year in Arizona. (1)

AUG. 17. Representatives of California and Nevada meet with Governor Hunt's appointees in Tri-State River Conference. Arizona refuses to withdraw its objection to building a dam near Boulder Canyon. Nevada and California walk out and report it is impossible to work with any Hunt-dominated committee. (3)

AUG. 26. Pima, Cochise and Santa Cruz counties report rapid development of agriculture through use of pumped water. (3)

AUG. 27. Picacho Dam breaks and thousands of acres in vicinity of Randolph and Picacho are flooded. (3)

AUG. 30. Governors of Colorado, Wyoming and Nevada urge Congress to oppose any development of power installations on the Colorado River by the lower basin states. Charge Arizona with bad faith. (3)

SEPT. 2. Federal government reports that 11,386 individuals and 477 corporations paid income taxes in Arizona. Collector announces heaviest tax was the $27,461 paid by Mrs. J. S. Douglas. Her husband, James S. Douglas, paid $16,345. Senators Ashurst and Campbell together paid less than $75. (1)

SEPT. 18. Governor Hunt warns U. S. that Arizona owns all the game within its borders and that this applies to forest preserves. (1)

SEPT. 18. U. S. withdraws two sections of Tucson land from public entry and designates them as site of an airfield for the city. (1)

SEPT. 19. Tucson gets a tornado and one inch of rain in 10 minutes. Much damage is done to government hospital at Pastime Park. Total rainfall is 2.47 inches in three days. (1)

SEPT. 20. Federal court jury hears case of seven farmers who suc United Verde and United Verde Extension mines for $62,000 damage done to crops by fumes; total verdict is $5,000. (1)

SEPT. 29. Arizona goes to the polls and votes to amend the State Constitution by rewriting the Workmen's Compensation Law. (1)

OCT. 2. Congressman Carl Hayden tells Arizona not to be bashful in asking U. S. aid for road building, despite protests of Easterners. (3)

OCT. 4. U. S. sues to obtain all water rights on the Gila in order to make sure the San Carlos dam will serve purpose for which it was built and supply the Indians with water. (1)

OCT. 13. Tucson Health Department submits survey of city and reports only half the main section of town has sewers or septic tanks; says outdoor toilets are a menace to health of community. (1)

OCT. 24. Fifty Mexican soldiers capture robbery suspect wanted by American police and shove him bodily across the border to waiting sheriff. (1)

OCT. 28. Federal Power Commission suspends any power development on the Colorado River until lower basin states get together on compact. (1)

OCT. 30. City of Phoenix decides to take over operation of its streetcar line until Jan. 1. (3)

NOV. 1. Special Irrigation and Reclamation Committee of U. S. Senate meets in Yuma and learns border city favors Boulder Dam and an All-American Canal into the Imperial Valley of California. (3)

NOV. 2. Special Senate Committee sits in Phoenix and is told Arizona will never ratify Colorado Pact until her rights are completely protected. (3)

NOV. 3. Governor Hunt signs proclamation announcing that the revised Workmen's Compensation Law is in effect and injunction suits are immediately filed. (3)

NOV. 7. Phoenix asks Southern Pacific to operate its streetcar line. (3)

NOV. 17. Western Division of the American Mining Congress meets in Chandler and denounces efforts of the government to raise taxes on mines. (3)

NOV. 20. Governor Hunt threatens to call out state troops to protect Arizona's right to control of the deer in Kaibab Forest. (1)

NOV. 30. Superior Court holds that Arizona's Workmen's Compensation Law is constitutional. (3)

DEC. 1. Second Tri-State Conference meets in Phoenix. California and Nevada make a bid for peace. No progress. (3)

DEC. 2. Indians in the Mohave-Apache Reservation complain to government that they are starving and need water for irrigation. (1)

DEC. 9. The Colorado River becomes an important problem in Congress; three new measures are introduced. (3)

DEC. 11. Secretary Herbert Hoover recommends the construction of a Boulder Canyon high dam project and suggests a contract be made by the government with some other agency for its completion. (1)

DEC. 17. California and Nevada reject Arizona's suggestions for settlement of Colorado River problem. Ask for another conference. (3)

DEC. 18. Tucson city council wires President Coolidge that it disapproves of the court martial of Colonel William Mitchell. (1)

DEC. 19. First action under new Arizona law making it a misdemeanor to give false information to a newspaper is brought by *Arizona Republican*. Defendant gets 30 day suspended sentence. (3)

DEC. 20. Twelve hundred boxes of dynamite explode at the United Verde Copper Mine and damage walls and window glass in Jerome to the extent of $20,000. (1)

DEC. 21. Swing-Johnson bill which provides for erection of Boulder Dam if compact is ratified by six states is introduced in both branches of Congress. (1)

DEC. 29. Arizona cattlemen are notified they have another six months of free grazing in the national forests. (3)

DEC. 31. Deposits in Arizona banks total $70,210,314. (27)

Total major minerals production in Arizona, $113,138,198. (16)

Total number of cattle in Arizona, 1,032,000; value, $32,508,000. (24)

State report on schools shows total daily attendance of 49,372 which includes 7,947 attending high schools; not in school, 16,664 children. (15)

1926 JAN. 1. Phoenix reports that building permits issued in 1925 totalled $3,183,000. (3)

JAN. 6. U. S. Department of the Interior asks Congress to appropriate $1,500,000 for Arizona projects and care for Arizona Indians. (3)

JAN. 22. U. S. Department of Agriculture announces new regulations governing grazing in national forests; ten year permits with the effect of contracts. (3)

FEB. 6. Senator Ralph H. Cameron of Arizona urges Congress to make sale of liquor to minors a prison offense. (1)

FEB. 11. Governor Hunt notifies U. S. Senate that if Boulder Canyon project on the Colorado is passed the State of Arizona will forcibly resist building of dam. (1)

FEB. 11. Mulford Winsor, president of the state senate, wins a private war with Governor Hunt when Supreme Court says governor must sign checks in payment of Winsor's work for code commissioner. (3)

FEB. 17. Using forged certificates, three rustlers ship 237 head of cattle out of Arizona and sell them in Los Angeles. (3)

FEB. 28. Automobile road is opened to within 12 miles of Rainbow Natural Bridge making it a tourist attraction. (1)

MAR. 1. Arizona Cotton Growers' Association starts lobbying in Washington for changes in immigration laws which will permit growers to bring in more Mexican labor. (3)

MAR. 2. Congress provides funds for a million dollar veterans hospital in Tucson. (1)

MAR. 3. U. S. Senate passes Lee's Ferry Bridge appropriation and specifies Navajo Indians must pay half the cost of the $200,000 structure. (3)

MAR. 4. Land Office rules that Tucson has prior claim to 30-acre tract of land on A-Mountain and it can remain a public park. U. S. takes position that land is more valuable for recreational purposes than for timber and mineral development. (1)

MAR. 4. Secretary Hoover of Department of Commerce tells House Irrigation Committee that there is little sense in Arizona's fight against the Colorado Compact and Boulder Dam. (1)

MAR. 5. Senator Ralph Cameron of Arizona introduces bill proposing construction of an irrigation and power development on the Colorado River at Glen Canyon as a substitute for Boulder Dam. (3)

MAR. 6. Governor Hunt tells public time will come when mines will no longer pay high taxes and Arizona must depend on income from Colorado River projects. (1)

MAR. 12. Landholders sue City of Tucson for running sewage into ditches and using it to irrigate municipal farms. (1)

MAR. 24. Clifton-Springerville highway through Apache National Forest opens era in which lumbering will become a permanent industry. (1)

APRIL 3. Tucson wins its campaign to get federal help in building a road to Ajo through Indian reservation. Government gives $125,000. (1)

APRIL 7. Five year shortage of water ends as heavy rains pour thousands of acre feet into reservoir behind Roosevelt Dam. (3)

APRIL 9. Tornado rips along 20 foot strip through eastern section of Phoenix, leveling six houses. (1)

APRIL 13. Governor Hunt refuses to attend conference of governors because Federal government criticizes Arizona's extravagances in spending of state funds. (1)

APRIL 20. Congressman Carl Hayden warns House Irrigation Committee that if Boulder Dam bill passes Arizona will fight it to the highest court. (1)

APRIL 21. Governor Hunt blasts Secretary Hoover for supporting Swing-Johnson bill and assails his competence as an engineer. (1)

APRIL 21. All river states except Arizona favor Boulder Dam bill but Senator Ralph Cameron warns U. S. Senate he will fight to the last against measure and threatens a filibuster. (1)

APRIL 23. Southwest Cotton Co. kills 84,000 prairie dogs and 2,000 gophers on 7,000 acres of land in Maricopa County. Similar campaigns carried on in other counties. (3)

APRIL 25. Boulder Dam battle in Senate reaches oratorical high when Senator Ashurst cries out against the injustice of making Arizona a desert. (1)

APRIL 25. *Arizona Daily Star* carries report of study which, it claims, shows Tucson now has 150 bootleggers against the 30 saloons it had in 1914. (1)

APRIL 29. Yuma County sheriff raids a dairy farm and finds more moonshine than milk. Haul includes 200 gallons of liquor, 750 gallons of mash, 75 gallons of wine and a 100-gallon still. (3)

MAY 5. President Coolidge authorizes the construction of a privately owned toll bridge across the Colorado River at Blythe. (3)

MAY 11. Board of Regents of the University investigates charges against President Marvin, the first step in opening a controversy which divides Tucson into two camps. (3)

MAY 12. Law catches cowboy who masterminded wholesale theft of cattle from Cochise and Pima County ranchers. Jury convicts and he gets one to fourteen year sentence. (1)

MAY 22. Lower House of Congress decides to delay action of Boulder Dam bill until next session. (3)

MAY 25. Mexico files protest with Governor Hunt over action of Phoenix police chief who ordered consulate flag either hauled down or flown below U. S. banner. (1)

MAY 26. Yuma city water supply is unsafe and high school uses tank wagons to bring in drinking water for students. (1)

MAY 27. First National Bank of Tombstone carries its last advertisement in the *Epitaph* and closes doors thereafter but the paper never mentions it again.

MAY 28. Yuma High School graduates 281 white students. Three days later it graduates 11 negroes. (3)

MAY 29. Phoenix citizens approve of $335,000 bond issue for water mains and sewer lines. (3)

JUNE 1. Maricopa sheriff and his deputies invade dense mesquite thicket near Buckeye and capture biggest still yet found in the county; three 500 gallon tanks, two tons of sugar taken. (3)

JUNE 2. U. S. District Court in Los Angeles enters Governor Hunt's war for control of the deer in the Kaibab Forest. Court rules forest service has the right to kill animals but withholds opinion on its right to admit private hunters. (3)

JUNE 3. State Supreme Court rules that judges cannot change or shorten a sentence once a defendant has been convicted and the sentence imposed. (3)

JUNE 6. Six children are trapped in Pantano ranch home by midnight blaze and burn to death. Lack of water renders neighbors helpless. (1)

JUNE 6. Maricopa Superior Court dismisses temporary injunction brought by taxpayer and rules Board of Education has right to hold a bond election to raise $80,000 for an athletic bowl at Phoenix Union High. (3)

JUNE 8. President Coolidge signs appropriation allotting $70,000 for use in fighting the boll weevil in Arizona. (3)

JUNE 9. Governor Hunt announces he will not run again. (3)

JUNE 11. Boys shake dice in rear of Tucson's St. Augustine Cathedral during high mass service and Bishop Daniel James Gercke, clad in all his vestments, boxes their ears and throws them out. (1)

JUNE 17. Arizona learns that Southern Pacific will shave five hours off its 68 hour run between Chicago and Los Angeles. (1)

JUNE 19. Dedication of Coronado Trail highway is held at Hannagan Meadows. (3)

JUNE 23. Aimee Semple McPherson, colorful Los Angeles evangelist who has been missing since May 18, ends two-state search when she staggers into Douglas with a tale of kidnapping, torture, ransom demands and imprisonment somewhere in the desert. (3)

JUNE 27. Shoulder blade of huge prehistoric animal is uncovered near Arivaca. Dr. Byron Cummings, professor of archaeology at the University, says it is probably a quarter of a million years old. (3)

JULY 4. Flagstaff celebrates the Fourth by trucking snow down from the mountains. Hundreds of tourists and settlers have a snowball battle. (3)

JULY 10. Governor Hunt reports that windows and doors of the din- a sixth term. (3)

JULY 10. Governor Hunt reports that windows and doors of the dining room in the state prison now have screens for the first time and that the place is very sanitary. (1)

JULY 16. By vote of five to three the Regents of the University refuse to sustain charges against President Cloyd H. Marvin and at the same time abrogate the faculty constitution. (1)

JULY 17. Governor Hunt defends bank policy but concedes 13 banks closed since 1923. [Some of these failures went unreported in the state press.] (1)

JULY 18. Board of Regents sustains President Marvin against charges brought by ministerial association. (3)

JULY 30. Old Salt River Canal, familiarly known in Phoenix as the "town ditch," passes into history as its water supply is diverted. (3)

AUG. 2. Cloudburst strikes Yuma; streets flooded and crops washed out. (3)

AUG. 6. Board of Regents reappoints President Marvin and the entire faculty. (1)

AUG. 7. Evangelist Aimee Semple McPherson identifies shack near Douglas where she says she was held by kidnappers. (3)

AUG. 12. City of Phoenix adopts a stringent liquor law hoping to dry up bootlegging. (3)

AUG. 16. "Double-header" trains pulls out of Phoenix hauling 95 carloads of cottonseed meal bound for England and Holland. (3)

AUG. 17. Lewis W. Douglas, candidate for nomination to Congress on Democratic ticket, tells a Bisbee audience that he stands for the drafting of capital, resources and manpower during war time. (1)

AUG. 18. Rt. Rev. Bishop Daniel J. Gercke offers sanctuary for 44 Mexican nuns seeking refuge from bitter warfare between Church and State in Mexican Republic. (1)

AUG. 19. Grady Gammage is made president of Northern Arizona Teachers' College. (3)

SEPT. 2. Gubernatorial campaign brings out the facts that assessed valuation of all taxable properties in Arizona increased 71 percent while the cost of government increased 187 percent, and that 15 percent of the tax burden was shifted from industry to the property owner. (3)

SEPT. 7. G. W. P. Hunt is again nominated for Governor, defeating E. E. Ellinwood on the Democratic ticket. (3)

SEPT. 21. Arizona Red Cross contributes aid to 50,000 people of Florida made homeless by hurricane. (1)

SEPT. 29. Heavy rain storms cripple southern counties. St. Mary's bridge washed out in Tucson. (1)

OCT. 1. Tucson alarmed by report that armed band of Yaqui is on the Ajo road 75 miles away. Indian agency at Sells says they are peaceful tribesmen on way to fiesta at Magdalena. (1)

OCT. 27. E. S. Clark, Republican nominee for governor, campaigns on the promise that if elected he will discharge Cloyd H. Marvin, president of the University of Arizona, immediately. (1)

NOV. 1. Boiling hot Arizona campaign for gubernatorial and congressional nominations results in inquiry into alleged slush funds. Copper tycoon admits having given between $35,000 and $50,000 to campaign of a Hunt opponent. (1)

NOV. 2. Gov. Hunt defeats Edward S. Clark for governor by 399 votes; Carl Hayden is elected to U. S. Senate; Lewis W. Douglas sent to House of Representatives. (1)

NOV. 8. Low price of cotton brings widespread hardship to growers in South and Southwest. (1)

NOV. 11. Attempt to cause a head-on collision between the Golden State Limited and Sunset Express on the Southern Pacific line near Gila Bend is foiled by alert engineer. (3)

NOV. 31. Galli-Curci, internationally famous mezzo-soprano, turns the first sod of the excavation for Tucson's Temple of Music and Art. (1)

DEC. 1. California bankers come to assistance of Arizona farmers who hold large supplies of surplus cotton in storage. (3)

DEC. 2. Maricopa County Farm Bureau complains to Interstate Commerce Commission that refrigeration rates on the new main line are altogether too high. (3)

DEC. 5. Arizona growers decide to hold cotton off market in effort to halt falling prices. (3)

DEC. 20. City of Nogales makes a bid for National Guard company. Promises to build armory. (1)

DEC. 24. U. S. pays Southern Pacific $1,000,000 to move 15 miles of track between Bowie and Globe to clear way for Coolidge Dam. (1)

DEC. 31. Deposits in Arizona banks total $72,167,850. (27)
Total major minerals production in Arizona, $113,536,288. (16)
Total number of cattle in Arizona, 917,000; value, $29,986,000. (24)
Town of Benson, Cochise County, incorporated. (18)

1927 JAN. 1. Seven earthquake shocks usher in New Year's Day at Yuma. Damage there is light but nearby Calexico and Mexicali suffer great disaster. (2)

JAN. 1. California, Nevada and Arizona delegates to Colorado River tri-state conference suspend deliberations. Disagree over Arizona's share of power revenue. (3)

JAN. 2. Flagstaff stages all-day celebration closing with grand ball to mark opening of new $300,000 hotel. (3)

JAN. 3. Legislature is called into special session to consider appropriation for Colorado River Conferences and the relief of State Highway Department which is deep in red. Adjourns without accomplishing anything except to irritate the governor. (2)

JAN. 6. Arizona bankers refuse to accept veteran's bonus insurance certificates as security for cash loans. Claim six percent interest is too low. (2)

JAN. 10. Eighth State Legislature meets in regular session. Friction between governor and legislature and alarm over Colorado River legislation being considered by Congress results in six special sessions. (14)

JAN. 12. Congressman Carl Hayden warns Congress that Arizona will fight to last ditch to stop Swing-Johnson Boulder Dam bill. State senators carry protest to President Coolidge. (2)

JAN. 18. State Treasurer reports to Legislature that State of Arizona has lost $450,000 in failures of state banks. (2)

JAN. 18. U. S. Treasury recommends expenditures of $811,000 in Phoenix and $725,000 in Tucson for new postoffices. (3)

JAN. 20. President Cloyd H. Marvin resigns at the University. Chancellor E. E. Ellinwood follows him. Robert E. Tally, president of United Verde Copper Co., succeeds Ellinwood. U. S. withholds aid to Agricultural College until campus turmoil is cleared up. (2)

JAN. 21. Legislature defeats resolution asking Governor Hunt to dismiss entire Board of Regents for its share in Marvin case. (2)

JAN. 21. Congressman Hayden carries Arizona's fight for Colorado River rights to Congress with bitter attack on California and eloquent plea for preservation of his state's sovereign rights. (3)

JAN. 23. State superintendent of public health orders all student gatherings at U of A., except classes and laboratory sessions, quarantined. Fears scarlet fever epidemic. Two known cases on campus. No additional cases are noted. (2)

JAN. 25. Five and one-half year audit of state highway operation, presented to legislature, claims gross irregularities create deficit of $1,209,342. (3)

JAN. 31. Dr. Byron Cummings is appointed temporary president of the University by Board of Regents. (2)

JAN. 31. U. S. Bureau of Reclamation announces that Salt River Valley led all Federal irrigation projects in California, New Mexico and Texas in cotton yield per acre in 1926. (3)

FEB. 12. Nine state senators, far ahead of their time, seek in vain to interest legislature in a dam and power plant at Glen Canyon. (3)

FEB. 16. Special fact finding committee of the Legislature investigates State Highway Department and declares it has been turned into a political machine by Governor Hunt with resulting loss to the state of $200,000. (2)

FEB. 17. Floods which wash out bridges over Agua Fria and Hassayampa rivers halt traffic on Phoenix-Gila Bend-Yuma highway. (3)

FEB. 18. Floods add 344,000 acre feet of water to Roosevelt Reservoir. (3)

FEB. 19. Grand Jury bars 13 "art" magazines from Tucson news stands. (2)

FEB. 22. Superior Court judge notifies Maricopa County supervisors that if they do not put the jail in a sanitary condition he will send no more federal prisoners there. (3)

FEB. 23. Filibuster in U. S. Senate blocks vote on Boulder Canyon bill. (3)

FEB. 26. Swing-Johnson Boulder Dam bill is lost in Congressional legislative jam. (2)

FEB. 28. Legislature sends Governor Hunt a compromise Colorado River bill providing for eight commissioners, four to be named by Governor, four by Legislature, and initial appropriation of $100,000. Governor Hunt approves. (3)

MAR. 2. Nogales business district has $250,000 fire. (3)

MAR. 2. Federal prohibition officials make 20 arrests in Tucson while the grand jury is in session. (2)

MAR. 3. Maricopa County is plagued by automobile owners who avoid high county tax by purchasing licenses in Pinal County. (3)

MAR. 14. U. S. District Court upholds right of Secretary of the Interior to cancel permits for Verde District Irrigation and Power District. (3)

MAR. 15. Senate bill legalizing use of voting machines in Arizona becomes a law. (3)

MAR. 16. Report of discovery of rich gold deposits near Winkelman starts rush for Dripping Springs Range. (3)

MAR. 19. Legislature takes recess while waiting for Governor Hunt to veto appropriation bill, then reconvenes and over-rides the veto. (3)

MAR. 19. Winkelman's gold strike dies early. (3)

MAR. 30. Second special session of State Legislature, called by Governor Hunt, declares reasons given by Governor for calling a special session do not establsh the existence of an emergency and adjourns after passing appropriation for legislative salaries. (3)

APRIL 1. Five thousand Valley residents help Glendale celebrate inauguration of its street lighting system. (3)

APRIL 1. Fifty-five rum runners plead guilty in Tucson after three-week drive by federal officers. (2)

APRIL 2. Cochise-Graham cattlemen act to halt rustling. Order their crews to ride armed on the ranges and not to spare the hot lead. (3)

APRIL 3. Horse Mesa dam and power plant go into operation and begin earning $3200 a day for Water Users' Assn. (3)

APRIL 10. Convicted of attempting to wreck Golden State Limited, prisoner gets 25-35 year sentence. (1)

APRIL 14. First through passenger train over the newly completed Southern Pacific of Mexico leaves Nogales for Guadalajara. (1)

APRIL 18. Legislature reconvenes after a month long recess but finds itself still deadlocked in arguments with Governor Hunt. (1)

APRIL 20. Globe celebrates 50th anniversary of founding and 12,000 Arizonans turn out to help, including Governor Hunt who entered town first in 1881 riding a burro and seeking his fortune. (3)

APRIL 30. Mrs. William Henry Brophy gives $250,000 and 25 acres of land to endow and build Jesuit college in Phoenix. (3)

MAY 5. Fire destroys 15 buildings in Globe. (3)

MAY 8. U. S. Army hold 38 Yaqui Indian warriors who flee across U. S. border after bloody battle with Mexican troops. (3)

MAY 9. Nogales hears armed Yaqui Indian fighters are marching on city and many Americans leave hastily by auto. Mexican troops entrench above Nogales, Sonora. (3)

MAY 10. Wife of manager of Slaughter ranch is captured by roaming Yaquis and held until her husband provides ransom of horses and clothing. (2)

MAY 11. Railroad and telegraph communications between Douglas and west coast of Mexico cut off by burned bridges and broken lines. Mexicans blame Yaquis. (2)

MAY 14. Nogales breathes easily again as Yaquis straggle across border in small groups and offer to lead U. S. troops to their cache of arms and ammunition. (3)

MAY 17. Three Federal Court judges rule that U. S. Government has the right to open the Kaibab to hunters, set the bag limits and do whatever else it deems necessary to protect the forest no matter what Governor Hunt or the State of Arizona may rule. (3)

MAY 19. U. S. closes the international border at San Luis south of Yuma because of political unrest and threats of rebellion in Sonora. American civilians patrol the fence with their own weapons. (2)

MAY 23. Santa Fe fast trains crash at Flagstaff. One death; scores are injured. (3)

MAY 25. Maricopa Grand Jury returns 47 true bills in its initial report. Most of the charges involve gambling or prohibition violations. (3)

MAY 26. Santa Fe hauls largest trainload of cotton shipped from Salt River Valley; 1,000 bales. (3)

MAY 31. Arizona votes to adopt two constitutional amendments which strengthen state's hand in development of Colorado River water. (3)

JUNE 3. University laboratories dissect 300 Tucson cats and fail to find one healthy specimen. All have tuberculosis. (2)

JUNE 4. U. S. and Mexican guards of honor join in paying national tributes to wife of President Calles as her casket is transferred at the border to Presidential special train on Southern Pacific of Mexico. (1)

JUNE 7. President Grady Gammage of Northern Arizona Teachers College objects to University hiring out-of-state teachers. (1)

JUNE 8. State Teachers College at Tempe gives its first Bachelor of Education degrees to 13 graduates. (3)

JUNE 18. U. S. Army inspector makes unfavorable report on Phoenix and Tempe National Guard companies. Adjutant General threatens to muster them out. (3)

JUNE 20. Arizona Colorado River Commissioners and Utah state officials meet in Salt Lake City and agree that building of Boulder Dam would give Mexico and California unfair division of water. (1)

JUNE 22. Arizona Supreme Court ends hot state battle by ruling that three cent gasoline tax law is legal. (3)

JUNE 23. Phoenix building permits during first half of year surpass total figure for entire year of 1926 by exceeding $3,000,000 mark. (3)

JULY 1. Reservoir fills and first water flows over top of Horse Mesa dam in a cataract higher than Niagara Falls. (3)

JULY 1. California Congressman announces he will introduce bill asking Congress to demote Arizona to a Territory. Charges that in its attitude on Colorado River water the state had "violated, annulled and renounced the constitution." (1)

JULY 2. Tucson grants its day laborers first pay increase in 20 years; makes pay scale $2.50 to $3 a day. (1)

JULY 8. Federal prohibition officers report that in first six months of the year they made 504 arrests for violations and seized 4,000 gallons of illegal liquor in Arizona. (1)

JULY 11. Arizona makes strong protest to Interstate Commerce Commission over paying freight rate of 5.28 cents a gallon on gasoline shipped from Los Angeles. (3)

JULY 12. Delay in re-opening Apache Trail, closed by storm damages, creates political row in Salt River Valley and Governor Hunt finds emergency exists. (3)

JULY 19. All Arizona warehouses for rent for storage of cotton or wool become public service corporations and must obtain licenses from Arizona Corporation Commission. (3)

JULY 23. Unhappy over division of tax receipts Willcox citizens hold mass meeting and vote unanimously for separation from Cochise County. (1)

JULY 25. Eighth State Legislature opens third special session, making four sessions in six months. Purpose is to provide relief legislation for State's creditors. (1)

JULY 26. Members of Legislature ask Governor Hunt to broaden special session business to include general highway legislation. Hunt refuses. (3)

AUG. 1. Seventeen hundred foot bridge over the Gila near Gillespie dam is opened for use. (3)

AUG. 2. U. S. Biological Survey reports destruction of 4,000,000 Arizona rodents in last fiscal year. (3)

AUG. 8. Price of cotton jumps $10 a bale as Dept. of Agriculture releases estimates of damage done by boll weevil. Arizona, off 15 percent, is second high in production. (3)

AUG. 11. Eighth Legislature closes third special session and opens fourth. Governor and Legislature finally reach agreement on highway relief bill. Legislature condemns Board of State Institutions for appropriating $75,000 to pay for Colorado River surveys. (3)

AUG. 22. California and Arizona Colorado River Commissions hold conference in hope of reaching accord. No progress. (1)

AUG. 23. California and Arizona, still fighting for Colorado River water, finally agree Arizona has full right to its own tributary streams. (1)

AUG. 30. Prescott, Seligman, Flagstaff and Kingman report ranges are green as lawns and that grass is in the best condition in years. (3)

SEPT. 4. Arizona's highway affairs tangled again when state treasurer announces he will not honor warrants drawn on Governor Hunt's emergency fund for emergency repairs of bridges and roads. (1)

SEPT. 12. Nogales reports that Americans operating mines in Mexico fear for their lives and have so notified U. S. Consul at Mazatlan. (3)

SEPT. 13. Dr. Homer LeRoy Shantz becomes president of the University of Arizona. (1)

SEPT. 15. Twelve hundred foot gash, varying from a few inches to five feet in width, suddenly opens in earth near Picacho. (3)

SEPT. 17. Phoenix discovers that the wooden mains bringing water from the Verde intake 30 miles away are in danger of immediate collapse. (3)

SEPT. 23. Charles A. Lindbergh lands his plane, "Spirit of St. Louis," at Tucson. Officials of three Mexican states join 20,000 Americans from all parts of Arizona in enthusiastic welcome. (3)

SEPT. 29. Tornado strikes Ruby and wipes out half the village. (1)

SEPT. 30. Arizona border breathes easily after Nogales report that 600 Yaqui Indians and their chief have surrendered to Mexican army in Sonora. (3)

OCT. 8. Arizona State Federation of Labor joins fight against Swing-Johnson Boulder Dam project and calls on American Federation of Labor to assist. (1)

OCT. 15. Miami sells its publicly owned light and water plant to privately owned company at Globe. (3)

OCT. 20. Phoenix advertises it wants to sell City Hall Plaza but 30 days pass without a bid. (3)

OCT. 20. Fire of unknown origin destroys big lumber plant at Ray. (3)

OCT. 21. Maricopa County Attorney stages series of swift raids and files direct information against 86 people charged with violation of prohibition laws. County jail is crowded. (3)

OCT. 21. Tucson realizes dream of years as it dedicates Temple of Music and Art. (1)

OCT. 22. Lengthy session of water commissions of seven states interested in Colorado River water proves futile. California will not change stand. (3)

OCT. 23. University dedicates its new $450,000 library building; boasts it has 60,000 volumes in its stacks. (1)

OCT. 23. Thousands gather at Mesa to attend four day ceremonies marking dedication of the new Mormon Temple. (3)

OCT. 24. Fourth special session of the Legislature reconvenes after two month recess. Sessions of the Eighth Legislature to date have cost Arizona $145,580. (3)

OCT. 26. Pima County Grand Jury reports that 46 Tucson business firms were omitted from tax rolls during last four years and that books also show defalcations amount to $32,000. (1)

OCT. 29. Nogales, Arizona, joins Nogales, Sonora, in denouncing John H. Udall, state prohibition director, for his charge that "every vice known to man is practiced on the other side of the line." Storm of criticism quiets when Udall says he meant "San Luis." (1)

OCT. 31. Following series of holdups and robberies Phoenix police take to patrolling the streets armed with shotguns. (3)

NOV. 1. Hopi Indian Reservation sends delegation to U of A to appeal for help in airing their charges that Indian agents allow white men to turn their cattle into Hopi lands and refuse to hear protests. (1)

NOV. 1. Yuma becomes Gretna Green of the Southwest as California three-day marriage law drives couples across the border. (1)

NOV. 4. U. S. Horticulture Board finds pink boll weevils in cotton fields near Willcox, Safford and Duncan and plans campaign against the enemy. (1)

NOV. 5. Fourth special session of the Legislature adjourns after merciless use of the axe on appropriations favored by the administration. (3)

NOV. 6. Casa Grande stages elaborate three day pageant before its ancient "great house." (3)

NOV. 9. Southern Pacific charges that Santa Cruz County tax rate is illegal and wins rebate. Private citizens immediately launch wave of similar efforts. Attorney general upsets plans. Rules tax rate is legal. (1)

NOV. 18. Mexican consul in Tucson warns his countrymen that peso is worth $0.47458 and not to take less. (1)

NOV. 22. Selim M. Franklin, father of the legislative measure which created the University, drops dead on Tucson golf course. (1)

NOV. 23. State permits 15 hunters to chase and kill buffalo in House Rock Valley. (3)

NOV. 24. Seven miners die when flames destroy one shaft of the Magma Mine at Superior. Damage is $500,000. (3)

NOV. 28. Tucson becomes terminal of first daily passenger air service from Los Angeles to Southern Arizona. (1)

NOV. 29. Colorado River changes its course below Yuma and U. S. gains 600 acres of Mexican land. (3)

NOV. 30. After delays, recriminations and complaints the scenic Apache Trail between Phoenix and Roosevelt Lake is opened to tourists. (3)

DEC. 2. Arizona wins attention as the first state to regulate and control airplanes engaged in carrying persons and property for compensation. (3)

DEC. 4. Town of Bowie announces oil has been found in commercial quantities at 1,400 feet. Hopes range from 1,000 to 7,000 barrels a day. (3)

DEC. 6. Town of Oatman has its second disastrous fire in two years; damage totals $100,000. (3)

DEC. 9. Two revised Boulder Canyon Dam bills are introduced in Congress. (1)

DEC. 10. Phoenix High School dedicates $80,000 stadium and becomes the envy of all Arizona school districts. (3)

DEC. 20. Arizona Colorado River Commission is invited to appear before Congressional Irrigation Committee and state is elated. (3)

DEC. 25. Coolidge publishes a full page advertisement pleading for 25,000 people to move into Pinal County and populate 1,000 new farms to be irrigated by the waters impounded behind Coolidge Dam. (3)

DEC. 25. Coconino County declares it is largest county in the nation; 18,623 square miles. (3)

DEC. 28. Marana remembers 1927 as year in which it made one bale of cotton to the acre for first time. (1)

DEC. 29. Value of Salt River Valley Water Users crops for the year placed at $21,188,747, an increase of $4,639,586 over 1926. (3)

DEC. 30. Tucson completes successful campaign to raise funds for lights at airport. (1)

DEC. 31. Deposits in Arizona banks total $82,464,680. (27)

Total major minerals production in Arizona, $98,780,957. (16)

Total number of cattle in Arizona, 835,000; value, $34,152,000. (24)

1928 JAN. 1. Tucson reports gain of $500,000 in building permits, 511 new telephones, $5,000,000 gain in clearing house transactions, 600 new gas meters, 1200 new users of electricity and a $6,000 increase in postal receipts over 1926. (1)

JAN. 3. Secretary of the Interior Land endorses the Swing-Johnson Boulder Dam bill. (1)

JAN. 7. Mulford Winsor, president of the Arizona State Senate, pleads with the Irrigation Committee of the U. S. House not to support Boulder Dam measure. (1)

JAN. 7. Promoters who promise to build a soap factory at Safford sell citizens stock and disappear with $54,000. (3)

JAN. 8. Salt River Valley becomes second only to California in lettuce crop. (3)

JAN. 11. U. S. Department of the Interior plans to spend $929,000 in Arizona for irrigation projects and National Park Service. (3)

JAN. 14. Arizona State Tax Commission reveals property value increase of $20,000,000 during year 1927. (3)

JAN. 18. Governor Hunt makes a poor showing when testifying before the U. S. Senate Committee on Boulder Dam. He fails to find answers to Senator Hiram Johnson's questions and *Arizona Daily Star* derides him editorially. (1)

JAN 19. City Planning and Zoning Commission tells council that Tucson must widen its streets. (1)

JAN. 20. Citizens of Mesa open their new community-owned hotel, "El Portal." (3)

JAN. 24. Chairman of Highway Commission warns Good Roads convention at Nogales that old gravel topped roads must give way to hard surface highways. (1)

JAN. 26. Prohibition Director for California and Arizona says the quality of bootleg liquor is so poor that consumption is falling off. (1)

JAN. 27. Arizona Anti-saloon League demands that Mexican border be closed every night. (3)

FEB. 7. Tucson troubles over the price of gasoline become a little war of words with dealers both admitting and denying they make a profit of six cents a gallon. Senator Ashurst asks for probe. (1)

FEB. 7. Gadsden Hotel in Douglas is destroyed by fire. Loss is $200,000. (1)

FEB. 8. Fire destroys four old business landmarks in Tombstone. (1)

FEB. 12. U. S. Commissioner of Reclamation approves Water Users Assoc. plan to hold bond election to finance erection of Stewart Mountain Dam to provide power for the Valley. (3)

FEB. 12. U. S. Bureau of Entomology reports that Santa Cruz valley is affected by pink boll weevil. (1)

FEB. 18. Mexico opens diplomatic relations with U. S. seeking to keep U. S. border ports open at all times. (3)

FEB. 21. Senator Ashurst offers bill giving Arizona and Nevada equal shares in 80 percent of the profits of Boulder Dam. (1)

FEB. 26. Arizona cotton growers ask Congress to suggest a new supply of labor before closing the door to Mexican laborers. (3)

FEB. 28. Government reports that 2,302 acres in federal irrigation project known as Salt River Valley averaged 21,000 pounds of citrus fruit per acre and that dollar yield was $1,450,000. (3)

MAR. 1. Tucson stockholders in El Conquistador Hotel seek to recoup losses by trading holdings for stock in new organization. (1)

MAR. 3. Oil well comes in at Pima, in Graham County. Flow is 100 barrels a day. (1)

MAR. 6. Restaurant owners and waiters' union ask Tucson Council to stop sale of meals at drug store lunch counters. (1)

MAR. 10. Arizona and California join in dedication of new bridge across the Colorado at Ehrenberg. (3)

MAR. 12. Chandler dedicates airport. (3)

MAR. 14. Tucson's dying mayor, John E. White, turns new "Lindy Lights" on for first time at city's airport. He dies following day. (3)

MAR. 22. Federal prohibition officers make sudden sweep through Maricopa county and arrest 25 alleged violators. (3)

MAR. 25. Tucson is informed government will add $260,000 to appropriation for veterans' hospital. (1)

MAR. 31. Senator Ashurst threatens to stage a filibuster against the Swing-Johnson Boulder Dam bill, which he calls "the most sinister, most adroit" effort ever made to over-ride the sovereign rights of a state. (1)

APRIL 3. Tucson and Pima County will give voting machines a modest test in two precincts. (1)

APRIL 7. Declaring their prior rights to subterranean water from the Santa Cruz are being endangered by farming corporations, one rancher and his wife sue 250 farmers. (1)

APRIL 7. State awards $780,000 contract for road improvement. This is the largest highway appropriation to date. (3)

APRIL 8. Tucson citizen who tries to dodge high cost of Pima County automobile licenses by using California plates is fined $121. (1)

APRIL 10. Water Users Association adopts a $2,700,000 budget. Share holders to receive $1,750,000 from power sales which is twice as much as their assessment. (3)

APRIL 14. Mexican and American fire companies at Nogales join efforts and try to save famous old brewery from flames but fire cannot be checked and loss is complete. (3)

APRIL 15. Arizona Pioneers' Historical Society and Southern Pacific erect stone shaft over the graves of Union soldiers who died in the skirmish with Confederate force at Picacho Pass, April 15, 1862. (1)

APRIL 21. Maricopa and Pima Counties battle before Supreme Court over their boundaries. (1)

APRIL 22. State health officer of New Mexico addresses Tucson mothers and scores them for feeding raw milk to their babies. (1)

APRIL 25. Prohibition agents capture two Maricopa stills with potential output of 400 gallons of liquor a day. (3)

APRIL 26. Secretary of Agriculture quarantines the cotton lands of Cochise, Graham and Greenlee Counties in fight against pink boll weevil. (1)

APRIL 28. Senators Ashurst of Arizona and Johnson of California quarrel, shout and pound desks in U. S. Senate Chamber over Swing-Johnson bill. (1)

APRIL 30. Sen. Smoot of Utah joins Ashurst of Arizona in filibuster against the Boulder Dam Bill in Congress. (1)

MAY 3. Governor Hunt goes to Washington to participate in Boulder Dam fight and informs Federal Trade Commission that California is spending huge sums in lobbying for the bill. (1)

MAY 9. City of Tucson argues, and University of Arizona debates, proposal to build a road to Mt. Lemmon. Main objection, "It will cost too much." (1)

MAY 10. University of Arizona Dean of Women rules that women students must wear stockings and cannot appear on campus in abbreviated costumes. (1)

MAY 13. News of auto deaths becomes common and newspapers give the stories first page treatment. (1)

MAY 16. Record cache of 700 bottles of home brew is captured in a private dwelling in Phoenix. (3)

MAY 17. The 400 Chinese living in Tucson unite and offer to help finance campaign of Chiang-Kai-Shek against Japanese troops. (1)

MAY 18. Ease with which prisoners escape from penitentiary at Florence becomes a minor scandal. Florence citizens say number has been between 36 and 40 in last three years. (3)

MAY 19. Tucson Labor Council asks Board of Regents to ban student cars from campus. (1)

MAY 26. Lower House of Congress passes Boulder Dam Bill. (1)

MAY 26. Three are killed and five are injured in construction work at Coolidge Dam. (3)

MAY 28. Coconino County supervisors convey title to Bright Angel Trail to the federal government. (3)

MAY 29. A Congressional Act authorizes appropriation of tribal funds for purchase of lands for the Fort Apache Reservation. (17)

MAY 30. Both houses of Congress vote to submit question of Boulder Dam to a board of five nationally known engineers. (1)

JUNE 1. Maricopa County prohibition agents have a busy day, pouring 1200 gallons of hard liquor and 1500 bottles of beer down the sewers and destroying 45 stills. (3)

JUNE 8. Flagstaff dedicates an airfield with an air circus and a banquet. (3)

JUNE 14. Automobile registration for the year shows that 45 percent of the 72,997 cars in Arizona are owned in Maricopa County. (3)

JUNE 14. Two sections of new Ehrenberg bridge over the Colorado swept away by high water. No ferries available. (1)

JUNE 15. Arizona delegation votes for Hoover at Republican Convention in Kansas City. (1)

JUNE 22. Four Chinese killers who murdered a fellow countryman at Kingman are hanged in State Penitentiary. (3)

JUNE 23. One hundred extra fire fighters are rushed to Tonto National Preserve as district continues to shrivel under dry, hot winds. (3)

JUNE 27. State superintendent of public instruction says that under the $25 per capita tax of Arizona, schools will receive $1,774,000 for the 1928-29 term. (3)

JUNE 28. Arizona delegates to the Democratic convention in Houston, Tex., deliver unanimous state vote to Alfred E. Smith for president. (1)

JULY 7. Early morning fire in Miami destroys $100,000 worth of International Smelting Co. property. (3)

JULY 9. State board of equalization assesses Arizona's producing mines at $218,277,252. (3)

JULY 10. Ranchers round up 14 carloads of wild horses and turn them over to a reduction plant. Captors say animals are useless for farm work and destroy forage needed for cattle. (1)

JULY 11. Tucson holds national airmeet which attracts nation's top aviators. (1)

JULY 12. Pima County Board of Supervisors sue county school superintendent for $16,000 she ordered spent on two rural schools. (1)

JULY 14. Melon shippers of the state denounce railroads for failing to keep April 1927 pledge to cut freight rates $30 a car. (3)

JULY 20. After imprisoning delinquent girls at Fort Grant with delinquent boys Arizona finally decides it needs a school for girls. Modest cost is $30,000. (3)

JULY 24. John H. Udall, Federal prohibition director for Arizona, abandons trailing bootleggers to seek Republican nomination for governor. (3)

JULY 25. Fire takes three lives and destroys five large tanks of oil and gasoline at Kingman. (1)

JULY 27. State superintendent of banks announces that state savings accounts total $23,350,383, which averages $500 for every man, woman and child in Arizona. (3)

JULY 28. Cloudburst waters run down slopes of Pinal Mountains and sweep through Miami, doing $500,000 damage in seven minutes. (1)

JULY 30. *Arizona Republican* gives free picnic for white children this date and similar picnic for negro children on Aug. 6. (3)

AUG. 11. Dedication of a hot springs bath house at Clifton draws "thousands" according to newspaper. (3)

AUG. 14. Scores of motorists are marooned on desert roads all night when heavy rainfall raises water in the Hassayampa River and its washes three feet. (3)

AUG. 15. Flood waters from mountains of Mexico swirl down on Nogales, Ariz., wipe out 30 houses and one bridge. (1)

AUG. 17. Herbert Hoover, candidate for President, comes out finally in favor of Boulder Dam project. (3)

AUG. 19. Law enforcing agencies in Maricopa county make joint raid and arrest 22 persons for violation of the prohibition act. (3)

AUG. 21. Pima Board of Supervisors is told by court it must contribute $80 per pupil for students in public schools, including the two rural schools built by the superintendent without their permission. (1)

AUG. 21. Chief of Apache Indians on San Carlos Reservation christens plane which Safford's Chamber of Commerce enters in transcontinental air race. (3)

AUG. 22. Five members of Maricopa ranch family die as high voltage line falls in their own front yard. (3)

AUG. 26. Cyclonic rain lasting nine minutes does $250,000 damage in Phoenix. (1)

SEPT. 2. In debt $100,000, Pima County is forced to pay its road gangs with time checks which don't appear on payrolls. (2)

SEPT. 6. After being down for two years, storm-wrecked bridge over the Hassayampa at Wickenburg is re-opened to traffic. (3)

SEPT. 9. Twenty-four planes competing in national air race swoop into Tucson's Davis-Monthan field. (1)

SEPT. 11. George W. P. Hunt wins Democratic nomination for governor for the eighth time. (1)

SEPT. 14. Fire destroys Yuma warehouse and 1,000 bales of cotton. (2)

SEPT. 21. Forest fire sweeps 640 acres of Tonto National Forest, 60 miles from Prescott. (1)

SEPT. 25. Pima County school superintendent recommends that rural schools make mascots of cows in order to provide milk for young children. (2)

SEPT. 28. Arizona miners get a 10 percent increase in pay; 15,000 men affected. Benefit to state is $25,000,000. (3)

SEPT. 30. Douglas makes bids for airline service as it completes modern 654 acre field. (1)

OCT. 4. Phoenix city commissioner denies uses of city hall plaza to Communist candidate for governor, William O'Brien, for address by vice-presidential candidate of Communist party, William Gitlow. (3)

OCT. 10. The Rt. Rev. Daniel J. Gercke delivers his first public expression on prohibition and says, "The prohibition law is fast becoming a dead letter and soon will cease to function at all." (1)

OCT. 11. Communist party candidate for governor attempts to hold a meeting on public school grounds in Phoenix and is arrested. (3)

OCT. 13. City treasurer of Tucson shocks city when he admits theft of $105,000 from the Southern Arizona Bank and Trust Co. (1)

OCT. 21. Yuma unveils statue of Padre Francisco Garces, pioneer missionary and martyr. (3)

OCT. 21. Newly developed fabric made from Pima long staple cotton appears in eastern markets. (3)

OCT. 22. Fifteen hundred ranchers, cowboys, political candidates and plain citizens gather at Sasabe to celebrate completion of road to Tucson. (1)

OCT. 23. Tucson business men and University band visit Florence, Casa Grande, Coolidge and Randolph on good will tour. (1)

OCT. 25. Federal Land Office announces that it will begin to distribute 69,000 acres of land near Yuma to veterans who wish to homestead. (3)

NOV. 1. Arizona expects that reductions of state and interstate freight rates will save shippers over $1,000,000 annually. (3)

NOV. 1. Pima County Bar asks Governor Hunt to call special session of Legislature and rewrite state's civil and penal code. (1)

NOV. 3. Supreme Court rules that Indians living on reservations as wards of the government cannot legally vote in Arizona. (3)

NOV. 6. John C. Phillips, Republican, defeats G. W. P. Hunt for governor. Voters adopt referendum providing partial exemption of property taxes for widows and members of armed forces. State gains 19,000 registered voters in four years. (1, 3)

NOV. 12. Opening day records for the State Fair are broken in Phoenix when 40,000 visitors attend. (1)

NOV. 18. Six year fight ends when Department of the Interior recognizes Tucson's claim to Sentinel Peak as valid. University "A" is saved. (1)

NOV. 19. Arizona loses in carrying the case of the Kaibab deer to the U. S. Supreme Court. The court suggests that the state and federal government get together. (1)

NOV. 19. Eighth Legislature opens its fifth special session and adjourns *sine die*. (1)

NOV. 21. State Supreme Court holds $75,000 fund appropriated by boards of directors of state institutions for Colorado River survey is invalid. (3)

NOV. 25. Fifteen companies take out leases in Benson area with hope of striking oil. (1)

NOV. 27. Police are called to the State Capitol when Governor Hunt and Senator Colter engage in a fist fight over Colorado River problem. (1)

NOV. 27. Biggest feed trough in the west is built at Canoa Ranch in southern Arizona; one third mile long, it will feed 1500 head of cattle at one time. (1)

NOV. 29. Legislature passes measure providing $6,250 with which to match U. S. fund for survey of the upper Gila. (1)

DEC. 5. Casa Grande Chamber of Commerce launches ambitious $1,000,000 development program. (3)

DEC. 6. Special Senate committee calls in three Phoenix reporters to find out how they are getting news from secret executive sessions. Newsmen won't talk. (1)

DEC. 7. Senator Hiram Johnson of California who leads fight for Boulder Dam measure announces he will compromise in amount of water for his state as proposed by Senator Hayden, Arizona. (3)

DEC. 10. Verde Irrigation District votes unanimously for pact with Salt River Valley Water Users. (3)

DEC. 11. U. S. Senate votes to accept compromise in Boulder Dam Bill giving California 200,000 acre feet less water than it wants and depriving Arizona of 200,000 feet it says it must have. Arizona wins exception of Gila River from provision preventing Federal Power Commission leasing water rights on the Colorado and its tributaries until Swing-Johnson bill becomes effective. (3)

DEC. 12. U. S. Senate agrees to limit speeches on Boulder Dam bill to 15 minutes. California and Arizona agree to settlement of Mexico's claims to water by tri-state pact. (3)

DEC. 15. U. S. Senate puts an end to hard and bitter eight-year war between Arizona and California by passing Boulder Dam bill with appropriation for $165,000,000. California gets 4,400,000 acre feet, Arizona 2,800,000, Nevada 300,000. Senator Hayden's amendment to protect Arizona's right to levy taxes on power generated by dam is defeated. (3)

DEC. 15. Arizona's largest hotel, the new Westward Ho at Phoenix, is opened with brilliant ceremonies. (3)

DEC. 21. President Coolidge signs the Boulder Dam measure, providing for the largest dam ever built to this date, capable of producing 1,000,000 h.p. of electric energy and storing 20,000,000 acre feet of water. (3)

DEC. 25. Cars of revitalized streetcar system in Phoenix make first trip on Christmas Day. (3)

DEC. 29. Legislature completes work on a new Arizona code in which it compromised on irrigation, education and the state militia, but voted down uniform textbooks, and voted for general salary increases for state officials. (3)

DEC. 31. Sixth special session of Eighth State Legislature convenes at 8:30 p.m. Adjourns *sine die* Jan. 1, 1929. Special committee appointed to investigate condition of dams in the state. (3)

DEC. 31. Deposits in Arizona banks total $96,116,168. (27)

Total major metals production in Arizona, $114,300,381. (16)

Total number of cattle in Arizona, 735,000; value, $36,382,000. (24)

1929 JAN 1. Eighth legislature ends its sixth special session at 3:45 New Year's morning. (3)

JAN. 1. Phoenix announces that building permits passed $6,000,000 mark in 1928. (3)

JAN. 5. Governor Hunt signs the new code as passed by the Legislature. Bill is the longest ever presented to an Arizona governor. (3)

JAN. 6. Town of Clifton opens modern hot springs bath house. Expects to reap fortune from tourists. (3)

JAN. 6. Orpheum Theater, largest in Arizona, opens in Phoenix. (3)

JAN. 7. John C. Phillips is sworn in as governor. (1)

JAN. 8. Lee's Ferry bridge across Colorado at Marble Canyon is opened. Bridge links Grand, Zion and Bryce canyons. (3)

JAN. 11. U. S. Department of Labor reports a $25,000,000 program of development for Arizona in coming year. (3)

JAN. 13. Wyatt Earp, controversial gunman, lawman, and gambler during Tombstone's early eighties, dies quietly in Los Angeles with his boots off. (1)

JAN. 14. Ninth State Legislature meets in regular session and before it adjourns sets up a Colorado River Commission and Arizona Board of Reservoir Control and Supervision. (3)

JAN. 15. Arizona Colorado River Commission authorizes attorney general to file suit in U. S. Supreme Court to stop enactment of Boulder Dam contract, then reverses self. (1)

JAN. 16. Governor Phillips' first message to legislature urges Tristate river pact between Utah, California and Arizona. (1)

JAN. 22. Arizona Good Roads Association recommends 15 year building program at total cost of $94,376,000. (3)

JAN. 26. Mexican Department of Public Affairs issues long and detailed list of abuses to which, it charges, Americans subject Mexicans hired for common labor and field work. (1)

FEB. 2. State Legislature passes bill empowering Gov. Phillips to appoint a new Colorado River Commission. (3)

FEB. 4. Mexico makes Nogales an official point of entry to United States for air travel. (1)

FEB. 7. Deadlocked since the first of the year over the question of selecting a successor to a vacancy on the City Council, the Council is left without a quorum and unable to adjourn when Acting Mayor of Yuma walks out. Council members threaten to have him arrested. (3)

FEB. 7. Governor Phillips decides to send new Arizona Colorado River Commission to Santa Fe for meeting with California and Nevada commissioners. (3)

FEB. 8. Apaches who own land being flooded by Coolidge Dam break up a parley with Federal representatives by shouting out list of white man's broken promises. (3)

FEB. 17. Arizona's auto fees and taxes for 1928 pass the $2,500,000 mark. (3)

FEB. 17. Tempe sells its municipally owned electric power and gas company to private interests for $162,000. (3)

FEB. 19. Colorado River Tri-state Conference meets and Arizona declares that not one drop of Gila River water shall be used to satisfy international treaty obligations with Mexico. (1)

FEB. 23. Arizona Biltmore, new $2,500,000 resort hotel, opens near Phoenix. (3)

FEB. 24. Heavy winds level newly opened Pima County Fair and the show is closed. (1)

MAR. 2. Arizona offers a Colorado water division plan to Tri-state conference which would give Montana 300,000 acre feet, California 4,700,000 acre feet and retain 3,500,000 feet for its own use. Proposal based on presumption Arizona will receive proper revenue from Boulder Dam. (3)

MAR. 7. Utah becomes sixth state to sign Colorado River Compact and thus completes ratification of Swing-Johnson bill and Boulder Dam. Arizona only state refusing to sign. (3)

MAR. 8. Yuma reports construction of Mexican government air field at nearby San Luis. (1)

MAR. 8. California rejects Arizona's proposal for division of Colorado water and suggests it accept Swing-Johnson bill. (3)

MAR. 9. Arizona mines announce third wage increase in five months. Wage boost of five percent tied to 19 cent copper. (3)

MAR. 10. Nogales reports that week-old Mexican revolution sparked by General Enrique Estrada has not interrupted business on the border but Bisbee asks for troops and Fort Huachuca stations cavalry and infantry units opposite Naco. (1)

MAR. 14. U. S. Border Patrol in Tucson district reports having apprehended 187 aliens in February. (3)

MAR. 15. Ninth Legislature adjourns after bitter fight to pare University appropriations to the quick, establishing county free libraries, making destruction, mutilation or removal of desert plants illegal, providing for an attempt to locate artesian water near Salome and asking U. S. to construct and maintain roads in national forests and on Indian lands. (3)

MAR. 16. Florence starts planting trees along its streets. (3)

MAR. 21. Mexican revolution sends refugees fleeing to Nogales, Ariz., where closing of business establishments throws hundreds out of work. Charity funds are exhausted. (1)

MAR. 24. U. S. Department of Justice sends investigators to Douglas to determine whether city officials sold guns and ammunition to Mexican rebels. (1)

MAR. 26. Without the sanction of the state or any right in international law, armed Mexican Federal troops are transported from San Luis across American soil to reinforce the Mexican garrison at Naco. Governor Phillips reports the incident to Washington. (1)

MAR. 26. Safford reports that Southern Pacific and San Carlos Apaches are having trouble over ending of 30 year agreement which gave the Indians free rail transportation on the reservation. (1)

MAR. 26. Tucson voters adopt new charter providing for city manager type of municipal administration. (1)

MAR. 27. Chief and captain of police in Douglas are charged with selling city owned machine guns and ammunition to rebel Mexican troops for $2,000 and turning only $500 over to the city treasurer. (1)

MAR. 28. Wall Street panics but news of collapse of stock market and impending depression is found only on the market pages of Arizona newspapers. (1, 2, 3)

APRIL 1. Leading mines announce five percent boost in wages, increasing the mining payroll of the state by $7,000,000. (3)

APRIL 4. Governor Phillips sends protest to Washington over proposal that Mexican federal troops be allowed to march across Arizona to reinforce troops at Naco. Says it is a violation of Arizona Constitution. (1)

APRIL 5. Anticipating border trouble, full regiment of U. S. infantry is hurried from San Antonio to Bisbee. (1)

APRIL 12. General Francisco Manzo and 15 staff officers desert their rebel troops in Nogales and seek refuge on the U. S. side of the international line. (1)

APRIL 20. California and Arizona delegates to Colorado River Commission hold session in Yuma, find they are hopelessly deadlocked and go home. (1)

APRIL 27. Tucson rushes loads of food to Sasabe to help feed non-combatant Mexicans displaced by border warfare. (1)

APRIL 30. Last rebel generals in Nogales, Sonora, surrender the city and 700 troops. Mexican tri-color flies again. Douglas reports Agua Prieta forces hold on. (1)

MAY 1. Cattle in the Clear Creek district near Winslow found to be affected by scabies and all herds are quarantined. (3)

MAY 2. Glendale sinks 16 inch well 1,000 feet and finds enough water to double the city's supply. (3)

MAY 2. State inspector reports that Salt River Valley closes lettuce season with yield of $3,250,000. (3)

MAY 3. Agua Prieta Mexican rebels surrender. (1)

MAY 3. Thirteen Lowell homes are wiped out by fire. (3)

MAY 8. Town of Buckeye is incorporated.

MAY 11. Fire burns for days in the Patagonia Mountains. Cattlemen drive herds to the lowlands. (3)

MAY 12. Yuma asks for a special session of legislature in hope of speeding up highway work. Governor refuses. (3)

MAY 13. Army withdraws regiment sent to guard Nogales during recent Mexican revolution. (1)

MAY 13. Small army of fire fighters continue to battle blaze in Patagonia Mountains and finally subdue it in time to save little town of Harshaw. (3)

MAY 15. Arizona cotton growers back congressional move to place heavy duty on Egyptian long staple cotton. (3)

MAY 17. Arizona cattlemen are disturbed by efforts of Iowa and North Dakota congressmen to have duty placed on Mexican cattle entering this country through border ports. (3)

MAY 17. Early morning dust storm sweeps in suddenly from the desert and unroofs business buildings in Buckeye. (3)

MAY 19. Arizona farmers put 230,000 acres in cotton. This is a gain of 30,000 acres over 1928. (3)

MAY 22. Billion dollar slump in quoted values of stocks creates chaos in the East. No reaction in Arizona press. (1, 2, 3)

MAY 27. Majority of 800 voters approves $625,000 bond issue in Tucson, including funds for controversial Broadway tunnel. (1)

MAY 30. Alarmed by spread of Mediterranean fruit fly, Governor Phillips calls a mass meeting of growers and tells them vigilance and money must keep out pest at any cost. (3)

MAY 31. Arizona opens a legal battle against Swing-Johnson bill and Boulder Dam after meeting California and Nevada delegations in Washington. (3)

JUNE 1. Bathtub beer makes its appearance in Arizona. Federals arrest a Phoenician for using his tub as a brewing vat. (3)

JUNE 4. California, Arizona and Nevada tri-state conference meets and California denies it ever agreed to exempt the waters of the Gila. Arizona says it is her river and she will never surrender any part of it. Conference dissolves. (3)

JUNE 10. Phelps Dodge Corporation announces that it will spend $1,000,000 on Copper Queen smelter at Douglas. (3)

JUNE 10. Arizona labor union protests to Board of Regents over awarding contract for building of new stadium to Los Angeles firm. (1)

JUNE 13. All time high reported in returns from 1928-29 citrus crop of Salt River Valley. Total sales $850,000, an increase of $200,000 over best previous record. (3)

JUNE 14. Six thousand people gather in the desert to attend formal dedication of Marble Canyon bridge across the Colorado. (1)

JUNE 15. Confronted by total of $190,000 in unpaid taxes, Pima county considers selling bonds to provide funds for running expenses. (3)

JUNE 15. Tri-state Colorado River parley is recessed until October while states consider Donovan formula which would give control of Gila to Arizona. (3)

JUNE 16. Phoenix claims to have a population of 70,000. (3)

JUNE 20. Bisbee spends a busy night fighting fires which destroy 10 garages and damage three residences. (1)

JUNE 25. Kingman dedicates an airfield. (3)

JUNE 25. The six months of grace provided in the act having expired, President Hoover signs the Colorado River Compact to which California, Colorado, Nevada, New Mexico, Utah and Wyoming have agreed. Arizona fights on alone. (3)

JUNE 30. Town of Chandler dedicates an airport. (3)

JUNE 30. U. S. Reclamation Service asks Arizona to agree to erection of a new diversion dam, five miles above Laguna Dam on the Colorado. (3)

JULY 1. Arizona School for the Deaf is finally divorced from the University. (1)

JULY 2. New immigration law causes confusion among Mexicans in Arizona. Many, fearing deportation, sell their homes at great sacrifice. [Actually all who entered previous to June 3, 1921, were immune from deportation.] (3)

JULY 3. Five hundred Mexican residents of Miami are made homeless and all their personal possessions lost in fire which destroys 43 dwellings and three business houses in Turkey Shoot Canyon. (3)

JULY 8. Salt River Valley shows gain of 50 percent in citrus acreage in one year. (3)

JULY 14. Phoenix leads nation's first 50 industrial class cities in increase in postal business for the last fiscal year. (3)

JULY 16. As result of new Arizona law compelling wholesaler to guarantee freshness of eggs he handles, all large food stores stop buying direct from farmers. (3)

JULY 16. News reports from Arizona counties show boards of supervisors hard at work cutting operating expenses to meet reduced revenues. (1)

JULY 20. State Motor Vehicle Division reports that it received $2,569,700 from four cent gas tax in fiscal year ending June 30. (3)

JULY 21. State rejoices over fact that Congress appropriates $2,127,000 for 48 Arizona projects varying from feeding Indian children to vast reclamation works. (1)

JULY 26. U. S. Internal Revenue Department rules that Salt River Valley Water Users Assn. is government concern and therefore not subject to income tax laws. (3)

JULY 29. Heavy rains which reach from Nogales to Holbrook create general havoc and cause two day delay in schedule of Santa Fe. (1)

AUG. 2. Passengers on transcontinental trains delayed by washouts clean out small towns' food supplies. Bowie has nothing left but coffee. (1)

AUG. 3. Cyclone, followed by electrical storm and heavy rain, does $50,000 damage on Yuma mesa. (1)

AUG. 6. Dam at Littlefield breaks. Damage is $200,000. (3)

AUG. 17. Maricopa County discovers that veterans' exemptions will reach total of $4,000,000 for the year. (3)

AUG. 20. Heavy rains wash cattle troughs, barnyard dirt and red soil into Winslow's reservoir. Water turns blue-green then red and taste is so foul citizens won't drink it. U. A. scientists are called. (1)

AUG. 22. Federal officers raid Gila County spots and find five women operating stills, making beer and storing large quantities of alcoholic beverages. (3)

AUG. 27. Airship Graf Zeppelin sails over Tucson on its world-girdling journey. Citizens take to rooftops to watch spectacle and century-old bell at St. Augustine Cathedral sounds a welcome. (1)

AUG. 29. Due to shortage of money in the general fund, Arizona begins paying bills with interest-bearing warrants. (3)

SEPT. 2. Veteran prospectors claim to have struck gold running $20,000 to the ton in old Mohave County claim. [No further news.] (1)

SEPT. 6. Pima canal is broached at night by heavy rains and people of Florence arise in the morning to find their city in the bed of a running river. (3)

SEPT. 6. Arizona banks begin discounting Maricopa warrants one percent. Supervisors send their funds out of state. (3)

SEPT. 13. As the University opens for another year administration boasts that library contains 67,000 volumes. (1)

SEPT. 17. U. S. Army artillery joins Nogales celebration of Mexico's anniversary by firing 21 gun salute. (1)

SEPT. 17. Final game of the Arizona League baseball race between Bisbee and Miami ends in a riot on the diamond after umpire refuses to call game because of darkness. (1)

SEPT. 20. U. A. Student body bans hazing, on or off campus. (1)

SEPT. 22. Mexico protests action of judge in trial which cleared four police officers of killing Mexican in Phoenix. (1)

SEPT. 23. Heads of state institutions and departments meet with Governor Phillips to consider methods of further curtailment of expenses. Governor says soothingly this is merely a routine affair. (3)

SEPT. 24. Maricopa County decides to recall funds which it placed in out-of-state banks and deposit the money in Arizona. (3)

SEPT. 24. Record flood ruins bridge on St. Mary's road in Tucson and cuts off highways east and west while Sunshine Climate Club is celebrating at a dinner. (1)

SEPT. 27. Two hundred horned toads are entered in Tucson Desert Derby. Entry from town of Willcox wins the race. (1)

SEPT. 28. Federal court at Tucson discourages violation of immigration laws by sending 18 men to prison for illegal entry. (3)

SEPT. 29. U. S. Marshal and eight deputies pack special car in Tucson with 36 federal prisoners convicted of assorted offenses. Destination is federal penitentiary. (1)

OCT. 4. Casa Grande stages three day "Prosperity Jubilee" to celebrate dedication of airport. (3)

OCT. 4. Yuma cotton growers protest to government that price of cotton is hammered down annually by including 2,500,000 bale carryover in statistics. Growers claim huge carry-over consists of old and worthless stock and demand probe. (3)

OCT. 6. Gila Apaches' weather prophets who predicted end of 8 year drought warn that one of the worst winters in the history of the Gila Valley is on the way. (3)

OCT. 10. Superintendent of state prison is fined $1,000 for contempt by judge of superior court. Inquiry shows prisoners lived free lives. Judge calls prison a "resort hotel." (1)

OCT. 11. Tucson's first skyscraper, the 11 story Consolidated National Bank Building [now Valley National Bank Bldg.] is opened and is visited by 33,000 people in two days. (2)

OCT. 12. U of A dedicates its new stadium. Tucson declares a public holiday. (1)

OCT. 12. Florence dedicates airport with aerial circus and speeches. (3)

OCT. 15. City of Douglas offers a site for the building and $100,000 if Cochise County supervisors will print its name on the ballots to be used in selection of new location for county seat. (3)

OCT. 15. Safford opens a new $100,000 hotel. (3)

OCT. 21. Federal Farm Board announces that it will lend cotton co-operatives up to 16 cents a pound on graded and classed cotton. (3)

OCT. 24. *Tucson Daily Citizen* gives two line, 8 col. head on page one to latest stock market crash in New York but makes no comment on reactions in Arizona or Tucson. (2)

OCT. 24. Tombstone launches its first Helldorado in celebration of fiftieth anniversary. (2)

OCT. 28. Another break on Wall Street sends prices crashing again. *Tucson Daily Citizen* comment is, "Only paper values have been wiped out." (2)

NOV. 1. Pink boll weevil is found in Maricopa and Pinal counties. Washington orders quarantine restrictions immediately with Tucson as the point for fumigation. (3)

NOV. 4. Truck carrying load of roofing nails from Tucson to Florence leaks its cargo along 65 miles of highway. Dozens of autos are crippled by punctures. (2)

NOV. 8. Automatic voting machines are used in Tucson election for first time. (2)

NOV. 12. Nevada, Arizona and California argue over who gets Boulder Dam power. Nevada offers to buy the entire output at 1.75 a kilowatt hour. (3)

NOV. 13. Los Angeles asks for complete control over power generated at Boulder Dam. (2)

NOV. 13. Eastern scientists who seek to excavate dinosaur imprint from rocks on Navajo Reservation are forbidden to proceed by Governor Phillips. (2)

NOV. 14. Arizona's Pima cotton growers get loan of $750,000 from Federal Loan Board. (2)

NOV. 14. Secretary of the Interior orders agents to prevent removal of dinosaur tracks on Navajo Reservation. (3)

NOV. 15. With stocks still plunging Phoenix Chamber of Commerce declares Phoenix and Arizona continue to hold positions as most prosperous area in nation. (3)

NOV. 15. Tucson launches drive for funds to preserve historic Ft. Lowell but money is tight and effort ends with building of an adobe wall. (3)

NOV. 20. Tombstone loses the county seat to Bisbee. (2)

NOV. 24. Phoenix business men are finally interviewed on financial condition of that city and the state. Unanimous opinion is that "optimism is justified." (3)

NOV. 24. Phoenix Red Cross drive for $2,500 falls short by $1,762. (3)

NOV. 27. Governor Phillips wires President Hoover that Arizona's building program for 1930 will be the greatest in its history. (3)

NOV. 27. Three cars crash on highway at Picacho due to dust. One killed, three seriously injured, nine treated for injuries. (2)

NOV. 27. Tucson realtors declare stock market crash has no effect in city. (2)

NOV. 30. Douglas citizens and police department threaten to raise army of 600 armed Americans and Mexicans to hunt down a lawless Apache band. Mexican cavalry expects to co-operate. (2)

DEC. 2. Despite strong campaign favoring their passage, Phoenix bond issues amounting to $4,823,000 are defeated in special election. (3)

DEC. 2. Arizona cattlemen share in $5,000,000 loan from Federal Farm Board. (2)

DEC. 4. President Hoover asks Congress to allot an extra $100,000 for Gila River irrigation project. (2)

DEC. 5. Globe-Miami airport is dedicated by Governor Phillips. (3)

DEC. 7. U. S. Prohibition agents turn liquor law violators over to state until dispute over board of prisoners is settled with Maricopa County. (3)

DEC. 10. Boulder Dam plans for sale of power fail to impress Colorado, New Mexico, Utah or Wyoming. They ask Secretary of Interior to call in a panel of experts. (3)

DEC. 13. Arizona declines bid to join upper basin states in conference on division of Colorado water. (3)

DEC. 17. Congress votes $280,000 for expansion of veterans' hospital in Tucson. (2)

DEC. 17. U. S. Forestry board offers to match funds of Arizona and Coconino County for highway through Oak Creek Canyon. (3)

DEC. 18. Shareholders of the Salt River Valley Water Users Assn. vote down plan for sharing of Verde River water with Verde River Irrigation and Power District and the U. S. Government. (3)

DEC. 21. Secretary Wilbur asks Arizona, California and Nevada if they care to confer on Colorado River prospects in the hope that Arizona lawsuit can be deferred or killed. (3)

DEC. 24. Arizona asks Utah to delay ratification of the six-state river agreement until this state can come to an agreement with California. (1)

DEC. 25. Governor Phillips tells Secretary Wilbur that Arizona will meet with California and Nevada again providing status quo of Boulder Dam Act is restored before parley begins. (3)

DEC. 28. U. S. Attorney General rules that Boulder Dam Act provides no revenues for states of Arizona and Nevada. (2)

DEC. 31. Arizona Edison Co. buys public utility plants of Winkelman and Chandler. (3)

DEC. 31. Deposits in Arizona banks total $92,956,443. (27)
Total major minerals production in Arizona, $155,567,133. (16)
Total number of cattle in Arizona, 770,000; value, $35,420,000. (24)
Town of Tolleson, Maricopa County, incorporated. (18)

1930 JAN 1. Tucson's city auditor takes office as its first city manager at an additional salary of $1 a year. (3)

JAN. 1. Record of arrests made by Phoenix police in 1929 shows increase of 4,448 over 1928. (3)

JAN. 2. Supervisors and sheriff of Maricopa County quarrel because the officer accepts federal prisoners at 75 cents a day. Supervisors want one dollar a day and threaten to make sheriff pay the difference. (1)

JAN. 3. Phoenix postmaster reports gain of 15 percent in business during 1929. (3)

JAN. 4. Tucson reports expenditure for new buildings totalled $4,500,000 for 1929. Banking transactions up $14,812,000. (2)

JAN. 6. Fourteen Arizona crops showed a 1929 gain of $2,000,000 in valuation over 1928. (3)

JAN. 6. Average number of men employed underground in Arizona mines during 1929 was 11,499. Thirty-two fatal accidents reported. (3)

JAN. 8. Tucson Community Chest reports that three out of four auto migrants want free food, fuel and oil. (2)

JAN. 7. Federal Farm Board warns cotton farmers they must not overplant if they expect government to continue loaning money to co-operatives. (3)

JAN. 9. State Agricultural Commission establishes a non-cotton zone in Maricopa and Pinal Counties hoping to eradicate pink boll weevil. Farmers send commission to Washington to ask payment for crops they can't grow. (3)

JAN. 11. Arizona Industrial Congress meets in Phoenix and assures people banks have ample funds for all requirements, utilities will spend $6,000,000 in coming year, and that industry, mining, and farming are strong. (1)

JAN. 12. State Motor Vehicle Division reports 124,161 automobiles were registered in Arizona during 1929. (3)

JAN 14. Old West lives again in Chandler when desperados battle Maricopa deputies, wound two and kidnap one. (1)

JAN. 14. Warden Lorenzo Wright of State prison in Florence blasts state policies which crowd 526 convicts into cells built to hold 272. (2)

JAN. 14. Business halts and schools close in northern Arizona cities when heaviest snowfall in 50 years makes roads impassable. (1)

JAN. 17. Governor Phillips names Senator Carl Hayden advisor to Arizona Colorado River Commission. (3)

JAN. 17. U. S. Department of State notifies Americans they must have Mexican permits if they want to hunt across the border. (1)

JAN. 17. Fifty men fight 16 miles of snowdrifts to rescue 17 people marooned in a small cabin north of Flagstaff. (2)

JAN. 18. Dozens of residents of Northern Arizona are stormbound by sub-zero weather and snow on highways. Flagstaff sheriff reports he can't clear roads on mercy missions because highway commission won't pay $3 an hour. (3)

JAN. 20. New tri-state Colorado River conference opens in Reno with Arizona in attendance. (3)

JAN. 22. Nogales loses electric power when plant goes into receivership. Petitions court for aid in obtaining light. (3)

JAN. 24. Governor Phillips issues a proclamation and names February as "Prosperity Month." (3)

JAN. 28. Mount Baldy in the Santa Ritas is formally named Mt. Wrightson in honor of Arizona's first newspaper publisher. (2)

JAN. 28. Senators Carl Hayden of Arizona and Key Pittman of Nevada tell delegates to tri-state Colorado Conference that if they fail to come to an agreement on distribution of river water, Congress will probably refuse money for Boulder Dam. (3)

JAN. 29. Federal grand jury returns 46 true bills in Tucson. Violation of immigration, narcotics and prohibition acts lead list of offenses. (2)

JAN. 30. Reno meeting of tri-state conference adjourns when California's Los Angeles and Imperial Valley groups cannot agree. No progress is made. (3)

JAN. 31. Fifteen hundred Navajos assemble near Flagstaff and begin sacred fire dance in the hope of saving life of 102 year old chief who lies on his death bed. (3)

FEB. 1. Rockefeller Foundation matches U. S. and state funds in grant to aid Arizona health program. (3)

FEB. 7. Tri-state River Commission meets in Phoenix and California complains that it is being offered less water than it needs while Arizona claims more than it can use. California continues to demand share of the Gila's flow. (3)

FEB. 7. Arizona Colorado River Commission declares that the state will never, under any circumstances, surrender water from the Gila to California. (1)

FEB. 11. Phoenix tries again to win voters to support water and sewage bonds totalling $3,450,000. Projects are defeated. (3)

FEB. 12. Arizona Taxpayers Protective Assn. is formed at Safford but breaks up in disorder when Maricopa objects that farm interests are slighted and withdraws. (1)

FEB. 13. Governor of California calls for harmony on division of Colorado river water between Los Angeles and Imperial Valley. (3)

FEB. 15. Outrageous fleecing of Nogales citizens by a carnival ends suddenly when county and border patrol officers halt the games, jail proprietors and operators of gambling games. (1)

FEB. 18. Arizona Wool Growers Assn. affiliates with National Wool Marketing Assn., established by Federal Farm Board. (3)

FEB. 19. Imperial Valley offers to let Los Angeles have half the Colorado River water it demands. (3)

FEB. 19. U. S. approves establishment of $100,000 national guard camp near Flagstaff. (3)

FEB. 20. Arizona women fail in efforts to prove Eva Dugan, convicted murderess, is insane. Jury says she must die. (2)

FEB. 21. State of Arizona hangs first woman: for murder. Eva Dugan dies on scaffold in State Penitentiary. (3)

FEB. 28. Federal grand jury at Phoenix brings in 36 indictments for violations of prohibition and narcotics laws. (3)

MAR. 2. Tucson milkmen stage a price war and public gets its milk for 14 cents a quart. (1)

MAR. 4. Calvin Coolidge, former President, dedicates dam named in his honor. Ten thousand people see colorful ceremony. (3)

MAR. 12. Stewart Mountain dam's power system is completed and placed in operation. (3)

MAR. 13. Lowell Observatory at Flagstaff announces finding ninth planetary member of the solar system after 25 year search. (1)

MAR. 13. Jane Addams of Hull House, noted social worker, breaks ground for new Y.W.C.A. building in Tucson. (2)

MAR. 14. City Planning and Zoning Commission lays out Phoenix to accommodate population of 226,000 inhabitants. (3)

MAR. 17. Southern Arizona highways, soaked by 48 hours of rain, become mudholes. (2)

MAR. 22. Department of the Interior announces it is willing to give Arizona 28 percent of Boulder Dam electric power. (1)

MAR. 26. Flagstaff waiter shoots down night marshal who catches him with gallon of whiskey in his car. (2)

APRIL 1. Apaches complain that waters backed up by Coolidge Dam have driven them out of their homes. (2)

APRIL 4. Arizona State School for the Deaf and Blind is closed by state because of lack of funds. Three months salary due teachers. (1)

APRIL 7. Papago Saguaro National Monument abolished. (26)

APRIL 7. Congress boosts aid to Arizona highway projects by $708,127. (2)

APRIL 11. Congress agrees on seven cent duty on long staple cotton. (3)

APRIL 12. Ajo dedicates a new airfield. (1)

APRIL 19. District census director pays off Tucson workers on basis of 22,000 population. Chamber of Commerce insists Tucson has twice that population, and organizes 150 volunteer workers to find them. (2)

APRIL 20. Special census agent in Phoenix asks help of business firms in obtaining complete list of residents. (3)

APRIL 21. Government engineers and geologists recommend 25 foot increase in height of Boulder Dam. (3)

APRIL 24. Dr. Homer Leroy Shantz is formally installed as president of the University of Arizona. (2)

APRIL 25. The term "Depression" begins to appear in Arizona headlines in references to condition of nation outside this state. (3)

APRIL 26. California interests sign contracts with U. S. Government to pay $21,000,000 in 50 year period for Boulder Dam power. (3)

APRIL 27. Census supervisor announces that population of Tucson is 32,198. (2)

MAY 1. Major copper companies throughout Arizona announce a five percent cut in wages because of four cent a pound reduction in prices. (3)

MAY 3. Arizona's Colorado River Commission berates federal government for entering into Boulder Dam contracts with California. (3)

MAY 13. State Highway Commission starts paring $10,000,000 budget down to $5,500,000. (3)

MAY 15. Driving a suspected cattle thief into a stone cabin in the Steamboat Mountains, Arizona deputy sheriffs try a new weapon and get their man with tear gas. (2)

MAY 16. Outlaws fire railway trestle between Miami and Globe in effort to wreck Southern Pacific train but engineer opens throttle and races through flames. (2)

MAY 21. Arizona succeeds in delaying Congressional action on President Hoover's request for $10,660,000 with which to begin construction of Boulder Dam. (3)

MAY 24. Arizona presents bronze statue of John C. Greenway to Statuary Hall in Washington, D. C. (2)

MAY 25. Salt River Valley Water Users Assn. is assured of 14 year extension in paying off its debt to the government. (3)

MAY 26. Sunset Crater is made a National Monument. (26)

JUNE 1. Pyromaniac tries to burn down Yuma; starts fires in four hotels. (2)

JUNE 2. Station KTAR of Phoenix brings first national broadcasting network (NBC) to Arizona. (3)

JUNE 2. Auto prices are cut and Ford sedans sell in Arizona for $495.00. (3)

JUNE 5. Census places population of Arizona at 418,000, a gain of 85,000. Maricopa County makes gain of 75 percent and totals 148,625. Pima County totals 44,858. (3)

JUNE 8. U. S. Attorney General holds contracts for sale of Boulder Dam power are valid. (3)

JUNE 12. Tucson celebrates opening of its greatly enlarged municipal airport. (2)

JUNE 16. Arizona press notes briefly that banks have been unable to halt slump of stocks to new low levels. (2)

JUNE 20. Yuma Valley Bank, largest bank in the city, closes and turns affairs over to State Banking Commission. (2)

JUNE 22. Cloudburst followed by hurricane winds drops two inches of rain on Tucson and rips roofs off houses. (2)

JUNE 22. Southern Arizona Bank files formal notice on Pima County to pay up on $125,000 of its registered warrants. (2)

JUNE 25. Phoenix tries again and despite depression, taxpayers finally vote for water and sewer bonds. (3)

JUNE 26. United Verde drops 825 men from its works at Jerome and Clarkdale. (3)

JULY 3. Assessed valuation of producing mines in Arizona drops $2,856,000 below previous year's total. (3)

JULY 3. Maricopa County supervisors vote to spend $5,000 for eradication of grasshoppers. (3)

JULY 7. First actual labor begins on Boulder Dam. (3)

JULY 8. Arizona Supreme Court upholds right of Cochise County to change county seat to Bisbee. (3)

JULY 8. Building of dams, canals and other projects works for the development of Verde River Irrigation and Power District is approved by Secretary of the Interior. (3)

JULY 11. For third consecutive day the Ray-Hayden district is flooded by rainstorm. Southern Pacific rails at Winkelman, Christmas and Ray are out. (2)

JULY 12. State auditor reports nearly half direct tax funds assessed by Arizona will go for school support. (3)

JULY 16. Yavapai County valuation drops $4,900,000. (3)

JULY 17. Tucson newspapers report employment is fair but quote no figures. (2)

JULY 18. Unemployment in the Jerome mines creates exodus of 280 Mexican miners and their families who leave in a body for Guadalajara, Mexico. (3)

JULY 23. Eastern Arizona has 16 consecutive days of storm and rain. San Francisco river is high and the washes are torrents. (3)

JULY 23. U. S. Department of Commerce makes Phoenix and Tucson stops on the "Fair Weather" airmail route from Birmingham to Pacific Coast. (3)

JULY 25. Twelve Arizona counties make a total gain of $9,863,000 in valuation over 1929. (3)

JULY 29. Superior court in Pima County serves notice on juveniles that widespread theft of bicycles must end and sends four culprits to Fort Grant reformatory. (2)

JULY 30. Tucson complains that Southern Pacific freight rates discriminate against it in favor of Phoenix, Gila Bend, and Ajo. (2)

JULY 30. Despite depression, Arizona comes through fiscal year of 1929-30 with $400,000 surplus. Four cent gasoline tax pumped $2,699,985 into the state's coffers. (3)

JULY 31. Arizona census leads Rocky Mountain states with gain of 23.7. (3)

AUG. 1. Citizens State Bank of Five Points closes its doors. (3)

AUG. 1. Heavy rains create flood which does great damage in Nogales, Son., and backs up into business section of Nogales, U.S.A. (3)

AUG. 3. Pima County supervisors cut school budget $150,000, and hear loud protests. (2)

AUG. 7. Cloudbursts again deluge twin cities of Nogales. Three die, adobe houses sink into mud, many homeless. Damage is $75,000. (2)

AUG. 7. Municipal economy pays off in Phoenix which closes fiscal year with $30,000 in cash and collectable assets of $62,000. (3)

AUG. 8. Rainy season is marked by cloudbursts which do great damage. Trestle gives way near Winslow and Santa Fe eastbound passenger train drops into wash; two dead, 39 injured. Twin cities of Nogales swept by wall of water which fills streets with debris. Hundreds homeless, four known dead. Red Cross rushes aid and Salvation Army sets up soup kitchen. (3)

AUG. 9. Nogales, Arizona, starts getting its electricity from Tucson. (2)

AUG. 22. Tucson proposes a road connecting Tucson and Yuma via Ajo. Engineer begins surveys. (2)

SEPT. 3. Federal Grand Jury in Los Angeles issues indictments for mail frauds including sale of so-called citrus fruit lands in Maricopa County. (2)

SEPT. 7. U of A. opens job bureau to assist needy students who must find work or leave college. Going wage is 35 cents an hour. (2)

SEPT. 7. Tucson campaigns for a Catalina Mountains highway costing $500,000. (2)

SEPT. 9. George W. P. Hunt wins Democratic nomination for governor over three rivals. (3)

SEPT. 10. Bond issue to build highway to Mt. Lemmon in Pima county is defeated two to one. (2)

SEPT. 17. Ignoring Arizona's pending lawsuit to halt building of Boulder Dam, Secretary Wilbur drives silver spike into first tie on branch railroad to damsite. (3)

SEPT. 17. U. S. Department of Labor surveys conditions in Arizona and reports mildly, "The supply of all classes of labor somewhat exceeded requirements." (2)

OCT. 1. Arizona Democrats meeting in convention denounce Republican tariffs but want a duty placed on copper. (2)

OCT. 6. U. S. Court in Tucson sentences 42 Mexicans to month in jail for illegal entry and tells them there is as much work in Mexico as in the United States. (2)

OCT. 13. Supreme Court grants Arizona's right to challenge validity of act authorizing Boulder Dam but refuses its plea that funds for initial work be held up. (3)

OCT. 14. Census Bureau reports that 32.9 percentage gain in number of Arizona farms during last decade leads the nation's: 13,260 farms now as compared to 9,975 ten years ago. (3)

OCT. 15. Saying he was grossly insulted by game commission, Zane Grey, famous for his Arizona books and stories, declares he is reluctantly shaking its dust from his feet. Thinks glories of the state are being sacrificed to commercial interests. (2)

OCT. 15. Seventy-three years from the date when the first coach of the famed "Jackass Mail" reached Tucson, first transcontinental mail plane arrives. (2)

OCT. 17. Farmers Commercial Bank of Somerton is forced to close. (3)

OCT. 21. Census bureau makes final compilation of its figures in Arizona and gives Tucson a total count of 32,506. (2)

OCT. 23. County Board of Health asks Maricopa County prosecutor to take action against cotton growers who maintain filthy labor camps. (3)

OCT. 26. State's second airmail line opens service at Winslow. (2)

OCT. 31. Extent of unemployment in Arizona gets its first headlines in news that Governor Phillips is promoting plan to register all those out of work. (3)

NOV. 4. Campaigning on the pledge, "Back to prosperity with the Democratic party," former Governor W. P. Hunt defeats incumbent John C. Phillips and becomes head of state in Arizona for the seventh time; wins by 2,644 votes. Legislature is solidly Democratic. (3)

NOV. 11. *Arizona Republican* changes its name and becomes *Arizona Republic,* forty years to the day from its first issue. (3)

NOV. 18. *Arizona Republic* announces purchase of *Phoenix Gazette.* (3)

NOV. 20. Phoenix opens a municipal woodyard which furnishes work, food and shelter for "worthy unemployed." City finances it with $3,000 appropriation. (3)

NOV. 23. Federal Grand Jury at Phoenix returns 77 true bills, most of them for narcotics and liquor violations. (3)

NOV. 26. U. S. Census Bureau reports that Maricopa County's irrigated acres increased by 101,242 in last decade. (3)

NOV. 27. Social service groups in Tucson distribute 50 Thanksgiving baskets. (2)

DEC. 2. Governor Hunt takes oath of office but will not enter on duties until first Monday in January. (3)

DEC. 4. Arizona is allotted nearly $2,500,000 for government work for Indian, reclamation and public parks service. (3)

DEC. 8. Tucson trade unions petition Governor Phillips to open armories and equip them with cots so that many unemployed will have warm place to sleep. Urge Arizona support Hoover's efforts to increase jobs. (2)

DEC. 14. Governor Phillips asks if he has authority to make an emergency appropriation and provide food and shelter for jobless people. He proposes to erect tent cities using National Guard equipment. Attorney General says "No." (3)

DEC. 15. State Highway Commission makes plans to put 2,000 men at work by Jan. 1. (2)

DEC. 16. Tucson Chamber of Commerce agrees with unions the time has come to make a survey of unemployment problem. (2)

DEC. 23. Children of Douglas gather canned foods for hungry people. (2)

DEC. 24. Acting in defiance of Arizona law which says a loaf of bread must weigh a pound, small bakers of Arizona produce 5-cent loaf for the jobless poor. Court upholds them. Says law is invalid. (2)

DEC. 24. Phoenix Jaycees give Christmas party and distribute gifts to 4,000 needy children. (3)

DEC. 25. Minor offenders in city jails are fed turkey dinners and released. (2)

DEC. 31. Total bank deposits in Arizona $79,855,684. (27)

Total major metals production in Arizona, $81,042,418. (16)

Total number of cattle in Arizona, 800,000. (24)

U. S. Census reports Arizona population as 435,523; a gain of 30.3 percent. (25)

Average attendance in elementary schools, 61,847; high school, 12,126. (15)

1931 JAN. 1. *Tucson Daily Citizen* declares outstanding accomplishments of the city in 1930 were, the coming of airmail, completion of the subways, erection of the Federal building, enlargement of the public school system and a $200,000 program to improve streets and lay the dust. (2)

JAN. 1. Colorado River Commission makes its final report to Governor Phillips. Recommends that attorney general be provided with a fund of $250,000 to carry on legal battles for protection of Arizona interests in the Colorado and its development. (3)

JAN. 2. *Arizona Republic* compilation of traffic deaths in 1930 places total at 190, an increase of 63 over 1929. (3)

JAN. 2. Tucson streetcar service to University ends and gives way to bus transportation. (2)

JAN 2. Establishment of trans-continental air mail service with stops in Phoenix, Tucson and Douglas is held to be one of the important Arizona advances in past year. (3)

JAN. 3. Tucson Chamber of Commerce opens small jobs campaign and urges citizens to give some employment to jobless, hungry workers. (2)

JAN. 5. Geo. W. P. Hunt assumes his duties as Governor without ceremony. (2)

JAN. 5. Senator Henry Ashurst introduces a resolution in U. S. Senate asking the President to begin negotiations for purchase of 10,000 square miles of Sonora and Lower California. [Ashurst introduced the identical resolution in 1919 without noteworthy result.] (2)

JAN. 7. Salvation Army in Douglas reveals that it fed 1800 hungry people during December. (2)

JAN. 8. Phoenix reports that building permits totalled $3,000,000 in 1930. (3)

JAN. 9. Chairman of Tucson Re-employment Committee announces "the astonishing fact that over 2,000 breadwinners are out of work and many of these with families to support have not had steady work in months." (2)

JAN. 10. Governor Hunt has words with U. S. Employment Service and withdraws Arizona from State-Federal Employment Bureau. (3)

JAN. 10. Gila County Supervisors petition State Highway Department to start highway construction as aid to jobless. (3)

JAN. 11. Senator Hayden notifies Douglas that it is to get customs inspection station. (3)

JAN. 11. Governor Hunt urges President Hoover to speed work on Federal Building in Phoenix and on forest roads to help relieve unemployment in Arizona. (3)

JAN. 12. Six Colorado Compact states ask U. S. Supreme Court to throw out Arizona's suit designed to prevent building of Boulder Dam. (2)

JAN. 13. Safford learns that Forest Service will spend $83,000 on highways in that area before July 1. (3)

JAN. 13. Members of the Southern Arizona Cattle Growers Assn. agree to report voluntarily 80 percent of their cattle to county assessor for taxation. (2)

JAN. 13. Town of Williams reports that protracted cold spell has frozen the ground so hard city water mains are bursting. (3)

JAN. 17. Arthur Brisbane, famous editor, pays visit to Tucson and predicts that mountain tops will be levelled off and made into landing fields to serve coming air age. (3)

JAN. 24. Yuma Legislators have dream of getting enough funds from Congress to turn the Colorado River into a canal 600 feet wide and 25 feet deep from Yuma to the Gulf. (2)

JAN. 25. Phoenix Social Center reports that relief work increased 32.5 percent in 1930 over 1929 and medical attention increased 25 percent. (3)

JAN. 25. First roadbuilding contracts under new clause, making employment of Arizona labor mandatory, are let on Yuma-Phoenix highway project. (3)

JAN. 26. Tucson citizens form an emergency group under Harold Bell Wright and raise $11,600 to pay for feeding hungry citizens. (2)

JAN. 30. Clarkston swept by $50,000 fire. (11)

JAN. 30. Governor Hunt signs $3,000,000 road bill, thus assuring federal advance aid of $1,170,000. (3)

JAN. 30. Delegation of 150 citizens from Cochise county wins appeal to Legislature for $300,000 highway appropriation to relieve serious unemployment. (3)

JAN. 31. Nogales files a formal objection to adoption of the slogan, "Tucson — Gateway to the West." (3)

JAN. 31. State raises gasoline tax from four to five cents. (3)

FEB. 1. Three Glendale and Phoenix bankers are indicted by grand jury charged with willful misapplication of funds of their defunct institutions. (3)

FEB. 3. Senate bill requiring 90 days legal residence in Arizona as prerequisite for divorce proceedings, is introduced as "a business proposition for the good of Arizona" and is defeated after stirring up a state-wide storm. (2)

FEB. 3. State Board of Health worries over spread of cerebro-spinal meningitis. Twenty-three cases reported in state. (3)

FEB. 8. Phoenix police open drive on crime. Bandits respond by holding up four stores in 15 minutes. (3)

FEB. 9. Robbers hold up Orpheum theater in Phoenix and escape with $4,000. (3)

FEB. 10. Standard scale for highway labor in Arizona is made $4.00 a day. (3)

FEB. 11. Governor Hunt urges all Arizona boards of supervisors to push highway construction and other public works as means of providing jobs for idle workers. (2)

FEB. 11. Governor Hunt announces he will call conference on crime correction. (3)

FEB. 14. Two days of steady and heavy rain raises Roosevelt Lake 17 feet. (3)

FEB. 15. Phoenix boasts that its 15,080 acre Mountain Park is the largest municipal park in the United States.

FEB. 20. Grand jury investigates crime and law enforcement in Phoenix and blames apathy of citizens for conditions. (3)

FEB. 23. Fifteen convicts break out of penitentiary at Florence. (2)

FEB. 25. Phoenix celebrates its 50th birthday with a Golden Jubilee parade, costume ball and rodeo. (3)

FEB. 28. Census supervisor reports that there are 2,037 radios in Pima County. (2)

MAR. 3. Arizona press headlines the news that eastern and midwestern banks which failed in 1930 are beginning to re-open. (2)

MAR. 4. City of Coolidge celebrates first anniversary of the dedication of Coolidge Dam. (3)

MAR. 4. A Congressional act authorizes appropriation of tribal funds for purchase of lands for the Fort Apache Reservation. (17)

MAR. 5. Title to Whipple Barracks transferred from War Department to U. S. Veteran's Bureau, thus assuring Prescott a permanent veteran's hospital. (3)

MAR. 7. Governor Hunt vetoes bill exempting private livestock dams from state regulation but 10th Legislature over-rides him. (3)

MAR. 10. At insistence of Governor Hunt the legislature cuts $364,000 from the appropriation bill providing for buildings at the University and Flagstaff Normal. (2)

MAR. 10. Arizona gets $343,800 in federal funds for Grand Canyon roads. Money will help ease unemployment situation. (2)

MAR. 12. Actual work on Boulder Dam begins. (2)

MAR. 15. After session marked by bitter political fighting the Tenth State Legislature adjourns. Its chief accomplishments are the creation of a Highway Patrol, a statewide survey of tax assessments, and the purchase with California of the toll bridge at Blythe. (2)

MAR. 20. Governor Hunt vetoes bill to substitute lethal gas for hanging in State Penitentiary. (2)

MAR. 20. Arizona State Teachers' College, Tempe, celebrates acceptance into membership of North Central Assn. of Colleges and Secondary Schools. (3)

MAR. 21. Engineers report Salt River project dams impound over 400,000 acre feet of water for first time in three years. (3)

MAR. 24. Utah and Arizona object to Presidential proclamation committing 2,000,000 acres of Colorado River lands to recreational uses. Governor Hunt says Secretary of the Interior is trying to gain control of power dam sites. (3)

MAR. 25. Governor Hunt slashes $429,450 from appropriation bill passed by Tenth Legislature. (3)

MAR. 26. Phoenix High School girl chooses possible solutions for unemployment as her theme and wins first prize. (3)

MAR. 31. Governor Hunt informs chairman of Federal Tax Commission that only seven of Arizona's 49 copper producing areas are operating. Asks for protective tariff. (3)

APRIL 1. Canyon de Chelly made National Monument. (26)

APRIL 2. Wickenburg reverts to its old days when the new Vulture mine is reported to have uncovered a vein identical with one in its famous predecessor. Town is swamped with miners and prospective developers. (2)

APRIL 5. Governor Hunt orders probe of Adjutant General's records. Says he has evidence of fraud. (3)

APRIL 10. Federal court issues perpetual injunction restraining Navajo County officers from interfering with Forest Rangers who are killing wild horses in forest areas. (3)

APRIL 14. Phoenix moves to fourth position in western building totals for March. Leaders are Los Angeles, San Francisco and Oakland. (3)

APRIL 14. Supreme Court of Arizona declares Phoenix ordinance prohibiting driving while drunk invalid. (3)

APRIL 17. Superintendent of Phoenix Indian School tells U. S. Senate sub-committee that his biggest problem is to protect male students against sale of solidified and denatured alcohol by whites. (2)

APRIL 18. Arizona national and state banks show loss of more than $10,000,000 in deposits over March of 1930 but state superintendent says they are in better condition. (3)

APRIL 20. Secretary Wilbur signs $48,890,995 contract for the construction of Boulder Dam by Six Companies, Inc. (2)

APRIL 20. Mayor of Tucson tells U. S. Senate sub-committee on Indian affairs that city wants to sink wells on the Papago Reservation. Committee says Congress will do nothing which will impair the rights of the Indians. (2)

APRIL 23. Tornado rips tent city at Boulder Dam to shreds, leaving 200 workmen without shelter. (2)

APRIL 24. U. S. Bureau of Public Roads releases $418,000 to Arizona, and highway department calls for bids on Wickenburg-Ehrenberg highway. (3)

APRIL 24. U. S. Senate sub-committee on Indian Affairs meets with Apaches of White River Reservation. Inquiry reveals that Indian Bureau is spending much of tribal money on highways. Senator Wheeler charges that the highways are for tourists — not Indians. (2)

APRIL 24. Governor Hunt seeks to bolster economy by ordering state departments to do their buying in Arizona. (2)

MAY 1. Citizens of Phoenix plant 2,000 young palm trees. (3)

MAY 4. Congressional sub-committee studies flood menace to Leupp Indian School and says unless proper controls are built waters of Little Colorado will sweep away 400 Indian children during a flood period. (3)

MAY 6. U. S. probe of Arizona Indian affairs reveals that Supais of the Grand Canyon need schools. (3)

MAY 9. Arizona Highway Commission awards road contracts totalling $723,838. (3)

MAY 12. University of Arizona's famous polo team leaves campus on invasion of the East. (2)

MAY 13. Senator Hayden urges stabilization of price of silver to hasten return of prosperity in Arizona. (3)

MAY 16. Lumberman's Club of Arizona urges tariff on copper. (3)

MAY 16. Prohibition agents and Tucson police break up whiskey ring by capturing 860 gallons of bootleg liquor. (2)

MAY 17. Nogales dedicates its new international airport. (2)

MAY 18. Governor Hunt asks all copper producing states to join Arizona in fight for protective tariff on the red metal. (2)

MAY 18. U. S. Supreme Court declares law authorizing construction of Boulder Dam is constitutional and Arizona finally loses its last chance to stop project unless she can later prove water distribution causes injury. (2)

MAY 19. U. S. District Attorney warns Arizona that he will apply federal padlock law against property on which liquor is found. (2)

MAY 21. Border patrol finds skeleton of 25,000 year old mammoth near Hereford. (2)

MAY 24. Prescott editor criticizes Yavapai County sheriff editorially and sheriff beats him up. (3)

MAY 25. Defeated in its attempt to stop building of Boulder Dam, Arizona prepares to ask Supreme Court to apportion Colorado River water. (2)

MAY 27. Phoenix school teachers take five percent cut in salaries to keep schools operating full time. Board of education says cut was voluntary. (3)

JUNE 4. Arizona's Future Farmers of America begin construction of a camp in the White Mountains. (3)

JUNE 5. Salt River Valley farmers claim they have withstood depression and are in better financial condition than any other farming community in the nation. (3)

JUNE 9. State Dairy Commissioner rules that Tucson dairies must take out state licenses if they are to continue in business. (2)

JUNE 11. Federal officers discover a $20,000 still, largest ever found in Arizona, near Jerome. (2)

JUNE 12. Grand Jury begins probe of Tucson whiskey ring by indicting police officer. (2)

JUNE 13. Tucson celebrates opening of East Broadway subway. (2)

JUNE 18. Construction of 90 mile tunnel from Little Colorado River in northern Arizona to upper Verde Valley is urged for purpose of irrigating 1,500,000 square acres near Phoenix and equal amount near Yuma. (3)

JUNE 19. Business depression moves State Tax Commission to reduce Southern Pacific and Santa Fe assessments $318,000. (2)

JUNE 22. Arizona Southwest Bank with branches at Tucson, Casa Grande, Coolidge and Douglas forced to close. Banks held $800,000 in deposits. (2)

JUNE 27. Southern Pacific and Atchison, Topeka and Santa Fe file transcript in their legal battle to set aside Arizona law limiting the length of trains. It contains 2,760,000 words. (3)

JUNE 30. Dr. Andrew Ellicott Douglass of the University of Arizona is honored for his research work in dendrochronology by Research Corporation of New York. Charles Evans Hughes presents citation. (2)

JULY 1. Arizona Tax Commission reveals that assessment value of Arizona mines has dropped $29,500,000 in one year. (2)

JULY 2. Arizona enjoys normal temperatures while East and Midwest are swept by blistering heat which takes hundreds of lives. Montana and North Dakota are declared drouth areas. (1)

JULY 4. State Supreme Court rules that drunk driving is not within the jurisdiction of police courts. (1)

JULY 4. Arizona-Nevada climate proves too hot for many workers on Boulder Dam and rigid medical examinations are prescribed for all job-hunters. (1)

JULY 8. Tucson ends fiscal year with $201 left in the treasury. (1)

JULY 10. Crime waves in Phoenix are reported to have caused 13,500 arrests in year ending June 30. July opens with four deaths from poisoned liquor. (3)

JULY 14. Workers strike on Boulder Dam but new laborers carry on under guards. (1)

JULY 15. Tucson's Salvation Army continues to furnish free food for drifters but no lodgings. (1)

JULY 16. County agents urge farmers to diversify their crops at least to the point where they can raise their own food for the duration of the depression. (1)

JULY 21. Because Governor Hunt vetoes bill carrying necessary appropriation, Arizona's 13 quarantine stations are without funds and are told to close. (3)

JULY 21. Arizona State Motor Vehicle Division authorizes copper license plates for automobiles. (3)

JULY 22. U. S. Department of Agriculture warns Arizona that if it persists in closing road quarantine stations as demanded by Governor Hunt the State's entire cotton crop will be quarantined to prevent spread of pink boll weevil. (1)

JULY 23. Tempe's new $500,000 bridge over the Salt River is opened for service. (3)

JULY 28. Governor Hunt refuses to call special session of Legislature and ask for funds for inspection stations. (3)

JULY 29. Under pressure Governor Hunt agrees to reopen two inspection stations and reconsiders calling a special session of the Legislature. (3)

JULY 30. Twin Nogales cities get three and one-half inches of rainfall in two hours and suffer much damage but heat wave is broken. (1)

AUG. 5. Southern Pacific's crack passenger train, "Argonaut," is derailed east of Yuma. Two are killed, 15 injured. (3)

AUG. 10. Workers strike at Boulder Dam and 1,400 lose their jobs. (3)

AUG. 11. Seventy-five residents of Mammoth leave home and retreat to hills as floods sweep down the San Pedro. Four dead. (1)

AUG. 11. Five are dead and property damage of $100,000 reported from southwestern Arizona which is swept by two day rain. (3)

AUG. 12. U. S. Forest Service says Arizona is practicing overgrazing to point where it becomes a menace. (3)

AUG. 19. Tourists sit glassy-eyed as Hopis open prayer for rain with annual snake dance, heavens open and everyone is soaked. (3)

AUG. 22. McNary school teacher who suffers a crippling attack of typhoid fever wins $27,500 in damages from lumber company which allowed its sewage to poison domestic water supply of town. (1)

AUG. 22. Arizonans protest proposed freight rate boost of 15 percent and say it would "be ruinous to state." (3)

AUG. 27. Governor Hunt still refuses to call special session of legislature. He fears idle lawmakers would sit down, do nothing and draw their pay for 60 days. (1)

SEPT. 1. Residents of "Potato Patch," a summer resort on summit of Pinal Mountains, change its name to "Ferndale." (3)

SEPT. 5. Pima County Supervisors charge Maricopa County supervisors with giving eastbound indigent tourists enough gasoline to get to Tucson. Maricopa indignantly denies charge. (3)

SEPT. 10. Governor Hunt appoints a director of unemployment relief, declaring the situation is "most acute." (Washington says problem of preventing distress during coming winter "is serious but presents no occasion for public alarm.") (3)

SEPT. 10. President Shantz tells grumblers who complain because U of A takes out-of-state students that if it could get 500 more who pay $150 tuition University would turn over a profit to the state. (1)

SEPT. 12. Organized charities of Tucson prepare to resist army of hoboes and hundreds of destitute tubercular patients who are heading for the Sunshine City. (1)

SEPT. 21. Security Trust and Savings Bank of Yuma fails to open for business. (3)

SEPT. 23. Governor Hunt assures fugitive Yaquis at Barrio Libre in Tucson that none will be forced to return to Mexico against his will so long as he does not become a public charge. (1)

SEPT. 30. U. S. Department of the Interior tells Arizona the illiteracy rate of its native white population dropped from 2.1 in 1920 to 0.5 in 1930 and that in the same period rating of Mexican residents dropped from 64.7 to 28.5. (1)

SEPT. 30. U. S. Department of Labor announces that Arizona has 2,000 men working on state highways. (3)

OCT. 12. Arizona cities check on number of needy unemployed through civic groups. (3)

OCT. 16. State Supreme Court rules that counties must pay jurors' warrants irrespective of whether or not there is money in the designated fund. (3)

OCT. 19. American Federation of Labor demands Congressional investigation of wages and labor conditions at Boulder Dam. (1)

OCT. 20. Bodies of two slain women are taken from a trunk in Phoenix and famous murder case opens with police broadcasting news of search for Mrs. Winnie Ruth Judd. (1)

OCT. 22. *Arizona Republic* reveals that Maricopa County has had 14 killings in the last six months. (3)

OCT. 26. Winnie Ruth Judd surrenders in California and Governor offers to sign papers for her return to Arizona. (1)

OCT. 31. State of Arizona to ask for separate trials for murder of two women alleged to be victims of Winnie Ruth Judd. (1)

OCT. 31. Program for copper tariff as proposed by Arizona congressional representatives is adopted in its entirety by governors of seven Western States. (3)

OCT. 31. Survey of a site for Glen Canyon Dam is completed. (3)

NOV. 2. Miami Copper Company files complaint in federal district court charging the State Tax Commission's methods are "whimsical, capricious, illegal and discriminating." (1)

NOV. 3. Apache who murdered Columbia University co-ed on White River Indian Reservation is caught after four months and confesses. (1)

NOV. 3. Pima County Health Department discovers Tucson has a milkman who is a typhoid carrier. (1)

NOV. 4. Completion of Phoenix-San Diego highway, 20 years in building, is celebrated in San Diego. (3)

NOV. 5. Three hundred small wood dealers in Phoenix protest a license fee of $60 a year. (3)

NOV. 12. Walter Douglas, former president of Phelps-Dodge, warns that copper industry must have protection of a tariff or it will die. (3)

NOV. 13. Arizona enters fourth consecutive day of rain and snowstorms. (3)

NOV. 14. Tucson, the "Sunshine City," awakens to find itself covered by thick fog. (1)

NOV. 18. Steward Observatory at University records spectacular display of 278 meteors from midnight to 5 a.m. (1)

NOV. 21. Arizona National Guard is told to save money by reducing number of drills. (3)

NOV. 24. Arizona border cities note with anxiety the collapse of the Bank of Sonora at Hermosillo and Nogales, Son. (1)

NOV. 27. Superintendent of Navajo Agency at Fort Defiance notifies Washington unless supply trains can reach snowbound Indians many of them must starve. Flagstaff reports 6,000 sheep, snowbound for a week, are starving on range. (1)

DEC. 2. Arizona, Montana and Michigan join in plea to Congress for protection from flood of African copper produced by serf labor. (1)

DEC. 3. Arizona Corporation Commission orders electricity and gas rates in Nogales cut from 15 to 25 percent. (1)

DEC. 4. State Highway Commission announces that highway contracts totalling $2,000,000 are under way in Arizona. (3)

DEC. 5. With winter weather on the way Tucson relief workers report emergency funds already exhausted. (1)

DEC. 8. American Airlines opens six daily plane schedules between Phoenix and Tucson. (3)

DEC. 8. Abandonment of army posts at Douglas and Nogales draws protest from Governor Hunt who tells Washington it is destroying district's "sense of security." (1)

DEC. 10. Citizens of Gila County meet at Globe and organize tax relief association. Charge taxes are "out of proportion to the increase of population and to the actual needs of good government." (3)

DEC. 11. Flash flood in the Salt River south of Phoenix endangers campers. Seven are rescued. (3)

DEC. 12. Snowstorms sweep northeastern Arizona. Three hundred persons snowbound at Presbyterian Mission in Ganado without fuel chop buildings and fences for stoves, while boys over 12 and teachers walk five miles through snow to cut wood. (3)

DEC. 16. Organized Tucson charities beg public for used clothing and shoes. (1)

DEC. 17. Tucson Chamber of Commerce studies a plan to give unemployed men 20 hours of work a week at 50 cents an hour. (1)

DEC. 18. Western Navajo Reservation Indians suffer from hunger in their hogans as U. S. Agents fight 10 to 12 foot drifts to deliver supplies. (3)

DEC. 19. Pima County ranchmen offer to contribute 4,000 pounds of beef as Christmas gift to needy families. (1)

DEC. 21. Copper Institute decides on voluntary curtailment of production to 26.5 percent of capacity to cut surplus and raise prices. (3)

DEC. 25. Organized charities, directed by Harold Bell Wright, distribute 1,200 Christmas baskets of food and toys to Tucson indigent. (1)

DEC. 28. Governor Hunt calls extra session of 10th Legislature. Principal purpose to consider means of relieving unemployment. Critics fear a "highway grab." (3)

DEC. 29. University's College of Law is elected to membership in Association of American Law Schools. (1)

DEC. 30. Legislature quarrels over length of session but because members need the pay finally agree to 14 days. (1)

DEC. 31. Legislature passes measure providing for weight fees on commercial vehicles and leaves Governor Hunt 35 minutes to sign it before New Year bells ring. (1)

DEC. 31. Total deposits in Arizona Banks $62,167,507. (27)
Total major metals production in Arizona, $40,114,694. (16)
Total number of cattle in Arizona, 824,000; value $18,375,000. (24)

1932 JAN. 1. Legislature works on holiday and gives auto owners an unwanted New Year present of a five cent tax on gasoline. (3)

JAN. 5. Legislature in turmoil when senate attempts to adjourn and house blocks move. (3)

JAN. 5. Mayor Henry O. Jaastad tries to cut working hours and pay of city employes but runs into provisions of city charter. (1)

JAN. 6. Legislature does not forget memorials to Congress. One asks aid in building bridge over Colorado at Parker and a second requests government use Boulder Dam funds to build Kingman-Hoover highway. (1)

JAN. 6. Unemployed Tucson men do $5,000 worth of work on University grounds for a pittance under Organized Charities Plan. (1)

JAN. 9. Work of the U. S. Border Patrol in Arizona leads to prosecution of 1,835 persons in 1931. (3)

JAN. 9. Special session of the Legislature adjourns after placing a tax on stores, killing an income tax bill and apologizing to newspaper men for having said their stories were unfair and their editorial comments biased. (1)

JAN. 10. Coolidge suffers a $50,000 fire. (3)

JAN. 14. Despite curtailment of work in mines, Arizona still leads nation in production of copper. (3)

JAN. 15. Chairman of Maricopa County Board of Supervisors advises Indian school superintendent that gainfully employed Indian boys and girls ought to be discharged and their jobs given to white children. Says Indians are government wards. (3)

JAN. 16. Six U. S. bombing planes are loaded at Winslow with food for frost-bitten, hungry Indians in snow-swept northern Arizona and New Mexico. (1)

JAN. 17. Army bombers drop five tons of beans, coffee, sugar, salt pork and dried fruit in snowbound Navajo Indian villages. (1)

JAN. 18. Harold Bell Wright, western novelist, writes open letters to winter visitors in Tucson asking for their help in feeding 250 families. (1)

JAN. 24. In a year of financial distress Arizona pays $1,330,921 in income taxes. (1)

JAN. 26. Four convicts open the escape season at Florence by making their get-away in empty oil truck. (1)

FEB. 4. Gordon Sawyer, vice-president of the Southern Arizona Bank in Tucson, is kidnapped. Bank offers $5,000 reward for arrest and conviction of abductor. (1)

FEB. 5. Two-day session of the Board of Regents of University and State Teachers Colleges, in which economy of operation is considered, results in suggestions that University be closed and Tempe turned into a vocational training school. (1)

FEB. 5. Kidnapped Tucson banker is found alive in the bottom of a dry well. (1)

FEB. 8. Coconino County sheriff is found dead, shot through the head, in Flagstaff taxicab. (1)

FEB. 9. Jury finds slayer Winnie Ruth Judd guilty of murder. Sentence means death. (1)

FEB. 24. Report that University of Arizona may be closed because of low level of state's finances causes concern in national educational circles. Board of Regents issues a formal denial. (3)

FEB. 25. Court sentences Winnie Ruth Judd to hang. She creates a scene, shouting that her two victims were not murdered. (1)

FEB. 26. Phoenix launches a "Create-a-job-Campaign." (3)

FEB. 28. State-wide citizen reconstruction committee starts Arizona campaign against money hoarding. (3)

MAR. 1. New Mexican law requiring all employees to be Mexican citizens affects Arizona. Expected to throw several hundred Americans out of work in Nogales, Sonora. (2)

MAR. 2. American Legion launches united action campaign to obtain 1,000,000 jobs for unemployed. Nation-wide total in first two weeks is 127,500. Arizona contributes 415. (1)

MAR. 6. U. S. Border Patrol charges that Mexico is getting rid of unwanted Chinese by running them across the border to the United States, which must pick them up and deport them. (1)

MAR. 9. Arizona highway patrolmen are ordered to watch Arizona roads for sedan thought to be transporting the Lindbergh baby. (1)

MAR. 13. Seventeen hundred unemployed register for jobs in Phoenix. (3)

MAR. 13. Fire destroys five business houses in Superior. Loss is $100,000. (3)

MAR. 21. Apache Indian range rider given life sentence for murder of Columbia University co-ed on White River Indian Reservation. (1)

MAR. 25. Speaking at Phoenix, National Commander of American Legion tells Arizona the lack of unity in fight against depression is greater menace than World War. (3)

MAR. 26. Secretary of Agriculture rules that farmers in irrigated lands may borrow money to pay their water bills. (3)

MAR. 30. Two thousand high school and junior college students take field in Phoenix to hunt jobs for unemployed men. (3)

MAR. 30. Senator Hayden tells Congress that Arizona will be bankrupt unless copper tariff is passed. (1)

MAR. 31. Faculty of the University of Arizona, although suffering from pay cut, votes for the second time to contribute $8,000 to the fund for the unemployed. (1)

MAR. 31. U. S. Department of Agriculture lends $50,000 to Arizona farmers for purchase of seed. (3)

APRIL 5. Major Arizona cities launch "Prosperity Week" to fight depression by boosting sales of products. (3)

APRIL 13. Arizona bankers take to the air via radio to assure people they can have confidence in banks. (2)

APRIL 13. Arizona Cattlegrowers Association heartily backs resolution before Congress favoring disposal of all remaining government lands to the states. (1)

APRIL 14. Phoenix banks refuse to cash state warrants but two Tucson institutions pay cash for paper despite depletion of state treasury. (2)

APRIL 15. Old Dominion Bank of Globe, Miami, Superior and Yuma is closed by state banking department. (3)

APRIL 19. Depression fails to stop Arizona pioneers from their annual reunion in Phoenix. Attendance reaches 2,400, and breaks the record. (3)

APRIL 21. Tucson distributes 1,316 loaves of bread and three and one-half tons of other food to its needy in one month. (1)

APRIL 24. Bisbee forced to cut 25 teachers from public schools faculty to balance budget with a saving of $120,000. (1)

APRIL 26. Board of Regents of the University whittles faculty salaries by 10 percent. (1)

MAY 1. Prohibition agents confiscate 400 gallons of whiskey and still with 100-gallon daily capacity, on outskirts of Tucson. (1)

MAY 4. Papago Indian steals blanket in which to bury body of dead brave. Tucson judge releases him on suspended sentence. (1)

MAY 4. Phoenix cuts police force 25 percent as economy measure. (3)

MAY 8. U. S. Department of the Interior says overgrazing on public lands by Arizona cattlemen is ruining ranges but that Department is without legal right to interfere. (1)

MAY 14. Arizona Good Roads Assn. outrages promoters of local projects by recommending that money be spent only on primary roads. (3)

MAY 16. Machine guns set up around penitentiary in Florence when plans for mass escape of prisoners are discovered. (1)

MAY 20. Joint house and senate committee of the Arizona Legislature recommends to Governor Hunt that colleges at Tempe and Flagstaff be abolished as one means of cutting the budget. (1)

MAY 22. Despite depression Arizona building record for April leads all western states except California. (3)

MAY 29. Governor Hunt refuses to call extra session of legislature to consider economy plans because he thinks nothing will be done. (1)

JUNE 2. Arizona packer contracts to furnish year's supply of beef and veal to U. S. Army forces in Hawaii for $275,000. (3)

JUNE 3. Record snowfall of 12 feet is reported for seven months ending April 30 in Northern Arizona. (3)

JUNE 5. Arizona Department Veterans of Foreign Wars discourages participation of members in bonus march on Washington. (3)

JUNE 6. President Hoover signs bill providing four cent tariff on copper and Globe miners stage a celebration; bells ring, whistles blow and guns roar. (3)

JUNE 6. Governor Hunt favors cancelling State Fair to save money. (3)

JUNE 6. Maricopa Board of Supervisors objects to highway commission policy of hiring only residents of counties in which roads are built. (3)

JUNE 8. Federal government collected $2,262,619 in taxes from Arizona in 1931 but plans to spend more than $16,000,000 here in 1932; a return of more than seven to one. (3)

JUNE 9. After an absence of 104 years the Franciscan order again occupies quarters in San Xavier Mission. (1)

JUNE 11. Supervisors cut Maricopa's assessed valuation of homes and farms from 23 to 25 percent to save owners heavy taxes. (3)

JUNE 17. Water Users Assn. adopts plan to give $3,500,000 credit to farmers of the Salt River Valley. (3)

JUNE 17. Bonus army, headed for Washington, marches from Phoenix to Tucson and is greeted by American Legion. Spends three days in city. (1)

JUNE 21. Supervisors ease bonus army out of Tucson by giving it $250 for gas and oil. Announce that any future "mob" will be escorted beyond the city limits. (1)

JUNE 21. Arizona counties quarrel over roads which highway commission expects to build. (3)

JUNE 24. Congress passes $2,300,000,000 unemployment relief measure. Arizona scheduled to receive $3,280,000 from federal road funds. (3)

JUNE 30. Pima County supervisors cut employees' wages from three to ten percent as economy move. (1)

JULY 1. Governor Hunt announces his candidacy for an eighth term. (1)

JULY 3. Arizona awakens to fact that four cent copper tariff which is at last assured will bring no benefits for a long time. Stockpiles so great they will last for months. (1)

JULY 7. Arizona's Senator Ashurst leads battle in U. S. Senate to save dry laws. (1)

JULY 8. Four foot wall of water from cloudburst sweeps through Nogales depositing thick layer of mud in homes and business houses. (1)

JULY 12. Hoover's threat of veto on huge unemployment relief bill forces Congress to rewrite measure, and Arizona is disappointed. (3)

JULY 15. Maricopa County cuts its school budget $566,500. Phoenix cuts pay of city employees 12½ percent. (3)

JULY 16. Globe and Miami cut budgets. Other Arizona communities do the same. (3)

JULY 19. Governor Hunt decides to ask Congress for $45,000,000 in federal aid under federal relief bill. Would build more highways and employ more unemployed. (1)

JULY 20. Ray-Hayden set peace-time record for copper shipment, sending $250,000 worth of ingots to French and Italian interests. (3)

JULY 21. School budget for Pima County is cut $145,000. Teachers' pay slashed. (1)

JULY 30. Special master in chancery asks Federal Board of Equity to enjoin the State of Arizona from enforcing the law which limits passenger trains to 14 cars and freights to 70 cars. (3)

JULY 30. Senator Hayden tells Arizona that it will receive a greater amount of federal funds per capita than any other state in the nation. (3)

AUG. 8. State Tax Commission cuts total assessed valuation of Arizona to $473,350,000, a drop of $201,400,000 from the 1931-32 valuation. Tax rate is set at $1.20, highest in Arizona history. (1)

AUG. 14. Steward Observatory at the University reports meteor showers have been very heavy, running as high as 200 to 400 an hour. (3)

AUG. 19. Phoenix taxpayers squirm under combined tax levy of $5.41. (3)

AUG. 27. Governor Hunt changes his appeal for government aid and asks $1,000,000 for "direct material relief," to be administered by local agencies. (1)

AUG. 29. Price of cotton soars, almost doubling in 60 days, and Arizona hopes worst of the depression is over. (3)

SEPT. 1. Fire destroys main dining room and cottages valued at $500,000 on North Rim of the Grand Canyon. (3)

SEPT. 6. Northern Arizona State Teachers College at Flagstaff decides to accept hay, potatoes, eggs, oats, or anything man or beast can eat in lieu of cash from students for board, room, and books. (1)

SEPT. 10. Federal employment bureau says there are 4,000 jobless men in Pima County. (1)

SEPT. 11. Reconstruction Finance Corporation grants Arizona $250,-000 for unemployment relief. (3)

SEPT. 16. For the first time in his long political career, George W. P. Hunt loses a primary election race in his try for an eighth nomination for governor. Dr. B. B. Moeur defeats Hunt on the Democratic ticket. (1)

SEPT. 22. Returning students at University arrive riding the rods or hiding in box cars. (1)

SEPT. 25. Arizona towns give Franklin D. Roosevelt a rousing welcome as he crosses state on his campaign for the presidency. (3)

SEPT. 28. For first time in 16 years Salt River Project will start its fiscal year Oct. 1 with more than one million acre feet of water behind its dams. (3)

OCT. 4. Arizona Supreme Court rules that state can vote on prohibition at November election. (1)

OCT. 6. State reveals that it has spent $56,700,000 on better roads in the last 20 years. (3)

OCT. 6. Reconstruction Finance Corporation lends Prescott $500,000 to improve its water supply. (3)

OCT. 19. Survey shows 24,075 acres of Salt River Valley land are citrus orchards. More than half the 2,000,000 trees are bearing. (3)

OCT. 20. U. S. government loans $880,000 to Salt River Valley cattlemen and farmers. (3)

OCT. 21. Arizona sends out warnings that it has all the labor of every description it can use and that outside jobless should avoid state. (3)

OCT. 26. Surplus copper stocks continue to grow in spite of the four cent tariff. (3)

OCT. 29. Arizona Education Association meets in Phoenix, opposes repeal of state prohibition law and favors graduated tax on incomes above $1,000. (1)

OCT. 29. Communist group in Tucson attempts to stage a hunger march but only its officers and 11 admirers show up. (1)

NOV. 5. Outlaws hold up bank in little town of Clemenceau and get away with $7,000. (3)

NOV. 9. Arizonans repeal state's 18-year-old dry law at the polls but prohibition will continue until Governor Hunt issues proclamation nullifying old measure. (3)

NOV. 9. Arizona votes two to one for Franklin D. Roosevelt against Herbert Hoover in presidential election. Dr. Benjamin B. Moeur elected Governor. (1)

NOV. 13. Despite his defeat, 5,000 people greet Hoover when his train halts for 10 minutes in Tucson. (11)

NOV. 13. Diversion channel at Boulder canyon is opened and mighty Colorado changes its course; first major step in project is completed.

NOV. 17. United Bank and Trust Co. of Tucson closes its doors. (1)

NOV. 22. Governor-elect Moeur lets his patients know he will continue his medical practice while serving his term. (1)

NOV. 23. City of Nogales deducts taxes from power company's bill for service and the company shuts off its current, leaving town in the dark. (1)

NOV. 26. Dr. R. B. Moeur, governor-elect, announces he will set an example of sacrifice by cutting his salary $1,500. He urges all state employes to do the same. (3)

NOV. 26. Tucson's Chamber of Commerce fights to "restore the freedom of mining prospectors" on the Papago Reservation. (1)

DEC. 1. Governor-elect B. B. Moeur gives state a sample of his thinking when he advises University to stop extension work to cut expenses. (1)

DEC. 2. Governor-elect Moeur summons presidents of state institutions of higher learning, tells them the pendulum of school costs has swung too far and that they must take drastic cuts in their budgets "without impairing efficiency." (3)

DEC. 8. Phoenix investigates what is called its early morning "smoke nuisance," traces pall to residences. (3)

DEC. 9. Darkened streets of Nogales are lighted again as city wins its tussle with power company which pays its franchise fees under protest, and turns on the current. (1)

DEC. 11. Copper and silver reach record low prices. (3)

DEC. 14. Despite desperate efforts of Douglas and Nogales to prevent abandonment of Camp Stephen D. Little and Camp Harry J. Jones, U. S. Army moves troops to Fort Huachuca. (3)

DEC. 17. Federal court jury holds that Indian's firewater known as "Tiswin" is a sacramental wine and can be made legally on reservations. (1)

DEC. 21. University says farewell to Governor Hunt by making him ex-officio member of the Board of Regents and on Dec. 30 granting him honorary Doctor of Laws degree. (1)

DEC. 24. Phoenix Junior Chamber of Commerce plays host to 6,000 under-privileged at Christmas Eve party. (3)

DEC. 24. Tucson's organized charities provide Christmas food for 1500 families. (1)

DEC. 28. Maricopa County Taxpayers Association demands 66 percent reduction in taxes on real estate. (1)

DEC. 29. Negro soldier runs amok at Fort Huachuca and kills two officers and their wives, wounds a third officer and is finally brought down by a rifle of a guard. (1)

DEC. 29. Maricopa County grand jury indicts Arizona Industrial Commission on charges of embezzlement and misapplication of public money. (1)

DEC. 31. Senator Hayden stages a hard battle in Congress to save army posts at Nogales and Douglas. (1)

DEC. 31. Total deposits in Arizona banks, $45,015,683. (27)

DEC. 31. Arizona copper mines feel effects of great depression. Production drops from 415,314 tons in 1929 to 288,095, falls to 200,672 tons in 1931, 91,246 in 1932 and 57,021 tons in 1933. Price falls from 12.92 cents a pound in 1927 to 5.555 in 1932. (27)

Total major metals production in Arizona, $13,535,935. (16)

Total number of cattle in Arizona, 835,000; value, $13,778,000. (24)

1933 JAN. 2. Dr. B. B. Moeur is inaugurated as Governor of Arizona. (1)

JAN. 5. Arizona lowers its flags to half-mast for one month's mourning for former president Calvin Coolidge (3)

JAN. 8. Women's Christian Temperance Union makes survey and lists Arizona as one of the few really wet states. (1)

JAN. 10. Few who had the time to read an almost solid 8 columns of type in the *Arizona Republic* could fail to understand that Governor Moeur's program was extremely long. (3)

JAN. 10. Eleventh Legislature opens session and receives Governor Moeur's initial message in which he recommends cut of $4,000,000 in state spending, abolishing highway department and cutting all salaries 20 percent. (1)

JAN. 11. Special legislative committee recommends closing colleges at Tempe and Flagstaff and consolidation of state's 68 departments into eight bureaus and five departments. (1)

JAN. 20. Flagstaff has rabies scare. Family pets are killed and owners take Pasteur treatment. (12)

JAN. 22. Director of University Employment Bureau begs people of Tucson to find employment for students who must earn way through college. (1)

JAN. 26. Bisbee City Council and Chamber of Commerce make stormy fight in Legislature against county road between Stein's Pass and Benson being made a state highway. (4)

FEB. 1. Two hundred Havasupai Indians and Indian officials are marooned in bottom of Grand Canyon by snow and relief parties are sent down with food. (2)

FEB. 5. State Board of Education decides that out-of-state teachers must pay $15 fee before they can teach in Arizona. Arizona natives pay $3.00. (1)

FEB. 7. State Senate moves to assume leadership in drive for a 10 cent tariff on copper in place of existing four cent rate. (2)

FEB. 8. Its lowest temperature in recorded history chills Tucson. Mercury drops to 17 above zero. (2)

FEB. 14. Arizona celebrates coming of age by closing city and county offices and holding special ceremonies in schools. (2)

FEB. 18. Phoenix parents and teachers inaugurate supervised recreation for children on 19 city playgrounds. (3)

FEB. 20. Tucson Boy Scouts canvass the city asking clothing for city poor. (1)

FEB. 23. President-elect Roosevelt announces that he will appoint Congressman Lewis Douglas director of the budget. (2)

MAR. 1. President Hoover signs proclamation setting aside Saguaro Cactus Forest near Tucson as a national monument. (2)

MAR. 2. Alarmed by California's "bank holiday" Governor Moeur and Legislature rush through similar suspension for Arizona banks. (2)

MAR. 6. Legal authority for issuance of script by banks and clearing house associations is established by legislative act and signature of governor. (3)

MAR. 9. Waiting word from Washington to reopen for business, Arizona banks are confused by Roosevelt's order continuing the holiday. (3)

MAR. 11. Tucson banks open long enough to cash government pay checks and make change for merchants. (2)

MAR. 14. Eleventh Arizona Legislature adjourns after adopting income tax, private sales tax and a $7,000,000 general appropriations bill. (2)

MAR. 14-15. Arizona banks reopen after "bank holiday." (3)

MAR. 15. Stringed orchestra plays "Happy Days are Here Again," in lobby as Consolidated National Bank in Tucson reopens for business. (2)

MAR. 28. Legality of Arizona's new emergency privilege-sales tax is taken to State Supreme Court. (3)

APRIL 2. Governor Moeur unveils monument on the Arizona-New Mexico line dedicating the Geronimo trail from Douglas to Cloverdale, N.M. (3)

APRIL 3. Banks at Florence and Willcox reopen. (3)

APRIL 7. Arizonans get their first taste of legal beer since prohibition. It is brought in by air. (2)

APRIL 8. Governor Moeur is informed that Arizona will receive $10,-000,000 in U. S. relief funds to be used largely in soil erosion work along the Santa Cruz. (2)

APRIL 10. Arizona reacts angrily to proposal that unemployed men from eastern states be sent into state to work on government reforestation program. (3)

APRIL 11. Constitutionality of the Arizona mortgage moratorium is attacked in Superior Court but is upheld. (3)

APRIL 19. Tucson goes dry again as beer shops post "sold out" signs in their windows. (2)

APRIL 23. After seven-day search, bodies of Carmel Giragi, publisher of the *Winslow Mail,* and his pilot are found near Winslow in wreckage of their plane. (3)

APRIL 25. Bandits hold up Valley Bank in Globe and escape with $34,000. (3)

APRIL 28. Rancher turned bandit is caught with half the loot taken from Globe bank. (3)

APRIL 29. State Supreme Court holds that privilege-sales tax law was not properly drawn and is unconstitutional. (3)

MAY 1. Arizona is informed by Washington that its recruits for reforestation jobs will have priority but must go to conditioning camp at Fort Huachuca first. (3)

MAY 10. Secretary of the Interior orders Boulder Dam contracts to stop paying workmen in script. (2)

MAY 13. Roosevelt administration drops name of Hoover from dam and calls it Boulder Dam. (2)

MAY 14. University of Arizona Regents drop 66 teachers and cut salaries of others from five to 15 percent in economy move. Tempe drops 11, gives leaves to three more and sees its president resign. (3)

MAY 18. State Land Board orders a cut of 50 percent in rentals of state-owned lands, 50 percent being .01½ cents. (3)

MAY 18. Governor Moeur warns that unless Legislature speeds up tax legislation and raises enough money to balance the budget, Arizona will lose out on "outright monetary gifts" resulting from Roosevelt's public works program. (3)

MAY 26. Coconino County people warned to be prepared to receive 1,100 men who will man five reforestation camps. (12)

JUNE 1. State Supreme Court affirms sale of defunct Arizona Bank. Depositors to receive 40 cents on the dollar immediately. (3)

JUNE 5. Eleventh Legislature convenes in special session. Governor Moeur asks it to alleviate state's distressing financial condition. (2)

JUNE 6. First concrete is poured at Boulder Dam. (2)

JUNE 9. Arizona House of Representatives votes 47 to 14 to give people a chance to vote for repeal of the 18th amendment. (3)

JUNE 12. Law limiting speed on state highways to 35 mph expires. (2)

JUNE 17. Hot weather drives legislative committees out of the State Capitol to the comfort of Phoenix air-cooled hotel parlors. (3)

JUNE 19. Two hundred representative citizens from northern Arizona counties reach Phoenix on a special train and demand a bigger share of highway funds than they have had. Their idea is $3,500,000. (3)

JUNE 22. Phoenix school board achieves saving of approximately $88,000 by discharging some teachers and cutting salaries of others. (3)

JUNE 24. Government allots $50,000 to Arizona for emergency relief. (2)

JUNE 26. Tucson bakers raise price of pound loaves of bread from eight to nine cents. (2)

JUNE 26. Legislature adopts income, sales and luxury tax measures and governor signs. (3)

JUNE 27. Eleventh Legislature opens second special session after passing luxury tax at insistence of the Governor. (2)

JUNE 29. State Auditor Ana Frohmiller announces 1,000 state employees will go without their salaries until legislation is interpreted to her satisfaction. (2)

JUNE 30. U. S. Attorney General announces dismissal of administrator and five aides of the prohibition administration in Arizona. Hundreds dismissed throughout the nation. (1)

JULY 1. Wage cuts for municipal employees ranging from $2.50 to $65 monthly ordered by Tucson city council. (1)

JULY 7. First death of a driver at hands of a hitch-hiker in Arizona occurs on Tucson-Nogales highway. (2)

JULY 9. One hundred homesteaders on abandoned Fort Lowell lands are given two-year extension on their payments. (1)

JULY 13. Senator Hayden wires good news to Arizona that it will receive $4,838,000 from government for good roads. (1)

JULY 14. In answer to government agricultural reduction campaign Arizona farmers withdraw 10,655 acres of cotton land and promise 12,000 more. (1)

JULY 17. Copper Queen smelter resumes operations in Douglas, calling 285 men back to work. (3)

JULY 23. Total Arizona assessed valuation for 1933 is $375,500,000, a drop of $98,000,000 in one year. (3)

JULY 27. Valuation of Arizona banks reported off $2,500,000. (3)

AUG. 2. Arizona Temperance Federation denied injunction against holding state vote on repeal of prohibition amendment. (1)

AUG. 4. The one surviving federal enforcement agent in Arizona pours the last of the bootleg liquor on the sands of the Salt River Valley. (3)

AUG. 7. Arizona business adopts NRA shorter work week schedules opening jobs in every community. (3)

AUG. 8. In landslide vote Arizona becomes 21st state to sanction repeal of national prohibition. Democratic voters nominate Mrs. Isabella Greenway for congressional seat vacated by Lewis Douglas. (3)

AUG. 10. Governor Moeur is informed that Public Works Administration has approved $6,211,960 for Arizona roads. Expect projects will provide work for 5,000 men. (1)

AUG. 11. U. S. approves Arizona's highway building projects for next 12 months and governor takes immediate steps to start projects. (3)

AUG. 18. Three quarters of a million dollars in taxes are slashed on city homes, ranches and farms in Arizona. (3)

AUG. 21. Local rainstorm drops 1.5 inches of rain on Tucson in 40 minutes, wrecking Drachman school and raising widespread havoc with highways. (1)

AUG. 22. Phoenix asks Federal loan of $1,436,000 to build sewers, drains and widen streets. (1)

AUG. 22. Tucson sentences unemployed and penniless transients to work on rock pile. (1)

AUG. 23. Yavapai supervisors cut state's valuation of United Verde Copper Co. properties. State orders its figures sustained. Supervisors refuse. Difference is $9,000,000 in mine's favor. (1)

AUG. 23. Government sets this as the deadline for ploughing under cotton crops. Maricopa farmers now wait receipt of $125,000 compensation. (3)

AUG. 30. U. S. Farm Credit Administration announces that four southwestern states, including Arizona, will receive $2,000,000 a month after Sept. 1. (3)

AUG. 31. Three hundred striking miners who fear arrest if they hold mass meeting in New Mexico cross the line to Lupton, Arizona. (1)

SEPT. 3. Maricopa Superior Court holds Arizona intangible tax law is unconstitutional. (1)

SEPT. 4. Two hundred workmen stage protest parade in Douglas as they refuse to sign 35 cent an hour wage for work on new Douglas-Tucson-Phoenix natural gas pipeline. (1)

SEPT. 5. Eleven thousand unemployed register at Arizona's re-employment offices. (3)

SEPT. 5. Arizona officially ratifies the 21st amendment to the Constitution repealing prohibition. (1)

SEPT. 6. Mexican Episcopal church in Salt River Valley charges cotton growers with paying starvation wages to pickers: 60 cents for a day's work of 100 pounds. (3)

SEPT. 14. Pima County Superior Court holds Arizona's new minimum wage law is unconstitutional. (3)

SEPT. 14. Salt River Valley Water Users make vigorous protest when Federal Farm Loan Appraisers cut estimates $40 an acre because of Water Users outstanding indebtedness. (3)

SEPT. 18. Public schools open and teachers are told they must accept their pay in warrants. (1)

SEPT. 20. State Tax Commission sets valuation of United Verde Copper Company's property in Yavapai County at $22,161,000. County assessor reduces figure to $13,185,000. Supervisors refuse to obey orders to convene and restore state's appraisal. County Superior Court supports supervisors. Tax commission retorts that mining company has taken $73,000,000 out of property in 25 years and paid less than $9,000,000 in taxes. (3)

SEPT. 21. Federal and state conciliators are sent to Douglas in effort to end labor trouble on new pipeline to Phoenix. (1)

SEPT. 22. Eighty percent of Coconino County potato crop is destroyed by a strange blight. (12)

SEPT. 22. Mesa co-operates in Arizona drive to support NRA and business houses score 100 percent record. (3)

SEPT. 23. Arizona wheat producers receive government loan of $4.25 an acre. (3)

SEPT. 24. Federal Public Works Administration charges that Arizona is "indifferent" to the opportunities offered under recovery program to relieve unemployment. (3)

SEPT. 24. Arizona notified Federal Government will provide 650,000 pounds of free pork for needy families. (1)

SEPT. 29. State board of arbitration sets wages of cotton pickers at 60 cents a hundred pounds for short staple and $1.00 a hundred pounds for long staple. Pickers' representative unhappy. (3)

SEPT. 29. Arizona orders children under 16 barred from cotton fields in compliance with state law. (3)

SEPT. 29. First transient men's camp in Arizona is scheduled for state fairgrounds in Maricopa County. (1)

SEPT. 30. Phoenix Chamber of Commerce complains that Senators Hayden and Ashurst are responsible for Arizona's failure to benefit properly from Federal Recovery Agencies. (3)

SEPT. 30. Old Flowing Wells ranch home is turned into hobo camp for young wanderers. (1)

OCT. 3. Mrs. Isabella Greenway is elected Arizona's first woman congressman. (1)

OCT. 3. Washington releases $3,000,000 for support of 30 Civilian Conservation Camps in Arizona during next six months. (3)

OCT. 3. By referendum vote Arizona changes method of administering capital punishment from hanging to lethal gas. (3)

OCT. 3. Federal Land Bank answers complaint of Salt River Valley landholders that appraisals are too low. Reports average loans run $80 an acre and some appraisals $600 an acre. (3)

OCT. 8. Chairman of Arizona Public Works board reports that federally approved projects will pour $15,000,000 into State during winter months and additional $21,000,000 may be expected. (3)

OCT. 8. Harold L. Ickes, Secretary of the Interior, asks Arizona, California and Nevada to speed up spending federal funds contributed for highway construction. (1)

OCT. 9. Enrollment at the University of Arizona touches 2,000 mark for first time. (1)

OCT. 16. Arizona — one of the last states to feel full effects of great depression — starts on road back. Twelfth Federal Reserve District figures show Phoenix leading great Pacific Coast cities. State gains 5.8 percent in August over same month in 1932. (3)

OCT. 21. Federal government gives Nogales $433,000 for flood control. (1)

OCT. 26. Salt River Valley relief officials decide to refuse public welfare aid to cotton pickers who would rather live on $12-$15 dollars a month dole than work in the fields for $1 a day. (3)

OCT. 28. Pima County Welfare Board begins serving lunches to hungry school children. (1)

OCT. 30. Southern Arizona Bank and Trust Co. refuses to pay its 1933 state taxes. Other big taxpayers watch developments. (1)

OCT. 30. Senator Hayden and Congresswoman Greenway complain to PWA that statistics on amount of federal aid given to Arizona are misleading. (3)

OCT. 31. University of Arizona prepares to conduct examinations of candidates who apply for right to practice the healing arts. (3)

NOV. 1. Indian tribal conference at Tuba City proves milestone in U. S. relation with tribes. Head of the Navajos says they are getting their first fair break in 200 years. (1)

NOV. 2. Arizona banks open legal warfare against state's taxing methods. (3)

NOV. 3. Corporation commission orders Yuma's electric rates cut from 19 to 28 percent. (1)

NOV. 4. Arizona Bankers Assn. meets and looks with doubt on government guaranty of bank deposits. One Phoenix banker defends it. (1)

NOV. 4. Public Works Administration (PWA) announces $4,000,000 initial allotment to begin construction of $18,912,000 Verde Irrigation and Power project which is to be the largest undertaken in the state. (1)

NOV. 5. Three Cochise Banks and Copper Queen branch of Phelps Dodge tax checks are refused by county treasurer who says they do not represent full amount due. (3)

NOV. 15. The new Verde River Irrigation and Power District, established in face of opposition by Salt River Valley Water Users Association, offers to negotiate amicable settlement of water rights. Salt River Project insists it will seek settlement of its rights on the Verde in the courts. (3)

NOV. 15. Navajos agree to government request that tribe's sheep be reduced from 1,400,000 to 600,000. One hundred thousand animals to be slaughtered and fed to distressed Indians in the northwest. (1)

NOV. 21. Civil Works Administration estimates it can and will put 11,000 men to work in the state. (3)

NOV. 22. First quarterly report of Arizona's new sales tax law shows $226,000 revenue. (1)

NOV. 22. Five hundred civil projects which will furnish work for 15,000 men are approved by Arizona Civil Works Board. (3)

NOV. 24. Six thousand men are dropped from unemployment relief rolls as projects are launched in 14 counties. (3)

NOV. 28. Tucson office of Civil Works Administration warns those on welfare that food and help of all kinds will be cut off if they do not register for CWA jobs immediately. (1)

NOV. 30. President Shantz of the University announces that government work projects coming up in Arizona will employ every unemployed and qualified engineer in the state. (1)

NOV. 30. Thanksgiving Day and 7,500 jobless men rejoice over being returned to a payroll. Hundreds of families sit down to holiday meal for first time in four years. (3)

DEC. 3. Fifteen thousand persons attend enormous Paradise Valley barbecue in celebration of federal grant for the Verde project. (3)

DEC. 9. College of Mines at University is authorized to place 60 Arizona engineers at work on geodetic survey. (4)

DEC. 10. Arizona Attorney-General files answer to suits brought by banks, mines and public utilities, charging that a conspiracy exists to "prevent due administration of the tax laws." (3)

DEC. 11. Apaches at San Carlos Reservation file vigorous protest with the government against white man's rule; claim they fear obliteration of all tribal customs, and demand virtually complete freedom. (3)

DEC. 11. Natural gas pipeline from El Paso reaches Tucson which celebrates by lighting a 40 foot torch. (1)

DEC. 18. Building and plant of the *Arizona Daily Star* reduced to ruins by fire. Paper continues to publish in the *Tucson Citizen* plant. (1).

DEC. 23. Small silver miners of Arizona cheer government's stabilization of silver. (3)

DEC. 24. Another effort is made to restore Fort Lowell, this time under the direction of the University, State Museum, and Arizona Archeological and Historical Society. (1)

DEC. 31. Total deposits in Arizona banks $45,309,355. (27)

Total major metals production in Arizona, $10,307,749. (16)

Total number of cattle in Arizona, 840,000; value, $12,944,000. (24)

1934 JAN. 4. Chino Valley Dam project gets a $100,000 construction loan from the government. (3)

JAN. 4. U. S. announces it will build $60,000 inspection station at Naco. (3)

JAN. 5. Governor Moeur pays a $25 fine for cutting through a funeral procession and speeding on Phoenix streets. (1)

JAN. 6. Phoenix gets additional $735,000 federal loan for civic improvements to bring employment to idle citizens, making total amount of its public works funds close to one million dollars. (3)

JAN. 7. Public Works Board refuses to spend $200,000 on a flood control dam at Charleston unless Arizona does its share. State has no funds. (1)

JAN. 7. Government makes $68,000 loan to Globe for improvement of water system. (3)

JAN. 10. Superior court orders state to reduce tax assessments of Arizona Bank 48 percent. (3)

JAN. 11. Natural gas pipeline reaches Phoenix from Texas. (3)

JAN. 16. State Supreme Court affirms conviction and judgment of kidnapper of Tucson banker; says he must serve life sentence. (3)

JAN. 22. Hard pressed Arizona finds it has rich source of income in its gasoline tax. Report for year 1933 shows return was $2,679,000. (3)

JAN. 25. Governor Moeur warns California it cannot build dam on Colorado at Parker without consent of Arizona. (1)

JAN. 25. Wanted by the FBI and law officers of several states, the notorious John Dillinger and members of his gang are captured in Tucson. (1)

FEB. 9. Tucson gets $150,000 from Federal highway funds for underpass on Stone avenue. (1)

FEB. 10. Civil Works Administration reports 8,000 Arizona families are dropped from relief rolls in last four months of 1933. (3)

FEB. 12. Federal Reserve Bank in San Francisco reports that Arizona leads the west in department store trade increases. (3)

FEB. 13. Phoenix and Maricopa County ask ouster of State Welfare Board on grounds they are not getting full share of federal aid. (1)

FEB. 19. U. S. Supreme Court considers Arizona's claim that other basin states must show cause why testimony for use in future Colorado River litigation should not be taken now and perpetuated. (1)

FEB. 22. *Arizona Daily Star* startles its readers by revealing that only two other cities in the U. S. pay as much for milk as Tucson's 16 cents a quart. (1)

MAR. 2. Mayor of Phoenix is arrested on charge of evading income tax payments. (3)

MAR. 5. Arizona floats bonds and retires $1,100,000 worth of registered warrants. (3)

MAR. 7. Arizona groups vigorously protest proposed NRA copper code, claiming it is detrimental to the industry. (3)

MAR. 8. Winds of 85 mile velocity unroof 25 buildings in Williams. (3)

MAR. 10. Governor Moeur sends two detachments of national guard up the Colorado to patrol Arizona shore where California wants to locate Parker Dam. (1)

MAR. 11. Basic Science Act passed by Eleventh Legislature is target of suits filed in Arizona courts. (3)

MAR. 21. United Mine Workers reject wage and hour terms in NRA copper code. (3)

APRIL 2. CWA activities which have employed 17,000 men come to an end in Arizona and Governor Moeur announces personal visit to Washington to urge fresh federal funds. Says need is for 24,000 jobs. (5).

APRIL 20. State finds more than $50,000 in errors in Yuma County records. (1)

APRIL 21. Copper industry is placed under NRA code, limiting domestic sales to newly mined metal. (1)

APRIL 25. Three hundred men search for six-year-old June Robles, kidnapped in Tucson and held for $15,000 ransom. (1)

APRIL 25. Arizona's minimum wage law is upheld by State Supreme Court. (1)

MAY 11. Tucson's first city hall building, built in 1881, is destroyed by fire. (1)

MAY 11. Aroused by activities of Arizona bootleggers, federals re-organize state enforcement unit and start drive on violators. (3)

MAY 12. State Corporation Commission orders Phoenix gas rates reduced 33 percent. (3)

MAY 13. Missing 19 days, Robles child is found alive in desert dug-out where she had been chained by kidnappers. (1)

MAY 16. Private citizen sues former Governor Hunt for improper expense account. Court orders Hunt to repay $329 he spent for photographs, books and a trip into Mexico. (1)

MAY 16. Citizens Building & Loan Co. of Tucson, with 1,000 depositors, fails owing $551,000. (1)

MAY 21. Forest fires sweep dry areas in the Bradshaws and the Rincons. (3)

MAY 22. Arizona loses point in Colorado River battle when U. S. Supreme Court denies her request to perpetuate testimony. (1)

MAY 22. First priests exiled by Governor of Sonora in Mexico's attack on Roman Catholic Church, enter the United States at Nogales. (1)

MAY 24. *Wickenburg Sun* established. (Personal letter)

MAY 24. Fifty-nine year old woman student at University sues Dean of Women who called her a "paranoic," for $25,000. After four day trial jury takes one ballot and exonerates dean. (1)

JUNE 1. Arizona is declared a drought area and Federal Emergency Crop Loan office is authorized to lend money for purchase of cattle feed throughout state. (3)

JUNE 5. Arizona Cattle Growers Assn. informs government 100,000 cattle are suffering from effects of drought. (3)

JUNE 5. President Roosevelt calls Washington conference of representatives of 15 drought-stricken states, including Arizona. Relief appropriations promised. (1)

JUNE 5. Ex-mayor of Phoenix is convicted of evasion of income taxes and is sentenced to three year term plus $2,500 fine. (3)

JUNE 8. President's conference on drought relief assures aid to Cochise, Graham and Greenlee Counties. (1)

JUNE 10. RFC loans Roosevelt Water Conservation District $1,227,500 to refinance bonded indebtedness. (3)

JUNE 10. Arizona's NRA Compliance Director reports to Washington that state needs $8,000,000 to relieve drought conditions. Graham, Greenlee, Mohave, Yavapai, Gila, Pinal, Pima, Yuma and Santa Cruz are designated as "drought areas." (1)

JUNE 10. Federal Relief Administrator allots Arizona $100,000 for drought relief. (3)

JUNE 13. Arizona rejoices over passage of silver bill by Congress. Bill provides for purchase of silver until it comprises 25 percent of the metallic stocks of banking currency. (3)

JUNE 14. G. W. P. Hunt announces he will campaign again for Democratic nomination for Governor of Arizona. (1)

JUNE 15. Cattlemen in eleven Arizona Counties are placed on emergency drought relief. (1)

JUNE 16. Congress passes Bankhead cotton bill which assures Arizona an allotment of 87,000 tax-free ginned bales from 1934 crop. This amounts to a gift to farmers of $400,000, but later figures set number of bales at 81,484. Maricopa, Pinal, Yuma, Graham, Greenlee and Pima Counties affected. (3)

JUNE 16. Governor Moeur wires President Roosevelt that Arizona is being discriminated against in matter of farm loans. Asks farm loan headquarters be set up in state. (1)

JUNE 20. Senator Hayden informs Arizona that it will benefit from government expenditure of $689,000 for highway and trail development in eight areas. (3)

JUNE 21. Government begins buying 18,000 head of drought-weakened cattle from Cochise and Graham County ranges. (1)

JUNE 30. Four states of the upper Colorado basin resolve that Arizona is entitled to no water from Boulder Dam until she ratifies compact already signed by six other states; approves awarding 750,000 acre feet of the stream flow to Mexico. (3)

JULY 3. Two idle copper mines, the New Cornelia at Ajo and the Miami Copper Co. at Miami, reopen on reduced schedules. Will employ 1,000 men. (1)

JULY 3. Mineralized ranges in southwestern Arizona are reopened to prospectors by the federal government. (1)

JULY 6. First lethal gas execution in Arizona takes lives of two brothers convicted of murder. (1)

JULY 10. Arizona suffers in nation-wide heat wave. Phoenix temperature breaks 39-year-old record with reading of 115. (3)

JULY 14. Single Maricopa taxpayer goes to court in effort to stop county purchase or use of voting machines. (3)

JULY 15. Yuma water supply intake threatened by sewage back-up caused by construction of temporary dam on Colorado by Imperial Irrigation District of California. Mayor protests. (1)

JULY 15. Prescott and Flagstaff report supply of city water greatly reduced. Flagstaff ships in from eight to eleven tank cars of water daily. Prescott plans two mile main to Granite Dells. (1)

JULY 19. Public Works Administration warns Phoenix that if it does not go into high gear on $1,900,000 municipal improvement program the government will cancel allotments to city. (3)

JULY 20. Pointing to fact that while Maricopa County pays 40.4 percent of the state gasoline tax, Phoenix Chamber of Commerce says county got but 10.9 percent of highway budget in last year. Calls program illegal. (3)

JULY 22. State Tax Commission cuts valuation of all counties except Coconino which is raised $7,709,000. (1)

JULY 25. Tombstone pleads with Arizona Corporation commission to compel Huachuca Water Company to improve its service and break drought from which town is suffering. (1)

JULY 28. Strike of stockyard workers in Chicago congests pens with cattle and government curtails buying beef in Arizona. (3)

JULY 31. Yavapai County Board of Supervisor raises assessed valuation of the United Verde Copper Co. from $8,662,000 to $17,638,000 and company files suit in district court asking for injunction. (3)

AUG. 2. Flagstaff seeks federal grant of $35,000 to meet drought conditions by sinking more wells. (3)

AUG. 3. Drought conditions in Arizona are so serious that Secretary of Agriculture modifies cotton contracts to help emergency need for livestock feeds. (3)

AUG. 7. State Corporation Commission rules that Huachuca Water Company must supply Tombstone's water needs for everything except the town swimming pool. (1)

AUG. 9. By Presidential proclamation silver is nationalized at 50.1 cents an ounce and Arizona is cheered. (3)

AUG. 12. *Arizona Republic* conducts a poll on question of whether Roosevelt "New Deal" has brought prosperity. Vote is 50-50. (3)

AUG. 12. State Tax Commission sets Arizona's valuation at $356,170,000 which is $30,701,000 less than 1933, and cuts tax rate to $1. (1)

AUG. 16. All preliminary work on public works program in Phoenix is halted while government seeks to discover whether bonds are valid. (3)

AUG. 18. Nogales stages greatest celebration ever held on the border, La Fiesta de la Plata. Honors silver champion Senator Key Pittman at reception attended by U. S. and Mexican dignitaries. Thirty-five pound silver tray is twin cities' gift to guest of honor. (3)

AUG. 18. University of Arizona gets $815,000 PWA loan for construction of seven new structures and remodelling one. (1)

AUG. 18. Anti-Alien Assn. holds a parade in Phoenix to advertise its objection to invasion of valley lands by aliens. (3)

AUG. 21. Arizona hears that presidential order commandeering the nation's stocks of monetary silver has poured 33,450,000 ounces of white metal into the treasury. Receipts from the mines reach 11,321,000 ounces. (1)

AUG. 22. U. S. Government enters alien land dispute in Salt River Valley. Fears Japanese reprisals. (3)

AUG. 22. President Roosevelt authorizes increasing lending ratio on cotton from 10 to 12 cents a pound. (1)

AUG. 26. Mesa merchant patrolman and burglar duel through store window in the dark with six-guns. Both die. (3)

AUG. 27. Night fire destroys five Tucson business establishments on Scott street including printing plant producing ballots for Pima, Santa Cruz and Pinal County primary. (1)

AUG. 28. Heavy rainstorms send the Gila river raging through the town of Duncan, driving 25 families from their homes and halting Southern Pacific trains. (1)

AUG. 31. *New York Times* prints story that Lewis Douglas, former congressman from Arizona, will resign as director of the budget because of lack of sympathy for Roosevelt spending policies. (1)

AUG. 31. Hundreds of men and women march on the State Capitol and demand additional relief, including free rent, fuel, milk and $10 a week for each single worker. Governor Moeur refuses them an audience and they threaten violence. (1)

SEPT. 1. Arizona building contractors and labor endorse the 30-hour work week advocated by President Roosevelt. (3)

SEPT. 6. Striking Federal Emergency Relief administration workers battle police in streets of Phoenix. County attorney refuses to issue warrants after police arrest 27 men charged with violence. (1)

SEPT. 3. Crowd of 10,000 swarm to Chiricahua National Monument to witness ceremonies opening new scenic highway through Wonderland of Rocks. (1)

SEPT. 7. Warrants are issued for 26 Phoenix rioters. Arizona National Guard is held under arms in anticipation of further violence. (1)

SEPT. 11. Governor Moeur defeats G. W. P. Hunt in race for Democratic gubernatorial nomination. (1)

SEPT. 18. Unknowns dynamite three irrigation ditches on Japanese-operated farms. U. S. State Department urges Governor Moeur take precautions against further violence. (1)

OCT. 3. Postmaster at tiny desert station of Picacho and his newly appointed successor end quarrel with gun battle and both lose lives. (1)

OCT. 3. Arizona and the Department of the Interior having agreed on a water contract for the state, Secretary Ickes warns Colorado Compact states they must file objections, if any, by Nov. 15. Proposed contract gives Arizona 2,800,000 acre feet of water. (3)

OCT. 4. Six members of the Colorado River Compact unite in fighting Arizona's demand for 2,800,000 acre feet of water from Boulder Dam. (1)

OCT. 4. Reign of terror is renewed in Salt River as enemies of Japanese farmers explode more bombs on farms. (1)

OCT. 4. Public Works Administration cancels $4,000,000 allotment promised for construction of a dam on the Verde River. Engineers report it will never repay cost of building. (1)

OCT. 4. Six Colorado Compact states protest vehemently to Secretary Ickes against Arizona receiving any Colorado River water until she signs Compact. (3)

OCT. 13. Five prisoners break out of Holbrook jail, lock deputy in a cell, steal all the guns in the sheriff's office, and escape in stolen car. (1)

OCT. 14. Paradise Valley residents burn effigies of Governor Moeur, Congresswoman Greenway and Secretary Ickes in protest against revocation of Verde Dam funds. (1)

OCT. 16. Lawmen track Holbrook jail breakers down in the Tonto Valley and capture them in gun fight. (3)

NOV. 2. Governor Moeur assures Japanese Consul that everything possible will be done to safeguard Japanese life and property in war being waged by Salt River Valley settlers against alien landholders. (1)

NOV. 2. University of Arizona boasts that its students come from 44 states and eight countries. (1)

NOV. 4. Governor Moeur wires U. S. Department of State that Arizona needs Department of Justice intervention in handling anti-alien situation. Says he cannot call out National Guard unless counties request it, and none have done so. (1)

NOV. 6. Governor Moeur is reelected as Roosevelt Democrats sweep Arizona. (1)

NOV. 12. Arizona's determination to bring a halt to building of Parker Dam reaches climax when Governor Moeur stations National Guardsmen on Arizona side of Colorado with instructions to prevent work there. (3)

NOV. 14. Secretary of the Interior Ickes orders work stopped on Parker bridge until "the respective rights of the states have been determined in an orderly manner." Governor Moeur calls back 100 Guardsmen. (3)

NOV. 15. Fifty Tucson women make plans to establish state's first birth control clinic. (1)

NOV. 17. Transcontinental bus arrives at Williams with 20 unconscious passengers suffering overdose of monoxide gas. (1)

NOV. 17. Valley National Bank announces that it will handle Arizona's current general fund warrants on a cash basis. (3)

NOV. 18. Report on Phoenix retail sales for the year shows monthly gains of from $5,000,000 to $10,000,000 over 1933. (3)

NOV. 19. Washington halts home loan service in Arizona and urges private financing. (3)

NOV. 21. Valley Bank and Trust Co. of Phoenix announces purchase of controlling interest in Consolidated National Bank of Tucson. (1)

NOV. 26. Eleventh Legislature meets in third special session to consider whether University will be allowed to accept $815,000 in government building loans. (1)

NOV. 27. State Supreme Court says Arizona's intangibles tax law is unconstitutional. (3)

DEC. 6. Legislature passes emergency bill which gives colleges, irrigation districts and municipalities chance to accept $5,000,000 in federal grants and loans. (3)

DEC. 6. Secretary of the Interior Ickes is angry at Arizona for holding up Parker bridge. He says state "is barking its own shins." (1)

DEC. 6. Although fought by the Salt River Water Users Assn., Legislature passes act giving Verde River Irrigation district more time in which to try to regain federal aid. (3)

DEC. 14. Arizona cotton growers vote to keep Bankhead Bill for another year. Only Pinal County is opposed. (1)

DEC. 17. Secretary Ickes hears Arizona's plea for water and upsets plan to give state 2,800,000 acre feet from Boulder Dam reservoir. Tells states to work out a contract on which all can agree. (1)

DEC. 23. Highway deaths reach 200 for the year. (3)

DEC. 25. George W. P. Hunt, seven-time governor of Arizona, dies at his Phoenix home at the age of 75. The body will lie in state in the capitol rotunda beneath the great seal of Arizona which he helped design. (3)

DEC. 31. Second earthquake in two days shakes Arizona. Phoenix, Nogales, Tucson, Florence and Coolidge report damages to buildings. (1)

DEC. 31. Total deposits in Arizona banks, $53,957,231. (27)

Total major minerals production in Arizona, $23,292,150. (16)

Total number of cattle in Arizona, 840,000; value, $13,717,000. (24)

Federal Indian Reorganization Act of 1934 restores lands of Papago Indian Reservation to exploration and location of mineral claims by outsiders. (17)

1935 JAN. 1. Governor Moeur picks New Year's Day to announce his budget in which he asks an increase of $442,500, but offers to cut interest on public debt and workers' salaries by $225,000. (2)

JAN. 5. State Superintendent of Banks pays $1,296,300 in dividends to depositors of First National Building and Loan Assn. in Phoenix, Old Dominion Bank in Globe, Intermountain Building and Loan Assn. in Phoenix, and the Citizens Building and Loan Assn. in Tucson. (2)

JAN. 5. Last act of retiring Maricopa County Assessor is to kill grove tax on citrus growers in the Salt River Valley. (3)

JAN. 8. Missing for 84 hours in the Superstition Mountains, Phoenix war veteran staggers out with gold nuggets in his pocket and holes in his memory. (2)

JAN. 11. State Highway Department announces it spent $3,285,752 for maintenance, betterment and construction of Arizona roads in the last six months of 1934. (5)

JAN. 21. U. S. Supreme Court rules that Arizona must show cause by Feb. 4 why it should not be prohibited from interfering further with work on Parker Dam. (2)

JAN. 22. Twelfth Legislature memorializes Congress asking for a 10 cent tariff on foreign copper. (5)

JAN. 22. University Agricultural Economist proves to Arizona farmers that total cash income of the farms of state in 1934 was 25 percent greater than in the preceding year. (2)

JAN. 23. Federal government spends $200,000 on aerial survey of 18,000 square miles of the Gila watershed to help identify its erosion problems. When finished map will cover a ballroom floor. (5)

JAN. 23. Valley National Bank announces it is earmarking $1,000,000 for homebuilding loans. (3)

JAN. 25. State Motor Vehicle Division reports net revenues from gasoline tax up 10 percent over previous year; Maricopa County contributes 38.9 percent of total. (3)

JAN. 29. Flagstaff pays Santa Fe Railroad $36,866 for hauling in 30,632,000 gallons of water during drought in second half of 1934. (4)

JAN. 30. Meeting in Phoenix, National Wool Growers Assn. makes a plea for a high protective tariff. (3)

FEB. 1. Three million pound gate at Boulder Dam is closed and the Colorado starts building a lake in the mountains. (2)

FEB. 2. State Association of Mayors merges with Arizona Municipal League. (3)

FEB. 2. Arizona cuts every relief case $1 a month to stretch its fading FERA funds. (2)

FEB. 4. All being quiet on the Colorado River front at the moment, Arizona senate fusses over probe of Colorado River Commission funds and considers abolishing that body. (5)

FEB. 5. It takes the combined efforts of city, state, and federal officers, but the bolted doors of the elaborate Chess and Checker Club in Phoenix are stormed. Gambling equipment and liquor are seized, and club members arrested. (3)

FEB. 5. Prescott's Townsend Old Age Pension Club holds a large meeting to listen to speakers expound the Townsend doctrine. (5)

FEB. 7. Young chiefs of San Carlos Indians fail to heed warnings of armies of ants which head for the hills, and floods drive their people belatedly to high ground. (5)

FEB. 8. Legislative flareup over Colorado River war chest dies out and appropriation measure providing for $69,000 is sent to Governor who signs it. (5)

FEB. 11. Supreme Court enjoins Arizona from interfering with work on Parker Dam, pending determination of U. S. application for permanent injunction. (2)

FEB. 11. Leading clergymen of Tucson denounce what they call "a wide-open town." (2)

FEB. 14. Phelps Dodge Co. gets control of United Verde Copper Co. (2)

FEB. 25. University sets a world record for cotton production on its experimental farms. One acre yields 2,190.8 pounds, or 4.6 bales. (3)

FEB. 25. Cattle-killing lion, which raids herds in Scott Basin near Prescott, is killed. Animal weighs over 200 pounds and measures 9 feet in length. Hunter claims lion is largest ever killed in state. (3)

FEB. 27. Yuma, finding it is host to a Communist writer and a Red dramatist, hustles both men out on the road to Phoenix. (3)

MAR. 2. Legislature gives Governor power to prohibit building an obstruction across a navigable stream. (5)

MAR. 6. Arizona Senate is told that God is "being wiped out of the hearts of Mexican children," and sends memorial to Congress asking investigation of alleged religious persecution in Southern republic. (5)

MAR. 6. Legislature approves Governor Moeur's request that Arizona send an "ambassador" to Washington and provides $7,500 for his salary and expenses. (1)

MAR. 11. Arizona lies under a blanket of snow stretching from the "strip" north of the Grand Canyon to Douglas and Nogales. (3)

MAR. 12. Central Arizona Light and Power Co. presents Phoenix and the valley with a $200,000 reduction in rates. (3)

MAR. 12. State Supreme Court affirms sentence of from 25 to 40 years' imprisonment for men who staged Tucson gas station holdup that netted $25. (3)

MAR. 20. U. S. Senate passes a bill giving Arizona the right to construct its end of bridge at Parker. State attorney general says the bill is unconstitutional. (3)

MAR. 21. Arizona's 12th Legislature adjourns after longest session in State's history — 67 days. Legislators increased the school levy per capita tax, cut $45,000 from general appropriations bill, wrote a new privilege sales tax, placed a luxury tax on liquor, tobacco and sports goods, established a State Board of Pharmacy, legalized sale of liquor and beer and dog and horse racing, and provided death penalty for kidnappers who injured captives. (3)

MAR. 21. Salt River Valley rejoices as lettuce prices jump from $1.50 to $2.85 a crate in ten days. (3)

MAR. 25. Governor Moeur reveals that state has $1,000,000, provided by acts of the Twelfth Legislature, with which to match government aid to the needy, plus a $25,000 income a month from sales and luxury taxes. (5)

MAR. 27. Federal Emergency Relief Administration operates a canning factory at Prescott to preserve meats and vegetables for families on relief. (3)

MAR. 27. State Supreme Court approves P.W.A. Loan of $815,000 to University. (1)

MAR. 31. Glendale farmer breaks world's records for production of Pima cotton. He averages 553.7 pounds to the acre on 30 acre tract. (3)

APRIL 12. Government's announcement of a 10 percent increase in the price of newly minted silver starts a scramble for leases of old silver mines. (1)

APRIL 12. Students of Arizona State Teachers' College at Tempe hold assembly and pray for peace as war clouds darken in Europe. (3)

APRIL 13. Travelling dust storm so dense it blots out moonlight moves west from the Mississippi Valley and envelops southern Arizona. (1)

APRIL 13. Globe schoolteacher creates consternation when she defies school board's order to quit and barricades herself in schoolhouse. (1)

APRIL 16. Windstorms carrying tons of topsoil from the great American dustbowl continue to darken Arizona skies but state suffers lightly in comparison with Colorado and New Mexico. (1)

APRIL 16. Eleven hundred Maricopa cotton growers co-operate with Agricultural Adjustment Administration in reducing acreage. (3)

APRIL 18. Phoenix relives the boom times of 1929 for one day when 50 foot lot on East Washington street is sold for $200,000 cash. (3)

APRIL 19. Water rights to the Gila River from point below the Pima Indian Reservation to the end of Duncan Valley in New Mexico agreed on by Arizona and New Mexico. (1)

APRIL 19. Arizona State Chamber of Commerce asks every chamber in the United States to urge Congress to continue protective tariff on copper. (3)

APRIL 21. Easter sunrise services on the brink of the Grand Canyon of Arizona are broadcast to the nation. (3)

APRIL 24. Arizona State Highway Commission votes to complete Highway 60, the state's transcontinental route, this year. (3)

APRIL 24. Arizona State Teachers' College, Tempe, celebrates its golden anniversary. (3)

APRIL 24. President Roosevelt raises government offer for newly mined silver to 77.57. (3)

APRIL 29. Arizona wins its first big victory in long campaign to hold its share of Colorado River water. U. S. Supreme Court reverses former ruling and says the state owns east bank of the river. (1)

MAY 7. Board of Regents reveals that it is paying University truck drivers more money than instructors with a master's degree. (1)

MAY 7. Arizona adds up its wants and asks for $139,119,808 in government funds for projects under the $4,880,000,000 "greater public works" program being planned by PWA. (3)

MAY 10. Mohave County gets seven CCC camps for summer which *Mohave County Miner* says will "be of great benefit." (13)

MAY 10. U. S. Reclamation Bureau agrees on development of 90,000 acres of Colorado River Indian Reservation and 150,000 acres of Yuma project. (1)

MAY 13. Senator Johnson, California, re-opens Colorado River fight by introducing bill which would give U. S. right to build Parker and 25 other dams. (1)

MAY 20. Governor Moeur issues proclamation appropriating $25,000 for use of the State Tax Department and Attorney General in prosecuting large corporations which refuse to pay delinquent taxes. (1)

MAY 24. President Roosevelt liberalizes PWA loans by cutting to 55 percent the amount states and municipalities must pay back, and dropping interest to three percent. (1)

MAY 27. Arizona agrees to let California erect Parker Dam, in return for right to build a dam at Headgate Rock which will water Colorado Indian Reservation lands. U. S. Senate accepts the compromise. (1)

MAY 30. Governors of Arizona and Utah meet at Boulder City and unveil memorial plaque to 89 men who lost their lives in the erection of Boulder Dam. (3)

JUNE 1. Members of the Phoenix City Commission object to accepting more federal funds for public improvement projects if city has to stand part of the costs. (3)

JUNE 2. Three carloads of dynamite are set off at the New Cornelia mine site at Ajo and 400,000 tons of rock are dislodged. (1)

JUNE 5. RFC approves a $10,610,000 refinancing loan to Salt River Valley Water Users Assn. Organization will save $2,500,000. (3)

JUNE 5. A Congressional Act transfers 75 acres of land in Arizona from the Veterans' Administration to the Department of the Interior, title to remain in the United States in trust for the Yavapai Indians (49 Stat., 332, c. 202). This is known as the "Yavapai Reservation." (17)

JUNE 6. Arizona Supreme Court rules that the Governor has no right to appropriate $25,000 for use in fighting delinquent big taxpayers. (1)

JUNE 7. State Educational Department reports a discrepancy of $600,000 between records of permanent school funds and actual amount in cash, bonds and investments. First answer is that bank failures and poor loans are responsible. (1)

JUNE 7. Northern Arizona rejoices over news that $1,065,742 is earmarked for Highway 66 which crosses Apache, Navajo, Coconino, Yavapai and Mohave Counties. (13)

JUNE 12. Striking Bisbee miners ask governor for food. Governor passes the plea on to Federal Relief Administration. (1)

JUNE 13. Colorado congressmen cause row before the House Rules Committee when they charge Arizona with "attempting to steal the birthright of the Upper Basin States." (1)

JUNE 16. Navajo tribesmen of Arizona and New Mexico vote to reject government's offer of home rule. (3)

JUNE 20. Fire destroys largest lumber mill in the state at Holbrook; loss is $250,000. (3)

JUNE 21. Bureau of Census reveals that despite the depression years the total number of Arizona farms increased by 4,651, bringing the total to 18,824. (3)

JUNE 24. Maricopa Superior Court rules that new privilege tax does not apply to farmers who need no license and need not pay tax. (3)

JUNE 25. Violence marks three weeks' old strike of Bisbee miners as guard shoots a worker. (3)

JUNE 25. Arizona copper men are informed that they have won their fight for an extension of copper tariff. Congress agrees to two more years. (3)

JUNE 26. Bisbee strikers, or sympathizers, stone bus. Nine are jailed. (3)

JUNE 30. Nogales has a gala day as it dedicates its new Federal Building. (1)

JULY 8. President Roosevelt backs Secretary Ickes' plan to spend $100,000,000 on reclamation projects. Plan gives Arizona $6,500,000. (1)

JULY 9. Valuation of Arizona mines is raised $18,196,000 by State Tax Commission. (3)

JULY 9. State Supreme Court rules that Phoenix ordinance making reckless driving illegal in city, is itself illegal. (3)

JULY 13. Federal Internal Revenue officials report 1934-35 fiscal year collection of corporation income taxes increased 68.7 percent over previous year. Advance called index to revival of Arizona business. (3)

JULY 14. Contractors' police dynamite one of two roads into Boulder Dam workings to prevent striking workmen from entering property. (3)

JULY 17. City of Phoenix buys Sky Harbor airport. (3)

JULY 19. Kingman joins towns which establish Townsend Old Age Annuity Clubs. (13)

JULY 20. Willcox and Benson citizens circulate petitions asking special election on proposal to form a new county, with Tombstone as county seat. (1)

JULY 22. President Shantz of the University gives signal which starts construction machinery on $815,000 campus building program financed by federal assistance. (1)

JULY 22. Phoenix fire department loses its mind as pranksters turn in 10 false alarms in three hours. (3)

JULY 24. Federal funds of $4,000,000 are provided for Water Users dam on the Verde River. (3)

JULY 26. City of Phoenix adopts occupational tax which it hopes dam on the Verde River. (3)

JULY 29. In Arizona's worst auto accident seven people are killed when car plunges off highway in Kaibab Forest. (1)

JULY 31. Safford district hard hit by cloudburst which roars out of the Graham Mountains down Cottonwood Wash. Pima and Thatcher suffer much damage to adobe homes. (3)

AUG. 1. Tucson postmaster sees sign of returning prosperity as postal receipts increase 13.16 percent in last fiscal year and 18.5 percent over pre-depression year of 1929-30. (1)

AUG. 1. Seven hundred men are recruited from Indian reservations and CCC camps to exterminate rodents on 1,500,000 acres of Arizona grazing lands. (3)

AUG. 2. Government establishes CCC headquarters in Tucson to direct force of 3,780 men who will be stationed in work camps from Yuma to Naco. (1)

AUG. 8. Mohave County officials start on 400 mile trail for Short Creek, into Utah and out again, to "The Strip" for purpose of prosecuting eight cases of alleged polygamy among Mormon settlers. (3)

AUG. 10. Fund of $1,200,000 for Federal Soil Conservation work becomes available to Arizona. (3)

AUG. 10. State Tax Commission fixes tax rate at 78 cents. Drop is due to two cent sales tax and increased taxes on mines and cattle. (1)

AUG. 20. Washington tentative set-up of road building funds reveals that Arizona will have total of $13,000,000 in two years. (1)

AUG. 22. Phoenix tolls city's bells in tribute to Will Rogers, cowboy humorist, who dies in Alaskan plane crash. (3)

AUG. 23. Settlers and cottagers along the peaceful Hassayampa River flee for their lives as mountain cloudburst brings down a wall of water swirling through Wickenburg. (3)

AUG. 29. Four passengers drown when bus is swamped by seven foot wall of water in an underpass near Dragoon. (1)

AUG. 31. Secretary Ickes orders work renewed on Parker Dam and Governor Moeur again threatens to call out the state troops. (1)

AUG. 31. Arizona prepares to cancel licenses of all car drivers and compel them to take new tests. Governor Moeur leads the way. (3)

SEPT. 1. Tucson is hit by a flood when Rillito and Santa Cruz overflow, drive lowland residents to high ground and take out two bridges. Tanque Verde bridge left high and dry. (1)

SEPT. 5. State Corporation Commission orders power rates reduced in Florence, Casa Grande, Coolidge, Bisbee and Douglas. (3)

SEPT. 6. Estimated on basis of government guaranteed price, Arizona cotton crop for the year will bring growers $7,000,000. (1)

SEPT. 6. President Roosevelt approves allocation of $2,000,000 for construction of first unit of Parker Dam. President makes it clear water will be used only by United States. (1)

SEPT. 7. Justice of the peace frees six Short Creek residents accused of polygamy while three others escape into the hills. (3)

SEPT. 7. Holbrook learns about tear gas when sheriff's tear gas gun is accidentally discharged in a pool hall. (3)

SEPT. 11. Mormon Church excommunicates 12 residents of Short Creek who advocate practice of polygamy. (1)

SEPT. 14. City manager of Phoenix announces all news about city departments must have his approval before released to the press. (3)

SEPT. 20. Copper mines boost production and job rolls are increased to 6,000. (3)

SEPT. 21. Three armed men hold up building contractor as he enters campus of the University of Arizona and rob him of $2,000 payroll. (3)

SEPT. 24. Maricopa Superior Court calls occupational tax established by Phoenix, in hope of $70,000 annual revenue, excessive and unconstitutional. (3)

SEPT. 28. PWA authorities authorize Arizona allotments totalling $1,385,000 of which $775,000 is for Indian irrigation works. Say the sum is "all Arizona can expect" of the $7,000,000 for which it asked. (3)

SEPT. 30. Latest hikes in PWA gifts to Arizona boost state's share to $4,004,000. Labor making jobs reach every section. (3)

SEPT. 30. President Roosevelt dedicates Boulder Dam. (1)

OCT. 11. Hundreds of Arizona and Utah residents gather at Lee's Ferry on the Colorado to join Latter Day Saints in celebrating historic crossing by early emigrants who went on to found Arizona's thriving Mormon communities. (1)

OCT. 11. Justice grinds relentlessly away at alleged polygamists of Short Creek; three accused are held for trial in Superior Court. (3)

OCT. 12. Governor Moeur urges that a concerted movement be launched in Arizona to increase home trade. Says state can hurry recovery by so doing. (3)

OCT. 13. Arizona has third highest auto death rate per 100,000 of population in United States with 44.85. California is fourth with 42.62. (3)

OCT. 16. Nogales is worried by news that several hundred rebel raiders in Sonora are advancing on the international line. (3)

OCT. 16. Washington reports more than $28,000,000 has been allotted to Arizona from the $4,880,000,000 works relief appropriation and there is more to come. (3)

OCT. 19. Phelps Dodge attorneys haul 3,000 detailed records of every Arizona real estate transaction over three year period into court as foundation for charge that company has been "discriminated against" by Pima County assessors. (3)

OCT. 20. Nogales and other points along international border relax as Mexican Federal troops halt insurrectionists. (3)

OCT. 20. Bureau of Agricultural Economics finds that Arizona farm wages average $50.75 a month; eighth in the nation. (3)

OCT. 30. Herds of 1,000 Mexican cattle imported into Arizona at Naco, Douglas and Nogales bring U. S. government high profits in duty fees. (3)

OCT. 30. Attorneys for Phelps Dodge, trying company case against Pima County, continue claim of discrimination; present evidence that Maricopa County is assessed at 60 percent of its value, Pima County at 55 percent. (3)

OCT. 31. Real estate appraisers and assessors testify in Phelps Dodge case that property in Arizona is always undervalued except in case of mines which are assessed for all assessors think they can get. (3)

OCT. 31. Work begins again on Parker Dam diversion channels and neither Arizona's army or navy are present. (1)

NOV. 2. Governor Moeur warns persons on relief that if they refuse to pick cotton there will be no WPA jobs for them. (3)

NOV. 4. Maricopa County opens drive to raise money for Will Rogers' memorial. (3)

NOV. 5. Proposal to divide Cochise County fails when petitions for a special election fall 300 short of sufficient signatures. (3)

NOV. 7. WPA expenditure of $700,000 for a dam to create a three mile lake in Sabino Canyon is authorized. (1)

NOV. 14. Arizona is taken off the dole by WPA which offers jobs to those who have been on relief. New Deal program now emphasizes recovery. (3)

NOV. 27. Seven weeks of testimony and legal wrangling in Phelps Dodge injunction suit with Pima County over $1,700,000 in taxes on the Copper Queen, New Cornelia, and Morenci properties, is adjourned over the Thanksgiving holidays to give all concerned a breather. (1)

NOV. 27. Maricopa County Board of Supervisors starts suit to halt efforts of State Board of Public Welfare to make County responsible for indigents. (1)

NOV. 30. A pontoon toll-bridge is opened across the Colorado, replacing Parker's famous ferries. (3)

DEC. 2. *Morning Sun* and *Arizona Sentinel* merged as *Yuma Daily Sun*. (6)

DEC. 5. Secretary Ickes shocks Arizona by suspending $24,000,000 Yuma project which is expected to irrigate 600,000 acres of land. (1)

DEC. 9. U. S. Supreme Court grants Arizona plea and gives California until Jan. 15 to show cause why Arizona should not be permitted to petition for a U. S. decree apportioning waters of the Colorado among upper and lower basin states. (1)

DEC. 10. Refusal of U. S. to bid on 20,000,000 ounces of silver knocks the bottom out of silver market. London market collapses. Silver crisis throws issue into Congress. (1)

DEC. 12. Stone Avenue underpass is presented to Tucson by the State of Arizona as hundreds watch ceremony. (1)

DEC. 12. City of Douglas gets $92,000 from WPA for an airport. (1)

DEC. 12. Governor Moeur urges citizens to threaten congressional representatives with defeat if they do not vote for soldiers' bonus. (3)

DEC. 13. Northern Arizona hails news that highway is opened over the top of Boulder Dam. (13)

DEC. 13. Two Short Creek polygamists are convicted and sentenced to serve 18 months in State Penitentiary. (3)

DEC. 15. Little Arizona town of "Christmas" loses its post office and will postmark no more mail. (1)

DEC. 18. State Attorney General orders arrest of all Parker Dam workmen laboring on Arizona side of the stream. Action seen as retaliation for Secretary Ickes' order suspending Yuma project. (1)

DEC. 19. Phoenix decides to experiment with a juvenile crime prevention department. (3)

DEC. 19. Governor Moeur wires Secretary Ickes that he regrets attorney general's order to arrest Parker Dam workers. (1)

DEC. 22. Arizona newspapers cheer announcement that Associated Press trunk line will establish a mainline station at Phoenix. (1)

DEC. 23. National Resources Board reports to President Roosevelt that the Santa Fe Compact has failed to settle basic controversies over the use of Colorado River waters. (1)

DEC. 27. Salt River Valley Water Users vote eight to one for ratification of contract with Department of the Interior for storage dam on Verde River, new spillways and sundry repairs. (3)

DEC. 31. State Supreme Court rules that newspapers must pay a sales tax on advertisements. (1)

DEC. 31. Total deposits in Arizona banks $63,707,870. (27)
Total public school enrollment, all grades, 77,993. Of this number 14,958 are high school students. (15)

1936 JAN. 1. Arizona sets new record with 216 auto fatalities in 1935. (3)

JAN. 2. Ranch hand is kicked and stomped to death at Eloy. Three CCC enrollees and discharged soldier are charged with crime. (3)

JAN. 2. Lacking even a volunteer fire-fighting group, Coolidge citizens stand by helplessly while flames destroy their leading hotel. (3)

JAN. 3. Arizona cattlemen and U. S. Department of the Interior quarrel endlessly over administration of Taylor Grazing Act. (3)

JAN. 4. Governor Moeur and other officials dedicate the last camp of Hadji Ali (Hi Jolly), famous pioneer camel driver, at Quartzsite. (3)

JAN. 6. President Roosevelt revives Yuma-Gila $2,500,000 reclamation project. Action due to personal intervention of President Homer L. Shantz of the University of Arizona. (20)

JAN. 6. American livestock industry leaders meet in Phoenix and denounce Canadian reciprocal trade treaty which cuts tariff one cent. (1)

JAN. 7. Sentiment of cattlemen attending national meeting of American Livestock Assn. is that their business has improved to a point where "a cow is worth stealing again." (1)

JAN. 8. State Attorney General's office says Arizona's auto responsibility law is so vague it is unenforceable. (3)

JAN. 9. Casa Grande learns that federal government will resettle 100 families occupying submarginal lands on 4,000 acres in San Carlos Valley. (1)

JAN. 15. Work begins on Imperial Dam. (23)

JAN. 15. City of Douglas stages march as protest against inclusion of Stein's Pass in the highway system. (1)

JAN. 16. Arizona State Tax Commission reports new excise tax brought in $4,000,000 in 1935. Made possible retirement $1,690,000 in registered warrants. (1)

JAN. 17. Phoenix police depopulate hobo "jungles" by loading 143 men and women into freight trucks and hauling them three miles out of the city with warnings not to return. Tucson reports its city jail is crowded with vagrants. (1, 3)

JAN. 24. Salt River Valley Project reports value of its crops increased $2,124,000 in 1935 over previous year while livestock increased $146,000. (3)

JAN. 26. State Safety Engineer warns public that auto accidents during 1935 cost Arizona $4,140,000, which is four times as much as is budgeted for highways. (3)

JAN. 27. Soldiers' Bonus Bill, providing payment of veterans' benefits due in 1945, is passed by Congress over Roosevelt's veto and Arizona vets celebrate. (3)

JAN. 27. U. S. Bureau of Mines says Arizona mines made a gain of 55 percent in 1935, for a total of $12,957,000. (3)

FEB. 1. Federal Emergency Relief Administration official visits Phoenix and wonders why the number of people on relief or work relief jobs does not diminish in face of rising employment by agriculture and industry. (3)

FEB. 2. With 2,742 students enrolled, University of Arizona notes it has a parking problem on campus. (1)

FEB. 3. Los Angeles sends 126 officers to Colorado River crossing points to give hoboes choice of staying in Arizona or serving terms at hard labor in California. (3)

FEB. 3. Seven workmen burn to death and 13 are injured in fire which destroys dormitory at Parker Dam worksite. (1)

FEB. 6. Secretary Ickes announces that the artificial lake behind Boulder Dam will be named for Dr. Elwood Mead, late reclamation commissioner, who was first to see possibilities of great public playground. (3)

FEB. 6. Florence High School basketball team captures three convicts who fled over the wall of Arizona State Prison. (3)

FEB. 7. California police turn 300 hoboes back into Arizona. (3)

FEB. 9. Federal Housing Commission reports that Phoenix building increases in 1935 gained 267 percent over previous year. (1)

FEB. 11. Los Angeles police take two score hoboes to the Arizona border and order them out of California. News photos in Los Angeles papers show more vagrants being herded into trains headed for Colorado River. (3)

FEB. 12. California police report they have prevented 662 hoboes from crossing into state from Arizona. (3)

FEB. 17. Apache County files 137 suits at St. Johns in attempt to collect $125,000 in alleged county shortages. (3)

FEB. 17. CCC workers complete work of cutting year-round road connecting Bright Angel and Kaibab trails at Grand Canyon. (3)

FEB. 18. Douglas loses its fight, and Stein's Pass road is added to the highway system. (1)

FEB. 24. Five Colorado River states start proceedings to have Arizona's petition for permission to sue for final decision on allocation of water thrown out by Supreme Court. (3)

FEB. 25. Governor Moeur pleads with President Roosevelt, urging that Home Loan Corporation be merciful to Arizona citizens who can't make payments on mortgages. (3)

MAR. 9. Transient claiming California citizenship sues Los Angeles police chief for blockade at Arizona border which denied him entry to California. (1)

MAR. 12. Arizona tells Supreme Court that California is "gambling with money furnished by U. S. Treasury" and is trying "to acquire the whole Colorado River." (3)

MAR. 13. Tucson School District No. 1 has serious budget troubles and so do teachers who are notified that one city bank will not cash their warrants and another will honor only its own depositors. (1)

MAR. 15. Monument is unveiled to Padre Eusebio Francisco Kino in Tucson. Dignitaries attending include General John J. Pershing, Dr. Herbert F. Bolton, famous western historian, churchmen and educators from Arizona and Sonora. (1)

MAR. 16. National Safety Council gives Miami citation for third straight year because it has had no fatal vehicle accident. (3)

MAR. 17. Thick clouds of soil from the dustbowl again cover Arizona. Bisbee residents find breathing difficult, visibility at Tucson is one-half mile, sky over Phoenix is a yellow fog, and mountains vanish in haze. (3)

MAR. 19. Old age pensioners in Arizona are rugged breed; only 249 die while 497 new ones are registered. (3)

MAR. 21. Tucson Welfare Board reports that with federal aid curtailed it cannot continue caring for indigent sick who drift in from all points of the compass. (1)

MAR. 23. Mrs. Isabella Greenway, only woman to represent an entire state in lower house of Congress, announces she will not be a candidate for re-election. (3)

MAR. 27. Four prominent Phoenix men found dead in Galiuro Mountains where their plane crashed. (3)

MAR. 31. Tempe has a primary election but no announced candidates; a do-it-yourself paradise for voters. (3)

APRIL 1. General John J. Pershing becomes a member of Tucson's Morgan McDermott Post, American Legion. (1)

APRIL 3. President Homer L. Shantz warns cacti collectors to stop stealing plants from University campus or go to jail. Says "they are people I would not trust around the corner with my dog's dinner." (1)

APRIL 4. Director of Federal Bureau of Prisons tells Congressional committee that 19 of Arizona's jails are sub-standard. (1)

APRIL 9. Collusion is charged by Secretary Ickes in bidding for Boulder Dam materials. (3)

APRIL 12. From the edge of the Grand Canyon national radio hook-up again carries Easter sunrise sermon across the nation to millions of listeners. (3)

APRIL 18. Arizona plans to spend $18,000,000 in federal funds in five years, fighting soil erosion in Gila, Graham, Greenlee, Cochise, and Pinal Counties. (1)

APRIL 29. National Emergency Council notifies Arizona the state has received $21,394,000 up to Feb. 29, in reconstruction loans, of which $8,147,000 has been disbursed. (3)

APRIL 29. President of the Carnegie Institution tells members of American Association for Advancement of Science meeting at the Grand Canyon that gorge below them is 1,000 million years old. (1)

MAY 1. President of Arizona Education Assn., speaking in Tucson at a state meeting, urges teachers to get out and battle politically. (3)

MAY 1. Phelps Dodge and Pima County reach a gentleman's agreement on taxes and the mining company makes partial payment of $234,844 without prejudice. (1)

MAY 1. Federal Prison Bureau removes all government prisoners from Pima County jail because of "lax administration." (1)

MAY 2. Tucson Democrats quarrel at Tucson convention. Wm. R. Mathews, editor of the *Arizona Daily Star,* is slugged from behind and knocked down by mayor of Nogales. Police rush in. Editor gets to his feet and gets in a last word and a laugh. Mayor apologizes. Convention breaks up without instructing delegates. (3)

MAY 8. Arizona Municipal League members advocate allocation of two-fifths of gasoline tax to cities. (3)

MAY 15. Townsend pension clubs in Salt River Valley stage a picnic at Casa Grande National Monument. (3)

MAY 18. Maricopa Superior Court mandamus seeking to redistrict county and cut number of representatives meets disapproval of State Supreme Court which says redistricting depends on votes cast for governor. (1)

MAY 20. City of Globe adopts an ordinance which makes it illegal to sell gasoline to intoxicated autoists. (3)

MAY 20. State Highway Commission makes Ajo-Gila Bend road a state highway. (1)

MAY 21. State Registrar of Contractors is denounced at Tucson meeting. Charge made that anybody with a hammer, saw, bag of nails and $15 can get a license, and that one out of every 237 people in Arizona has done so. (1)

MAY 22. State Liquor Control Department bans sale or purchase of empty liquor and wine bottles. (1)

MAY 24. Civilian Conservation Corps announces that its workers have completed erosion control works on 165,000 acres of Arizona and New Mexico land. (3)

MAY 25. U. S. Supreme Court refuses Arizona permission to bring suit for a final adjudication of rights to Colorado River water but leaves the door open. (1)

JUNE 1. Lower House of Congress passes bill amending Arizona enabling act, to allow 10 year grazing leases on state lands. Existing limit is three years. (3)

JUNE 6. First barrel of tequila made in the United States is produced at new San Andres distillery in Nogales. (3)

JUNE 9. Arizona veterans learn that they will receive $8,000,000 in bonus payments this month. (3)

JUNE 10. Townsendites hold a tumultuous state convention in Phoenix and predict monthly $200 old age pension plan will be adopted nationally within a year. (1)

JUNE 10. State employee breaks his wooden leg on the job and sues for compensation. State must decide whether wooden leg is a limb under the compensation law. (1)

JUNE 12. Salome (where she danced) is damaged by costly fire. (3)

JUNE 13. Florence marks the neglected grave of its straight shooting marshal, Pete Gabriel, with a bronze plaque. (3)

JUNE 13. Prescott installs lighting on U. S. 89, using sodium vapor lamps. (3)

JUNE 13. State Supreme Court rules that the basic science law, under which medical profession has operated in Arizona for three years, actually never existed. (1)

JUNE 17. Arizona World War veterans begin receiving their bonus bonds. (1)

JUNE 18. Million dollar project for Headgate Rock project on the Gila is stricken from the western reclamation program by President Roosevelt in effort to rescue master plan from complete defeat. Gila project is saved. (1)

JUNE 18. Transcontinental freight and passenger traffic on the Santa Fe is cut when fire destroys bridge across the Rio Puerco. (3)

JUNE 19. Western reclamation program containing $31,000,000 aid for 15 projects passes Congress. Arizona gets $2,750,000 for work on the Gila and Salt Rivers. (3)

JUNE 21. Arizonans develop the home evaporative cooler, as amateurs vie with professionals in installing the contraption. An era of better living on the desert predicted. (1)

JUNE 24. State Welfare Board asks Arizona counties to subscribe $100,000 for indigent relief in coming fiscal year. (1)

JUNE 24. State Supreme Court upholds constitutionality of Arizona law providing execution by lethal gas. (1)

JUNE 25. Battle opens between private utilities and Boulder Dam Power Transmission Assn., as Tucson citizens organize a local association. (1)

JUNE 27. Tucson banks decide to accept teachers' pay checks under certain conditions. (1)

JUNE 27. Arizona Superintendent of Public Health warns public to add a pinch of salt to every glass of cold water during summer hot spell. (1)

JUNE 30. Arizona, at the close of the fiscal year, finds it falls short of being in the black by only $45,000. First time since statehood. U. S. deficit for the year $4,400,000,000. (1)

JULY 1. Navajo medicine men steal jug of holy water from Pueblo tribe's mountain spring and hurry back to Ganado to use it in prayer for rain. (1)

JULY 1. *Arizona Historical Review* calls Camp Grant attack "brutal murder of women and children." (1)

JULY 2. Secretary Ickes approves $4,500,000 contract for construction of Bartlett Dam on the Verde. (3)

JULY 5. Contestants have a tough time at Prescott's annual Frontier Days; ten injured, one fatally. (3)

JULY 10. Short Creek colony of Mormons designates a day of prayer for release of two members sentenced to 18 months in penitentiary for polygamy. (3)

JULY 13. Last legal hanging in Arizona takes place in rugged canyon below Coolidge Dam when federal marshal hangs a San Carlos Apache convicted of the murder of his wife and child. Execution is bungled and the Indian is 33 minutes dying. (3)

JULY 14. Two are killed and a third man injured when ammonia pressure tank blows up in Phoenix. (3)

JULY 14. State Supreme Court rules that Arizona's Industrial Compensation Law is constitutional. (3)

JULY 17. Arizona's practice of halting touring motorists at the State border until they prove ownership of their cars, raises such cries of frustration that the vehicle department decides to give drivers benefit of the doubt. (1)

JULY 18. State accepts mobile tuberculosis unit presented by American Legion for preventative work among school children. (1)

JULY 23. State Highway Department announces sales and revenue taxes on gasoline in the last fiscal year totaled $3,565,758, a gain of 14.4 percent over 1934-35. (3)

JULY 26. Torrential rains sweep central and southern Arizona from Phoenix to Douglas. Damage is high. One dead, several injured. (1)

JULY 28. Arizona gets only $174,000 in first approval of projects under new PWA program. Williams and Mesa benefit. (1)

JULY 31. Heaviest rainstorm in five years does much damage in Kingman. (3)

AUG. 1. Resettlement Administration plans projects near Casa Grande, Florence and Phoenix which will move 100 families off sub-marginal lands. Estimated costs, $476,000. (3)

AUG. 1. Survey shows CCC has 9,000 men working on Arizona projects. U. S. reports it has spent $26,092,000 on programs in state. (1)

AUG. 4. Resident of the Arizona Pioneer Home reaches the age of 105 and says his years are due to his meanness. (3)

AUG. 4. Buckeye farm wife, struck on both hands by sidewinder rattlesnake, dies in Buckeye hospital. (3)

AUG. 7. Tumacacori Monument between Tucson and Nogales gets $50,000 from park service for a new building. (1)

AUG. 8. U. S. Office of Education announces that Arizona is to get $80,719 for vocational education in 1937. State must match 50 percent of the grant. (3)

AUG. 11. A new municipality is born as 87 citizens vote on incorporation of South Tucson. Measure carries by 17 votes. (1)

AUG. 14. Governor Moeur reports that in last three and one-half years the Arizona State Banking Department has returned $4,000,000 to depositors in defunct banks. (1)

AUG. 15. State Superintendent of Public Health announces great progress made in public health work during past fiscal year. State receives $300,000 in grants from Rockefeller Foundation and government aid. (1)

AUG. 15. Maricopa County Superior Court Judge campaigns for re-election with strong endorsement of the Townsend Plan. (1)

AUG. 16. City of Tucson discovers that its new underpass on Stone Ave. becomes a lake after a heavy rain. Council names it Lake Elmira, after Elmira Doakes, a Safford school student who was first to swim it. (1)

AUG. 19. Arizona property owners' tax burdens lighten as state fights way back towards prosperity. Eleven counties reduce their tax rates. (1)

AUG. 26. Parker's new $40,000 PWA high school, completed Aug. 21, is struck by lightning and burns. (1)

AUG. 29. Four largest Arizona copper producers announce five percent increase in wages. (1)

AUG. 31. Arizona cotton growers read news of Mississippi experiments which may mean bright future for them: mechanical cotton picker. (1)

AUG. 31. Social Security Board celebrates its first anniversary and notes that in seven months it has contributed $100,000 to the needy in Arizona. (3)

SEPT. 4. Fifty-two candidates enter the race for city constable in Tucson. (3)

SEPT. 6. Figures for first eight months of the year show Tucson building permits are $624,115 greater than same period of 1935. (1)

SEPT. 8. Governor Moeur defeated for renomination on the Democratic ticket by Judge R. C. Stanford. Republicans name Thomas E. Campbell, two-time governor. (1)

SEPT. 10. Tucson and Pima County apply to U. S. to construct 250 foot high dam in Sabino Canyon. (1)

SEPT. 11. President Roosevelt presses a button in Washington, twelve mammoth valves at Boulder Dam open to generate its first electric power. (1)

SEPT. 12. Board of Regents makes public its intention of asking higher salaries for University teachers whose pay has been cut twice during depression. (3)

SEPT. 14. Miami Justice of the Peace signs 11 warrants for Globe high school boys charging them with a misdemeanor after they destroy Miami High School "M" on Schome Hill. (3)

SEPT. 19. Pima County Welfare Board has trouble convincing able-bodied men and women that the days of the dole are past and there are no more free groceries. (1)

SEPT. 21. Harry Hopkins, WPA administrator, dedicates $200,000 stadium at Arizona State Fairgrounds in Phoenix. (1)

SEPT. 22. Phoenix City Commission votes to ask Public Works Administration to finance paving of three streets. (3)

SEPT. 23. Salt River Valley plants 10,000 acres in lettuce. (3)

SEPT. 25. Federal Court rejects suit of Standard Oil seeking to prevent "price-fixing" prosecution under Arizona's anti-trust laws. (3)

OCT. 1. Governor Moeur calls special session of Legislature to meet Nov. 5 and enact social security legislation. (1)

OCT. 5. Townsend Plan for old age pensions becomes an issue in Arizona race for governor. (1)

OCT. 7. Arizona cattlemen ask U. S. Collector of Customs to show a little more courtesy to Mexican cattlemen than is customary. (1)

OCT. 11. Social Security officials report U. S. Government is now contributing to the following Arizona activities: aid to dependent children, aid to the needy blind, crippled children, child welfare, public health, maternal and child health services. (3)

OCT. 13. Bureau of Internal Revenue reports Arizona paid income taxes of $1,203,941 in fiscal 1936. (3)

OCT. 15. State Attorney General refuses to sign applications for exchange of state and federal lands covering 309,066 acres. His objection: stockmen are not getting a square deal. (3)

OCT. 15. Arizona State Nurses Assn. is told by state epidemiologist that tests show half of the 2,500 school children in Yavapai County react positively to skin tests for tuberculosis. (1)

OCT. 18. Secretary Ickes divides jurisdiction over Boulder Dam between Reclamation Bureau and National Park Service. (3)

OCT. 20. Eleven hospitals in seven Arizona cities are approved by American College of Surgeons. (3)

OCT. 21. Alf M. Landon, Republican candidate for President, enters Arizona and speaks in Phoenix. (1)

OCT. 23. University of Arizona receives another loan grant from the government. It will build a dormitory and dining hall with $482,000 provided by PWA. (1)

OCT. 25. Counsel for Arizona Colorado River Commission and Attorney General recommend that the state ratify the Colorado River Compact. (3)

NOV. 1. Analysis of last federal farm census shows cash income from Arizona farm crop and livestock production increased 100 percent between 1932 and 1935. (3)

NOV. 2. Ground is broken in Phoenix for General Motors $100,000 plant. (3)

NOV. 3. District judge hands down decision in Phelps-Dodge tax suit and ends nine week trial with decision that mining company must pay state $4,000,000 in contested taxes.

NOV. 3. Coldest weather of the year keeps many Northern Arizonans from the general election polls. (2)

NOV. 3. Arizona votes heavily for Roosevelt. Democrats carry state and county tickets with avalanche of ballots. R. C. Stanford elected governor. One Republican left in legislature. (1)

NOV. 5. Twelfth Legislature meets in special session. Governor Moeur urges boost in liquor taxes to finance old age pension plan. (1, 2)

NOV. 7. Douglas schoolgirl cuts copper ribbon and opens new Douglas underpass; part of $300,000 highway widening project. (3)

NOV. 8. Completion of the Williams-Verde Valley District highway connecting Jerome and Williams is celebrated at Perkinsville. (3)

NOV. 10. It is announced at the University that the State Park Board will begin restoration of Fort Lowell "within a short time." (3)

NOV. 11. Engineers of the U. S. Surveying team working northeast of House Rock Valley find a rattlesnake den and kill 121 reptiles. (3)

NOV. 13. Survey of public health conditions in Arizona results in a scolding from American Public Health Assn., which threatens to recommend federal government aid be withdrawn. Pima County gets the highest score, 627 points out of a possible 1,100 while Maricopa is lowest with 266 points. (3)

NOV. 16. Surveys of cattle ranges in Pima, Cochise and Santa Cruz Counties show they are overstocked 12 percent. (2)

NOV. 18. WPA project launched which will pave streets of University campus. (1)

NOV. 19. Dr. Byron Cummings, Director of the State Museum, says that Arizona is stupid in its dealings with Indians and its refusal to use their labor potential. (2)

NOV. 24. Long drawn out criminal proceedings in famous June Robles kidnapping case apparently come to near end when suspect charged with sending extortion letter to parents is discharged by federal judge. (2)

NOV. 25. Special session of the Twelfth Legislature adjourns. It had passed a basic science bill, unemployment compensation act and established a commission, and had petitioned the U. S. Secretary of State to enter into diplomatic conversations with Republic of Mexico on possibility of getting Arizona a port on the Gulf of California. (1)

NOV. 26. Phoenix postmaster reveals that 12,000 employees of business and industry are covered by the old age benefits provided by Social Security Act. (3)

NOV. 26. U. S. Census bureau reports that the retail sales in 5,214 Arizona stores during 1935 showed a gain of 59 percent over sales in 1933. (3)

NOV. 29. Mayor John H. Udall of Phoenix threatens to take over the police department and run it himself if something is not done to break up gambling ring. (3)

DEC. 1. Secret committee of 500 women is organized in state to clean up "corruption and neglect of duty" among public officials. [No further notice found.] (2)

DEC. 1. Seventy-five hundred miners, mechanics and smelter workers employed by major companies get pay raise; second since September. (2)

DEC. 2. Speaking in Tucson, Sen. Carl Hayden favors retention of high taxes until national debt is retired at rate of $6,000,000 or $7,000,000 a year. (2)

DEC. 3. Another angle of Robles kidnap case is closed when government says it has no jurisdiction since girl was not taken across state's borders. (2)

DEC. 4. Tucson city council struggles with new sociological problem — what to do with the growing number of house "trailers," a word heretofore considered unpleasant. (2)

DEC. 6. Widely promoted "no accident week" is not a success in Yuma. Two women are injured first day, one man killed second day, a woman killed the third day. Campaign collapses. (3)

DEC. 9. Citizens flee when seven tons of dynamite loaded on a truck trailer catch fire in the heart of Jerome. Dynamite blazes merrily, never explodes. (2)

DEC. 9. Pima County Medical Association holds annual election and discusses community medical cooperatives. Reporters are barred. (2)

DEC. 9. Southside residents appear before Tucson city council and register such vigorous objections to establishment of a trailer park there that council refuses application. Same issue of the *Citizen* carries dateline story from Detroit with news that construction of home trailers is now a $100,000,000 industry. (2)

DEC. 17. State treasurer reports that for the first time in its history Arizona is operating on a cash basis. (1)

DEC. 18. Federal Grand Jury again considers evidence in Robles kidnapping case and fails to make charges. U. S. Attorney asks that case be dismissed. (2)

DEC. 22. Phelps Dodge brightens Christmas for its Ajo workers with rebates of $65,000 on purchases made at co-op store. (3)

DEC. 22. Price of copper rises to 11.62 cents in a year which has seen price increases add $2,000,000 to the income of Arizona mines. (2)

DEC. 22. Colonel Frank Knox, Republican candidate for vice-president, speaks in the new stadium in Phoenix and says it is example of New Deal waste: $85,000 worth of stadium and $115,000 worth of dedication." (3)

DEC. 23. Washington statistics show that Arizona received nearly $2,000,000 a month in federal relief money during 1936. Exact total is $21,706,988. (3)

DEC. 26. Two escaped Utah convicts confess having kidnapped a Nogales salesman and holding up a Tempe station agent. Court has no Christmas mercy. They get 20 years. (1)

DEC. 27. Determined to run vagrants out of town, Phoenix police pick up 23 undesirables and give them choice of hitting the road or working on it in chains. (3)

DEC. 28. Work begins on 24 homes being built in Glendale by Resettlement Administration. (3)

DEC. 29. Sudden blizzard maroons 300 Navajo Indians in Arizona's Painted Desert. Planes drop food. (1)

DEC. 30. Members of the Arizona Colorado River Commission recommend that attorneys and engineers make still another report on situation. (1)

DEC. 31. Copper closes the year with an advance to 12 cents. (2)

Total deposits in Arizona banks, $76,445,522. (27)

BIBLIOGRAPHY

Figures in parentheses following each entry in the *Chronology* indicate source from which information was taken.

(1) *Arizona Daily Star,* Tucson

(2) *Tucson Daily Citizen*

(3) *Arizona Republic,* Phoenix

(4) *Bisbee Daily Review*

(5) *Prescott Courier*

(6) *Yuma Daily Sun*

(7) *Florence Blade Tribune*

(8) *Phoenix Gazette*

(9) Nogales *Oasis*

(10) Nogales *Herald*

(11) *Ajo Copper News*

(12) *Coconino Sun*

(13) *Mohave Miner*

(14) Arizona. Laws, statutes, etc. *Session Laws,* 1913-1936.

(15) Arizona. State Department of Education. *Report of the Superintendent of Public Instruction.* 1913-1936.

(16) Elsing, Morris J. and Robert E. S. Heineman. *Arizona Metal Production.* Arizona State Bureau of Mines, Bulletin 140. 1936.

(17) Kelly, William H. *Indians of the Southwest: A Survey of Indian Tribes and Indian Administration in Arizona.* Tucson: University of Arizona Bureau of Ethnic Research, 1953.

(18) League of Arizona Cities and Towns. *Directory of Arizona City and Town Officials.* Phoenix. 1959.

(19) Lutrell, Estelle. *Newspapers and Periodicals of Arizona, 1859-1911.* Tucson: University of Arizona General Bulletin No. 15, 1950.

(20) Martin, Douglas D. *The Lamp in the Desert.* Tucson: University of Arizona Press, 1960.

(21) McGowan, Joseph C. *History of Extra-Long Staple Cottons.* El Paso: SuPima Association of American and Arizona Cotton Growers Association, 1961.

(22) Parsons, Malcolm B. *The Colorado River in Arizona Politics.* Master's thesis, University of Arizona, Tucson, 1947.

(23) Peplow, Edward H., Jr. *History of Arizona.* N. Y.: Lewis Historical Publishing Company, 1958. 3 vols.

(24) U. S. Agricultural Economics Bureau. *Livestock on Farms, Jan. 1, 1867-1919.* Washington: 1938.

(25) U. S. Bureau of the Census. *Decennial Census Reports,* 1920, 1930.

(26) U. S. National Park Service. *Proclamations and Orders Relating to the National Park Service.* 1947.

(27) Valley National Bank. *Arizona Statistical Review.* 1945.

INDEX

Benson
1924: Mar. 30, Oct. 22, Dec. 1
1926: Dec. 31
Bisbee
1917: Jan. 3, June 26
1923: June 2
1929: Nov. 20
1930: July 8
Bisbee Deportation
1917: July 12, 14, 17, Sept. 16,
  Nov. 24
1918: June 21, July 7
1919: July 11, 22, Aug. 25, Sept.
  9, 16
1920: Jan. 20, 21, Feb. 7, 26,
  Mar. 2, 4, 5, 9, 12; 24, 29,
  Apr. 30, May 10
"Blacklist law"
1918: May 10
Board of Control
1913: Apr. 7
Board of Pardons and Parole
1914: Dec. 15
1915: Mar. 12, May 28
Board of Regents
1918: Jan. 19
1922: July 29
1923: Sept. 11
1926: May 11, July 16, 18, Aug. 6
1927: Jan. 21, 31
1932: Feb. 5, 24, Apr. 26, Dec. 21
1933: May 14
1935: May 7
1936: Sept. 12
Board of Trade
1915: Nov. 20
Bonus march
1932: June 5, 17, 21
Border, Mexican
1915: Mar. 4, Nov. 26
1916: May 10
1917: Jan. 27
1918: Aug. 28
1919: Dec. 27
1920: Feb. 11, Mar. 6, Apr. 19,
  July 9, Aug. 30, Dec. 1
1921: Jan. 13
1924: July 2, 22
1927: May 19
1928: Jan. 27, Feb. 18
Border Patrol
1913: Apr. 14
1925: Aug. 9
1929: Mar. 14

1931: May 21
1932: Jan. 9, Mar. 6
Boulder Canyon Project
1921: Apr. 10
1922: Mar. 16, June 21, Oct. 17
1925: Aug. 17, Nov. 1, Dec. 11, 21
1926: Feb. 11, Mar. 4, 5,
  Apr. 20, 21, 25, May 22
1927: Jan. 12, Feb. 23, 26,
  June 20, Oct. 8, Dec. 9
1928: Jan. 3, 7, 18, Feb. 21,
  Mar. 31, Apr. 30, May 3, 26, 30,
  Aug. 17, Dec. 7, 11, 12, 15, 21
1929: Mar. 7, May 31,
  Nov. 12, 13, Dec. 10, 25, 28
1930: Jan. 28, Mar. 22,
  Apr. 21, 26, May 3, June 8,
  July 7, Sept. 17, Oct. 13
1931: Jan. 12, Mar. 12,
  Apr. 20, 23, May 18, 25,
  July 4, 14, Aug. 10, Oct. 9
1932: Nov. 13
1933: May 10, 13, June 6
1934: June 30, Dec. 17
1935: Feb. 1, May 30, July 14,
  Sept. 30, Dec. 13
1936: Feb. 6, Apr. 9, Sept. 11,
  Oct. 18
Buckeye
1929: May 8
Bureau of Mines
1915: Mar. 4

Calumet and Arizona Company
1913: June 2
Cameron, Ralph
1920: Oct. 23, Nov. 2
1921: Apr. 28, Oct. 24
1922: May 1, 17
1924: Aug. 31, Sept. 17, Oct. 1
1925: Feb. 6
1926: Mar. 5, Apr. 21
Camp Verde Indian Reservation
1914: Aug. 1
Campbell, Thomas E.
1916: Nov. 7, Dec. 16, 30
1917: Jan. 3, 27, 29, 30,
  Feb. 7, 28, Mar. 24, Apr. 19,
  May 2, June 5, July 5, 22,
  Aug. 1, Dec. 18, 22, 25
1918: Jan. 8, Nov. 5
1919: Jan. 6, 7, Feb. 6,
  Mar. 11, 25, Aug. 16
1920: Apr. 11, July 12, Aug. 22,
  Sept. 21, Nov. 2, 25, Dec. 23

Fires *(continued)*
Douglas
  1919: Dec. 29
  1928: Feb. 7
Florence
  1923: Dec. 22
forest
  1916: June 27
  1923: June 22
  1924: May 11
  1925: May 23, 31
  1928: June 23, Sept. 21
  1929: May 11
  1934: May 21
Globe
  1920: July 10
  1927: May 5
Grand Canyon
  1932: Sept. 1
Holbrook
  1935: June 20
Kingman
  1928: July 25
Lowell
  1920: Oct. 11
  1929: May 3
Maricopa
  1913: Apr. 29
Miami
  1928: July 7
  1929: July 3
Nogales
  1921: Nov. 9
  1923: Apr. 20, Oct. 13
  1927: Mar. 2
  1928: Apr. 14
Oatman
  1921: June 27
  1927: Dec. 6
Pantano
  1926: June 6
Parker
  1936: Aug. 26
Parker Dam
  1936: Feb. 3
Phoenix
  1914: Nov. 17
  1917: Oct. 5, Dec. 19
  1919: Apr. 19
  1921: Sept. 23
Ray
  1913: Aug. 15
  1927: Oct. 20

Rio Puerco
  1936: June 18
Salome
  1936: June 12
Superior
  1927: Nov. 24
  1932: Mar. 13
Tucson
  1920: Oct. 10
  1933: Dec. 18
  1934: May 11, Aug. 27
Yuma
  1921: Dec. 6
  1925: Jan. 25
  1928: Sept. 14
  1930: June 1

First
Arizonan to die in action in
  World War I
  1918: May 28
Arizonan to graduate from
  West Point
  1916: June 18
birth control clinic, Tucson
  1934: Nov. 15
city manager, Tucson
  1930: Jan. 1
Indian to vote
  1924: Sept. 4
licensed radio station
  1922: June 21
movies, talking, Phoenix
  1913: Nov. 16
prisoner of war, World War I
  1917: May 3
Red Cross chapter
  1916: June 29
transcontinental air mail
  1930: Oct. 15
voting machines, installed in Tucson
  1929: Nov. 8
woman hanged
  1930: Feb. 21

Flag, State
  1917: Jan. 9, 27

Floods
Agua Fria River
  1927: Feb. 17
Bisbee
  1917: Aug. 12
  1922: Aug. 22
Cave Creek
  1915: Jan. 30
Dragoon
  1935: Aug. 29

Floods (*continued*)
Duncan
 1934: Aug. 28
Ehrenberg
 1928: June 14
Florence
 1929: Sept. 6
Gila River
 1915: Jan. 30
Globe
 1919: July 14
Hassayampa River
 1919: Nov. 29
 1927: Feb. 17
 1928: Aug. 14
Hayden
 1930: July 11
Mammoth
 1931: Aug. 11
Maricopa
 1914: Dec. 26
Miami
 1928: July 28
Nogales
 1922: July 8
 1928: Aug. 15
 1930: Aug. 1, 7, 8
 1932: July 8
Paradise Valley
 1913: Sept. 2
Phoenix
 1916: Sept. 10
 1921: Aug. 22
 1922: Jan. 3
 1928: Aug. 26
Picacho
 1925: Aug. 27
Ray
 1914: Sept. 22
 1930: July 11
Safford
 1935: July 31
Salt River
 1914: Feb. 21
 1931: Dec. 11
San Carlos
 1935: Feb. 7
Santa Cruz River
 1914: Dec. 23
 1925: July 4
Tucson
 1921: July 1
 1926: Sept. 29
 1929: Sept. 24
 1935: Sept. 1

Verde River
 1919: Nov. 29
Wickenburg
 1935: Aug. 23
Winslow
 1929: Aug. 20
Yuma
 1916: Jan. 23
 1926: Aug. 2
Florence
 1913: Feb. 27
 1917: Apr. 13
 1924: Dec. 22
 1929: Mar. 16
Food supplies
 1917: Oct. 29, Nov. 1, 26,
  Dec. 1, 7
 1918: Feb. 3, Apr. 1, 11, 13,
  June 1, 19
 1919: Aug. 10, 14, 15, 16, 18, 25,
  26, 30, Sept. 20, 21, Oct. 4, 14,
  Dec. 6, 27
 1920: Mar. 20
 1921: Oct. 22
 1935: Mar. 27
Fort Apache
 1922: May 9
 1928: May 29
 1931: Mar. 4
Fort Grant
 1913: Mar. 29
 1914: Apr. 5
 1915: Aug. 11
 1928: July 20
 1930: July 29
Fort Huachuca
 1914: Apr. 22, 23
 1917: Apr. 7
 1920: Dec. 16
 1923: Feb. 25
 1932: Dec. 14
 1933: May 1
Franklin, Selim M.
 1927: Nov. 22

Gabriel, Pete
 1936: June 13
Gambling
 1916: Nov. 2
 1918: Aug. 17
 1922: Jan. 22
 1924: July 2
 1927: May 25
 1930: Feb. 15
 1935: Feb. 5

1936: Nov. 29
Gammage, Grady
1926: Aug. 19
1927: June 7
Garces, Francisco
1928: Oct. 21
Gercke, Daniel J.
1923: June 21
1926: June 11, Aug. 18
1928: Oct. 10
Gila River
1922: May 10
1924: May 10, June 5
1925: June 19, Oct. 4
1928: Nov. 29, Dec. 11
1929: Feb. 19, June 4, 15, Dec. 4
1930: Feb. 7
1935: Jan. 23, Apr. 19
1936: June 18, 19
Gila River Indian Reservation
1913: June 2
1914: Aug. 27
1915: July 19
Gilbert
1920: July 6
Glen Canyon Dam
1921: June 3
1922: Aug. 5
1926: Mar. 5
1927: Feb. 12
1931: Oct. 31
Globe
1914: Feb. 9
1917: July 5, 22, Aug. 7,
   Oct. 10, 22
1918: Feb. 16
1919: Jan. 8
1923: June 24, Dec. 27
1927: Apr. 20
1934: Jan. 7
Graf Zeppelin
1929: Aug. 27
Grand Canyon
1919: Feb. 26
1920: Apr. 30
1931: Mar. 10
1935: Apr. 21
1936: Feb. 17, Apr. 12, 29
Bright Angel Trail
1924: Aug. 31, Sept. 17, Oct. 1
1928: May 28
Great Western Power Company
1913: May 2
Greene Cattle Company
1923: Feb. 2

Greenway, Isabella
1933: Aug. 8, Oct. 3
1936: Mar. 23
Greenway, John C.
1918: June 21
1930: May 24
Grey, Zane
1930: Oct. 15

Hangings
1915: Apr. 23, Dec. 10
1917: May 6
1922: Jan. 13
1928: June 22
1930: Feb. 21
1931: Mar. 20
1933: Oct. 3
1936: July 13
Harding, Warren G.
1920: Aug. 22
1921: May 11
1922: Aug. 13, Sept. 23
1923: Aug. 2, 10
Hayden, Carl
1913: Sept. 8
1918: Nov. 5
1924: July 22, Dec. 6
1925: Oct. 2
1926: Apr. 20, Nov. 2
1927: Jan. 12, 21
1928: Dec. 7, 15
1930: Jan. 17. 28
1931: May 13
1932: Mar. 30, Dec. 31
1936: Dec. 2
Hayden
1923: Sept. 12
Health, public
1913: May 22
1920: Jan. 29, June 23, Aug. 7
1923: July 15, 29
1925: Oct. 13
1930: Feb. 1, Oct. 23
1931: Aug. 22, Nov. 3
1936: July 18, Aug. 15, Oct. 15,
   Nov. 13
see also Epidemics
Hi Jolly (Hadji Ali)
1936: Jan. 4
Highways
1920: Nov. 30
1921: Jan. 1, 13, Feb. 23, Mar. 11,
   Oct. 11

1930: July 23, Oct. 15
1931: Jan. 2
Poston, Charles D.
1925: Apr. 26
Poultry
1924: Dec. 29
Prescott
1913: Apr. 2, Dec. 23
1931: May 24
1932: Oct. 6
Prison, State
1913: Feb. 27
1915: Sept. 15
1926: July 10
1928: May 18
1929: Oct. 10
1930: Jan. 14
1931: Feb. 23
1932: Jan. 26, May 16
1934: July 6
1936: Feb. 6
Prohibition
1913: May 30
1914: Dec. 24, 31
1915: Feb. 14, Nov. 10, 18
1916: Jan. 5, Feb. 13, June 17
1917: Jan. 3, 25, Aug. 9, Nov. 9,
    Dec. 14
1918: Apr. 2, May 24
1919: Nov. 11, 12, Dec. 15
1920: June 11
1921: June 29, Dec. 29
1922: Jan. 17
1923: Oct. 13, Nov. 10, 23,
    Dec. 17
1924: Jan. 8, Feb. 19, May 22,
    July 11, Oct. 29
1925: Jan. 8, Feb. 20, July 8
1926: Apr. 25, 29, June 1,
    Aug. 12
1927: Mar. 2, Apr. 1, May 25,
    July 8, Oct. 21
1928: Jan. 26, Mar. 22, Apr. 25,
    May 16, June 1, Aug. 19,
    Oct. 10
1929: June 1, Aug. 22, Dec. 7
1931: Apr. 17, May 16, 19,
    June 11, 12
1932: May 1, July 7, Oct. 4,
    Nov. 9, Dec. 17
1933: Apr. 7, June 9, 30,
    Aug. 2, 4, 8, Sept. 5
1934: May 11
Prostitution
1918: Feb. 14, Aug. 17

Radio
1922: June 21
1923: Mar. 6
1924: Oct. 24
1930: June 2
1931: Feb. 28
1936: Apr. 12
Railroad accidents
1915: Aug. 27
1920: July 9
1923: Sept. 21
1926: Nov. 11
1927: May 23
1930: Aug. 8
1931: Aug. 5
Railroads
1913: Mar. 6, Apr. 25
1915: Apr. 28
1919: July 1
1921: Dec. 18
1922: Apr. 30, July 7, 31,
    Aug. 15, 17
1923: Dec. 28
1924: Apr. 22, July 26
1930: May 16
1931: June 19, 27
El Paso and Southwestern
1913: Jan. 7
1924: Sept. 30
Santa Fe
1917: Jan. 5
1922: Aug. 13
1923: Sept. 19, Oct. 1
Southern Pacific
1914: Feb. 13, Sept. 4, Dec. 26
1921: Jan. 13, 24, Aug. 4
1923: Oct. 1
1924: Feb. 20, Sept. 30, Oct. 2,
    Dec. 17
1925: Jan. 5
1926: June 17, Dec. 24
1929: Mar. 26
Southern Pacific of Mexico
1916: June 19
1927: Apr. 14
Tucson, Phoenix and Tidewater
1914: June 8
Recall
1915: Nov. 30, Dec. 23
1916: Mar. 31
Red Cross
1916: June 29, July 1
1917: Feb. 5, Dec. 11, 14
1918: Feb. 13
1926: Sept. 21
1929: Nov. 24

1921: Apr. 20
1931: Jan. 5
1936: Nov. 25
Sentinel Peak
1915: Dec. 11
1926: Mar. 4
1928: Nov. 18
Shantz, Homer L.
1927: Sept. 13
1930: Apr. 24
1931: Sept. 10
1933: Nov. 30
1936: Jan. 6, Apr. 3
Shenandoah (Navy dirigible)
1924: Oct. 24
Shootings
1913: June 9
1914: Aug. 21
1917: May 29
1918: June 9
1921: Jan. 13
1922: May 15
1930: Jan. 14, Mar. 26
1934: Aug. 26, Oct. 3
see also Murders
Silver
1931: May 13
1932: Dec. 11
1933: Dec. 23
1934: June 13, Aug. 9, 18, 21
1935: Apr. 12, 24, Dec. 10
Smith, Alfred E.
1928: June 28
Smith, Marcus A.
1914: Aug. 8
1920: Nov. 2
Smuggling
ammunition to Mexico
1920: May 8
bullion into U. S.
1914: Dec. 15
cattle into U. S.
1916: June 1
guns to Mexico
1913: Oct. 3, 13, 23, 27, Dec. 3, 11
opium into U. S.
1920: Sept. 27
whiskey into U. S.
1919: May 16
see also Border Patrol
Somerton
1918: Dec. 31
South Tucson
1936: Aug. 11

Spear, J. W. (Uncle Billy)
1924: May 7, 17
Speed limit
1913: Apr. 8
1933: June 12
Speed records
El Paso-Phoenix
1919: Nov. 2
San Diego-Phoenix
1923: June 3
Tucson-Nogales
1913: May 3
Tucson-Phoenix
1916: May 9
Stanford, R. C.
1917: Feb. 7, May 2
1936: Sept. 8, Nov. 3
Stewart Mountain Dam
1928: Feb. 12
1930: Mar. 12
Storms
1916: Dec. 25
1922: Mar. 13
1923: Sept. 12, 19, Dec. 12
1924: Dec. 18
1925: Sept. 19
1929: Puly 29
1930: Jan. 14, 17, 18, June 22,
       July 23
1931: Nov. 27, Dec. 12, 18
1932: Jan. 16
1933: Feb. 1, Aug. 21
1936: July 23, 31, Dec. 29
see also Floods
Streetcars
Phoenix
1913: June 24
1925: June 15, Oct. 30, Nov. 7
1928: Dec. 25
Tucson
1931: Jan. 2
Strikes
1915: Sept. 19, Oct. 4, 17, 21, 28,
       Dec. 10, 24
1916: Jan. 6, 25, Dec. 20
1917: May 24, 29, June 5, 26,
       July 2, 6, 12, 22, Oct. 1, 22
1918: June 23
1919: Oct. 30
1922: July 17, Aug. 13, 15, 17
1923: June 24
1931: July 14, Aug. 10
1935: June 12, 25, 26, July 14
see also Disorders, civil

enrollment
  1920: Feb. 3
  1923: May 31
  1933: Oct. 9
faculty
  1922: Mar. 4
  1924: Dec. 11
  1932: Mar. 31, Apr. 26
finances
  1919: Feb. 6, 19
  1922: Apr. 1
  1931: Sept. 10
library
  1927: Oct. 23
  1929: Sept. 13
Observatory
  1916: Oct. 19
  1922: July 17
parking
  1936: Feb. 2
presidents
  1917: Nov. 17
  1919: Nov. 6
  1920: May 1
  1921: Sept. 27, Oct. 8
  1922: Jan. 4
  1926: May 11, July 16
  1927: Jan. 20, 31, Sept. 13
  1930: Apr. 24
  1931: Sept. 10
  1933: Nov. 30
  1936: Jan. 6, Apr. 3
students
  1915: Oct. 21
  1920: Sept. 13
  1921: July 26, Sept. 2
  1928: May, 10, 19
  1929: Sept. 20
  1930: Sept. 7
  1932: Sept. 22
  1934: May 24, Nov. 2
summer schools
  1920: June 4
  1923: June 2
World War I
  1917: Mar. 29, Apr. 6
  1918: Aug. 17
  1920: Jan. 20
  see also Board of Regents

Vagrants
  1920: Jan. 16
  1921: Oct. 9
  1931: July 15, Sept. 5, 12

  1933: Aug. 22, Sept. 29, 30
  1936: Jan. 17, Feb. 3, 7, 11, 13,
    Mar. 21, Dec. 27
**Verde River Irrigation and
  Power District**
  1927: Mar. 14
  1928: Dec. 10
  1929: Dec. 18
  1930: July 8
  1933: Nov. 4, 15, Dec. 3
  1934: Dec. 6
Verde Valley
  1913: Jan. 1
von KleinSmid, Rufus B.
  1917: Nov. 17
  1919: Nov. 6
  1920: May 1
  1921: Sept. 27, Oct. 8
Voting machines
  1927: Mar. 15
  1928: Apr. 3
  1929: Nov. 8
  1934: July 14

**Walnut Canyon National
  Monument**
  1915: Nov. 30
Water, artesian
  1913: Jan. 3
  1914: Jan. 11
Wickenburg
  1931: Apr. 2
WICKENBURG SUN
  1934: May 24
Wildlife
  1916: May 7
  1920: Dec. 16
  1922: Nov. 3
  1923: Sept. 19
  1924: Nov. 19, 29, Dec. 18
  1925: Nov. 20
  1926: Apr. 23, June 2
  1927: Nov. 23
  1935: Feb. 25
  see also Kaibab Plateau
Willcox
  1915: May 1
  1927: July 23
Wilson, Woodrow
  1917: Feb. 3, July 13
  1924: Feb. 6
Winkelman
  1914: Dec. 31
  1927: Mar. 16, 19

Winsor, Mulford
    1920: May 10
    1925: July 21, Aug. 3
    1926: Feb. 11
    1928: Jan. 7
Women
    1913: Apr. 29, Aug. 19
    1914: Aug. 19
    1915: Sept. 20
    1919: Jan. 21, 29
    1920: Feb. 12, Dec. 11
    1923: Feb. 3, 13
    1936: Dec. 1
Workmen's Compensation Act
    1921: July 19
    1925: Sept. 29, Nov. 3, 30
World War I
    1917: May 25, Sept. 9, Oct. 19,
        Nov. 20, 22, 30, Dec. 7, 11
    1918: Aug. 25, Sept. 12
    1919: Feb. 6
    Armistice
        1918: Nov. 11
    "Boches"
        1917: Apr. 19
    Council of Defense
        1917: Apr. 19, Nov. 7, 10, 29
        1918: Nov. 13
    draft dodgers
        1917: Sept. 22
    draft quota
        1917: July 13, Aug. 1
        1919: Mar. 23
    espionage
        1918: June 29
    First Arizona Regiment
        1917: Aug. 25
    first prisoner of war
        1917: May 3
    food supply
        1917: May 30, June 2, Oct. 29,
        Nov. 1, 10, 26, 29, Dec. 1, 7
        1918: Feb. 3, Apr. 1, 11, 13,
        June 1, 19, Sept. 13
    liberty loan drive
        1917: June 14, Oct. 25

        1918: Apr. 19, 21, Oct. 20
        1919: Mar. 12, May 14
    loyalty parade
        1917: Apr. 1
    national lottery begins
        1917: July 20
    registration for service
        1917: June 5
    "slackers"
        1917: Aug. 28
    Tucson loses Army Cantonment
        1917: May 18
Wupatki National Monument
    1924: Dec. 9

Yaqui Indians
    1914: June 18
    1920: Aug. 30, Oct. 9
    1926: Oct. 1
    1927: May 8, 9, 10, 11, 14,
        Sept. 30
    1931: Sept. 23
Yavapai County
    1923: Nov. 3
Yavapai Indian Reservation
    1935: June 5
Y.M.C.A., Tucson
    1913: Jan. 7
Yuma
    1913: Dec. 13
    1914: Apr. 28, Dec. 31
    1921: June 11
    1924: Jan. 16, Dec. 12
    1926: May 26
    1927: Nov. 1
    1928: Oct. 21
    1929: Feb. 7
    1931: Jan. 24
    1934: July 15
    1936: Dec. 6
YUMA DAILY SUN
    1935: Dec. 2
Yuma Indian Reservation
    1924: May 1
Yuma Irrigation Project
    1935: May 10, Dec. 5, 18
    1936: Jan. 6